THE LIMIT

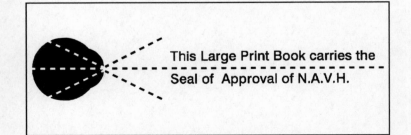

This Large Print Book carries the
Seal of Approval of N.A.V.H.

THE LIMIT

LIFE AND DEATH ON THE
1961 GRAND PRIX CIRCUIT

MICHAEL CANNELL

THORNDIKE PRESS
A part of Gale, Cengage Learning

GALE
CENGAGE Learning®

Detroit • New York • San Francisco • New Haven, Conn • Waterville, Maine • London

GALE
CENGAGE Learning®

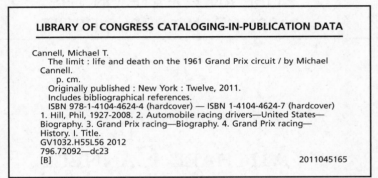

LIBRARY OF CONGRESS CATALOGING-IN-PUBLICATION DATA

Cannell, Michael T.
   The limit : life and death on the 1961 Grand Prix circuit / by Michael Cannell.
     p. cm.
   Originally published : New York : Twelve, 2011.
   Includes bibliographical references.
   ISBN 978-1-4104-4624-4 (hardcover) — ISBN 1-4104-4624-7 (hardcover)
   1. Hill, Phil, 1927-2008. 2. Automobile racing drivers—United States—Biography. 3. Grand Prix racing—Biography. 4. Grand Prix racing—History. I. Title.
   GV1032.H55L56 2012
   796.72092—dc23
   [B]   2011045165

Published in 2012 by arrangement with Twelve, an imprint of Grand Central Publishing, Hachette Book Group, Inc.

For Evie and Cricket

CONTENTS

Speed provides the one genuinely
modern pleasure.

— Aldous Huxley

In Morte Vita
(In Death There Is Life)

— the von Trips coat of arms

Phil Hill leads a procession of Ferraris on the notorious banking at Monza, site of the 1961 Italian Grand Prix. "This was a duel in the sun," a correspondent wrote, "and the pace was too hot to last." (Cahier Archive)

PROLOGUE

They began arriving a day in advance. The loyal Ferrari following — the *tifosi* — rolled up in caravans of Fiats and battered motorbikes to camp among the chestnut groves that spread more than six hundred acres around the boomerang-shaped racetrack in Monza, Italy. By the glow of evening campfires they raised cups of grappa to the great drivers, the *piloti* who once thundered around the terrible banked turns of the Autodromo Nazionale looming at the edge of the woods like a concrete cathedral.

Most of those *piloti* were gone now. Between 1957 and 1961 twenty Grand Prix drivers died. Many more suffered terrible injuries. By some estimates, drivers had a 33 percent chance of surviving. In the days before seat belts and roll bars, they were crushed, burned, and beheaded with unnerving regularity. One driver retired after winning the championship only to die three months later in an ordinary car accident near his home.

The survivors raced on, in spite of the ominously long death roll. Inside the *autodromo* half a dozen teams and thirty-two drivers warmed up for the 267-mile Italian Grand Prix, the climactic race of the 1961 season, with the spotlight focused squarely on Ferrari teammates Phil Hill and Count Wolfgang von Trips. The next afternoon, on Sunday, September 10, they would settle their long fight for the Grand Prix title, racing's highest laurel. One last race remained, the U.S. Grand Prix at Watkins Glen, New York, but Monza was expected to decide the back-and-forth battle between the two men.

Von Trips held a four-point edge, and he had earned the advantageous pole position with the fastest practice laps. His easy, agreeable manner gave him the air of an inevitable winner. He had the comportment of a champion. On the other hand, he had crashed twice at Monza over the previous five years. Either could have ended his career — or killed him. He had recovered, but the accidents clung to him like a curse. By comparison, Hill had won at Monza a year earlier, and he had set several lap records. If von Trips was the erratic star,

Hill was his rock-steady complement. Like any great sports story, it was a pairing of opposites.

The two men had traded checkered flags all summer as the Grand Prix made its way through six European countries. Their contest reached manic proportions, just as Borg vs. McEnroe and Ali vs. Frazier would in the following decades. It played large on the front pages of European newspapers. "This was a duel in the sun," the *Times* of London wrote on the eve of the race, "and the pace was too hot to last."

Neither man was Italian, which suited Enzo Ferrari, the reclusive white-haired *padrone* of the Ferrari empire. Every time an Italian driver died the government launched a meddlesome investigation and the Vatican made thunderous condemnations.

The rivalry was made vivid by their polar personalities — the American technician versus the German nobleman, loner versus bon vivant, backstreet hot rodder versus Rhineland count. Each would be the first from his country to earn the title after the war. Each considered himself a nose faster.

The location only heightened the suspense. The Italians called Monza the Death Circuit, in part because the banked turns catapulted errant cars like cannonballs. The sloped surface was coarse and pock-marked, and it exerted a centrifugal pull the fragile Formula 1 cars were not designed to handle. (The British teams had boycotted Monza in 1960 because they judged the banking too perilous.) More dangerous still, the long straights allowed drivers to touch 180 mph, and to slipstream inches apart. A series of tight curves, known as *chicanes,* had been installed to slow the cars, but it was still a track to be driven flat out. As much as any racetrack in the world, it conjured racing's heroics and horrors. To the north, it curved into a silent forest that was haunted by its many victims (or so went the legend).

The sun rose on a perfect cloudless Sunday with pennants snapping in a brisk breeze. The racetrack was bathed in soft September light. The pale outline of the Alps was visible to the north, glimpsed between a pair of Pirelli scoreboard towers. By afternoon the *tifosi* had gathered thirty deep at trackside railings, singing and drinking Chianti. They were jubilant in the promise of seeing the Italian cars humble the British — the hated Brits who had dominated the podiums over the previous few years with a new breed of lightweight, agile cars. Now the Italians were again ascendant, the British in retrograde. The anticipation was exceptional, even by the feverish standards of Grand Prix.

Down below, in the pits, mechanics clenching spanner wrenches and screwdrivers scurried around a fleet of low-slung single-seat cars painted national racing colors — red for Italian teams, green for Great Britain, silver for Germany — with no corporate logos to obscure them. Within a few years media handlers and sponsorship deals would inundate Grand Prix, setting it on its course to becoming the formidable business it is today, but in 1961 racing was more about nationalism than money. Though never stated explicitly, it was animated by dark, hawkish undercurrents. Ancient grudges were avenged with checkered flags. Young men died in the most advanced machinery their countries could devise, as they had in World War II.

The memories of the war, now sixteen years past, were increasingly overtaken by Cold War apprehension. Two weeks before the Monza race, Communist officials had sealed the border between East and West Berlin with concrete and barbed wire.

Almost overnight it became a hair-trigger world fraught with spy planes and satellites, intercontinental H-bombs, and an emergent space race. Phil Hill recognized the sport's ominous undercurrent. He and von Trips were, he said, gladiators in "an age of anxiety." For his part, von Trips knew that the pageantry of a Grand Prix title would provide a unifying lift for his fellow Germans. Countries have a way of creating the hero they need, and von Trips fit the part.

The two men cleared their minds as mechanics rolled their red cars into formation. They lowered themselves into reclined seats made to their specifications, their legs reaching through the fuselage for pedals. Their shoulders pressed tightly against wraparound windscreens and their gloved hands clenched and unclenched small leather-padded steering wheels. Gauges jumped to life as the engines fired. Finely wrought Italian cylinders thrummed in staccato and a hornet shriek of exhaust resounded off the heaving grandstands. Smoke billowed behind them. They were alone now, each in their own world. If they went too slow they'd lose, too fast and they'd die. Within moments they would be engaged in a solitary pursuit of the sweet spot drivers called the limit.

Phil Hill after the 1950 Pebble Beach Cup, the last-to-first dash that converted him from mechanic to driver. (Pebble Beach Company)

1
AN AIR OF TRUTH

Phil Hill hated the dinners most of all. The vile dinners with his parents cursing each other across the long table in their Santa Monica dining room. Shouting, taunting, springing from their chairs and spilling wine. Hill sat in stony silence with his siblings, too shaken to touch the pot roast or fried chicken put in front of them. Even as their parents fought, the children were required to maintain perfect table manners.

It always happened the same way. In the afternoon Hill would hear the faint chime of piano keys, the major and minor chords chasing each other as his mother worked out arrangements for the hymns she composed for publication. At 5 p.m. sharp his father left his job as postmaster general of Santa Monica and drove to the Uplifters Club, a hard-drinking enclave of civic stalwarts and businessmen, where he was known for making extemporaneous political speeches over a series of whiskeys. After more drinks — sometimes a lot more — he headed home in a darkening mood.

Julia, the black cook, climbed the tiled stairs of their home on the edge of Santa Monica to tell Hill and his younger brother Jerry and sister Helen that they would eat with the grown-ups that night. They dreaded it. Their father was a devoted Roosevelt Democrat, their mother an avid Republican. Meals ended in political quarrels enflamed by booze. Later Hill would sleep with his hands covering his ears to muffle the screaming downstairs.

When Hill was fourteen his father came home drunk and hit his mother. Hill pushed between them and hit him back. "It was the first time I ever struck my father," he said. "I had this feeling of power over him, finally. I remember it was a good feeling."

It should have been an ideal childhood. The Hills were pillars of Santa Monica, a thriving community on the edge of Los Angeles with a palm-shaded promenade overlooking a broad beach where children swam and played ball in the California sunshine. They lived in a Spanish-style house on 20th Street with creamy stucco walls, exposed beams, and dark wood floors. Shirley Temple lived next door. It was the picture of California comfort.

The setting was no solace to Hill. He grew up wretchedly disconnected from his domineering parents and painfully unsure how to fit in to his surroundings. He was slightly built and sickly, and he stood aloof from the boys patrolling the neighborhood. When polio broke out in 1936, his mother hired a tutor to homeschool Hill and his siblings for a year. He was further confined by a sinus condition that required a tube inserted in his nose. He was too clumsy to find escape in sports. "I was awful," he said. "When we played baseball I was always the poorest member of the team — the fact that I was cursed each time I came to bat didn't help me play any better." His only contentment was playing the piano. It was not just the music that captivated him, but also the reliable mechanical play of key, hammer, and damper.

His mother was too preoccupied with her own musical pursuits to pay much attention to family. She stayed up late listening to an Edison Victrola and writing hymns, including a popular song called "Jesus Is the Sweetest Name I Know." She also wrote religious tracts refuting the claim that Prohibition had a biblical basis. By her reading of the Bible, God endorsed drinking.

And drink she did. In the mornings she slept it off while a chauffeur delivered Hill and his brother to school. "Jerry and I hated to let the other kids see us," he said. "This was during the Depression, and we felt just awful being taken to school like a couple of royal princes, complete with Buster Brown haircuts."

Hill's father, Philip Toll Hill Sr., was a disciplinarian with the rigid mindset of a lifelong civil servant. He came from a long line of stalwart northeastern burghers and businessmen, all of whom attended Union College in Schenectady, New York. He followed in their path, then became a navy lieutenant in World War I and city editor of the *Schenectady Gazette* before taking a sales job with Mack Truck in Miami, where he married Lela Long, a farm girl from Marion, Ohio, with musical ambitions.

Philip T. Hill Jr., was born on April 20, 1927. Four months later the family fled Miami as a hurricane bore down. Lela had lived through one hurricane, and she refused to face another. The family drove across the country to Los Angeles, where Hill's father briefly worked as foreman of the L.A. Grand Jury, then became postmaster general of Santa Monica.

He was a remote figure who ruled the

household with regimentation. His children addressed him as "sir." He trained his sons to greet women with a bow and a crisp click of the heels. In 1935, he sent eight-year-old Hill to the Hollywood Military Academy. "Be a good little soldier," his father told him. Hill was anything but soldierly. His one interest was the most unmilitary activity available: playing alto horn in the school band.

Hill found his salvation in the family garage. The story of his childhood is bright with automotive impressions — the elegant tangle of wires under the hood of his mother's shiny Marmon Speedster; the Oldsmobile a family friend let him drive around the block, his back supported by pillows and his feet grazing the pedals; the 1928 Packard his parents drove up the coast road to Oxnard for picnics, with Hill egging his father on. "I remember going down one of those hills seeing 80 on the speedometer," he said. "And stuff was blowing out of the car and my mother was screaming bloody murder — and I loved it."

When Hill and some friends were driven home from a birthday party in a green 1933 Chevrolet sedan, he paid each passenger twenty-five cents for the privilege of sitting beside the driver and shifting gears. They laughed at his determination as they held out their tiny palms to collect the coins. "I was born a car nut," he said. "Really a mental case."

It was common for boys to fall for the full-figured cars of that era, but Hill verged on infatuation. Staring out at San Vicente Boulevard, he would challenge neighborhood boys to shout out the make and year of approaching cars faster than he did — '39 Chrysler Royal, '40 Chevy Coupe, '23 Dodge. They rarely beat him. He could spot a hundred models dating back to the 1910s. "It was as if I was trying to divorce myself from the presence of the people around me," he said, "and focus myself only on the cars."

The only adult who encouraged Hill was his aunt, Helen Grasselli, a wealthy Cleveland socialite. After divorcing her husband, a successful chemical manufacturer, she came west and settled in a house down the block from her sister. Helen had no children of her own, so she doted on her niece and nephews, buying them gifts and taking them on vacations in Miami. She favored Phil in particular, in part because she shared his fascination with cars. She let him sit on her lap and handle the oversized wooden steering wheel of her Pierce-Arrow LeBaron

Convertible Town Cabriolet as they cruised empty canyon roads. It was a car of stately luxury with an outdoor seat for chauffeurs and a wood-lined passenger cabin furnished with a lamb's wool rug and a beaverskin lap robe. "Phil was in awe of that car," said George Hearst Jr., grandson of William Randolph Hearst and a classmate of Hill's at the Hollywood Military Academy. "We all were."

Before the development of automatic transmissions and power steering, driving was an act of physical athleticism. Climbing the Sepulveda Pass through the Santa Monica Mountains one day, Helen grew impatient as Louis, the chauffeur, ground through a ponderous series of ill-timed gearshifts. She shoved him aside and took the wheel. When Hill was twelve, he and Helen spotted a black Model T Ford in a used car lot while walking down Figueroa Street in downtown Los Angeles. "It had only 8,000 miles on it and everything was original," he later said, "but they wanted an outlandish price for it — $40." His aunt bought it for him and arranged for its delivery that evening. "I peeled back the curtains and there it was, shuddering back and forth in the street below, with that familiar whine of the planetary box, and unmistakable sound in low and reverse," he said. "The salesman told me, 'Now, you get low by pushing the left-hand pedal down, high by letting it out. The middle pedal is for reverse and the throttle is on the right side of the steering column. Have you got that, boy?' "

Hill's father disapproved, and he ordered his son to stay off public roads. Fortunately for Hill, his friend George Hearst Jr. owned a slightly later version, the Model A. The boys drove the private roads of the Hearst estate in Santa Monica Canyon, and they staged races on a quarter-mile horse track on the property, skidding their way around the dirt oval.

"I learned a hell of a lot about the dynamics of cornering from that old Model T," Hill said. Even then he knew how to pull back from the edge of recklessness. "I was enthralled with cars and power and speed, but I already had a certain saving caution. I did not, for example, 'bicycle' that Model T — in other words, corner it on two wheels, as some characters I knew often did with their cars."

Hill learned how to handle the Ford, and he learned how to fix it. When the connecting rod for the pistons or crankshaft broke, Louis the chauffeur showed him how to replace it. While the neighborhood kids played baseball, he roamed junkyards looking for bargain cylinder blocks and carburetors. He could not stop his parents' drinking and fighting, but he could mend a busted throttle. Just as the children of Narnia slipped an oppressive home by stepping through the wardrobe, Hill found enchantment under the hood. He absorbed himself in the intricate language of carburetor, clutch, camshaft, and cylinder heads. He had found an escape to an ordered and predictable world where every pedal and piston had a clear purpose and responded to his touch.

"I've always expressed myself via the automobile," he said. "I guess I sensed that I was in an insane environment and that my only escape was in something that had structure. Cars gave me a sense of worth. I could do something — drive — no one else my age could do. I could take cars apart, too, and when I put the nuts and bolts back together again and the thing worked, no one could prove me wrong. That kind of technology was fathomable, made sense in a way people never did. Cars are easy to master; they hold no threat; and, if you're careful, they can't hurt you like people can."

Pooling money from his allowance and a

part-time job pumping gas, he bought a succession of cars, including a 1926 Chevy and a 1940 Packard convertible. He acquired them at a time when teenage boys, particularly Californians, expressed disdain for the fake chrome styling of Detroit by turning showroom models into hot rods, "hopping them up" with rebuilt transmissions, lightened flywheels, extra carburetors, superchargers, and half a dozen coats of shining lacquer. It was a subversive creativity, as graffiti and hip-hop would be to later generations. The kid who once breathed through a tube and could barely swing a Louisville Slugger had found his gift. He tested his handiwork on San Fernando Road and the side streets of Santa Monica, which in the 1940s were relatively empty and unpatrolled by police.

Teenagers met at stoplights and squealed away in clouds of smoke, their chrome exhaust pipes amplifying the throaty roar. "There was no problem in finding out whether a driver who pulled up beside me wanted to drag," Hill said. "We had our little signals. If one guy revved his engine in a subtle way, and that was returned, then the drag would be on. My left foot would be trembling on the clutch in anticipation as I waited for the moment when I let it in and took off."

Leadfooters and throttle stompers met at the Piccadilly drive-in on Sepulveda Boulevard or Fosters Freeze malt shop in Inglewood to eye each other's hop-ups and talk to girls. Hill was shy, but handsome in the manner of California hot rodders, with a ripple of dark hair and muscled hands stained with grease. Gas rationing had ended, and Hill and his friends chased each other on coast roads and twisty canyon drives. The wind blew their hair. Girls laughed in the backseat.

On weekends he drove a hundred miles over the mountains to the flat expanse of dry lakebeds near Muroc and El Mirage, where teens and war veterans congregated beyond the reach of police. They rolled into the desert in the evening, their headlights winding through the mesquite and sagebrush, and gathered around bonfires with beer and bedrolls. They started their engines at dawn, before the sun warmed the flats.

The Southern California aircraft industry had produced a generation of young men adept at welding and lathe work. From their garages and backyards came a fleet of lowered and lightened hot rods — fenderless, hoodless, and roofless. They were uncomfortable but fast, skimming the hard-packed sand at 125 mph and kicking up thirty-foot rooster tails of chalky dust.

One by one, or in pairs, they peeled across the desert, reaching speeds as high as 125 mph or so before hitting what they called "the traps." A stopwatch triggered when they crossed a rubber hose and stopped when they hit a second hose a quarter mile away. Timers seated at a makeshift table calculated their speed and shouted it to onlookers standing by in the hot rod uniform of Sinatra-slick pompadours and flapping shirttails.

Hill stacked issues of *Autocar, Motor Sport,* and other British magazines in his bedroom. At night he studied the grainy photographs of his faraway heroes — Juan Manuel Fangio, Luigi Villoresi, Alberto Ascari — leaning into curves on dusty Sicilian hills or rampaging down Adriatic straights. The images were like dispatches from a foreign war, their drama magnified by remoteness.

Hill had never seen specimens of that world up close until a boy named Donny Parkinson started showing up on the lakebeds in a Bugatti or BMW. Parkinson's father was a prominent architect — he designed the Los Angeles Coliseum and City Hall — and a prodigious car collector. Parkinson, who would later marry Hill's sister, invited Hill to borrow from the family's automotive library, and to inspect their considerable stable of foreign cars. Hill passed his hands over the Italian leather seats and German steering wheels without much hope of ever seeing that world first-hand.

In fact, his future was altogether unclear. His friends Richie Ginther and George Hearst were drafted in advance of the Korean War, but the military rejected Hill because of his sinus condition. So he worked for a while on the opposite end of the war, as a nose-gun assembler at the Douglas Aircraft plant in Santa Monica. His father wanted him to attend Union College, but Hill defied him by enrolling at the University of Southern California where he half-heartedly studied business administration, a subject Helen urged because she expected him to someday handle her estate.

He joined Kappa Sigma fraternity, attended sorority parties, played folk songs on a guitar, and cruised fraternity row in Helen's Pierce-Arrow. He did everything expected of a pledge, but his heart was not in it. Try as he might, he could not summon his father's gusto for hobnobbing and back-slapping. Even after moving into the frat house he would slip away a few nights a week to stay in the bedroom he kept at Helen's house. He had long since abandoned his parents' home.

Hill called his college career "a bust." He was a lackluster student and an indifferent frat brother, but he could not come up with an alternative. In the late 1940s California was bursting with opportunities, but he was adrift. "From the time I was a little boy, people would ask me: 'What do you want to be, Phil?' I couldn't tell them," he said. It didn't help that his brother Jerry was the classic California boy — blond, self-assured, athletic, and popular with girls.

Hill listened hard for a calling, but heard only pistons. Car mechanics was the one subject that stirred him, but grease monkey did not seem a plausible occupation. Mechanics were dropouts. It was considered a job of last resort.

Nonetheless, Hill jumped when a job presented itself. In June 1947, after Hill's second year of college, Hearst referred him to a mechanic named Rudy Sumpter who needed help in the pit crew of a midget car owned by Marvin Edwards, a manufacturer of automotive springs. Hill abruptly left school and began working for Sumpter. "My parents were apprehensive," he said, "but they didn't seem to get through to me."

From the college quadrangle to the midget pits: It's hard to imagine a more radical change of scene. The midgets were stumpy little scaled-down cars built strictly for racing and usually sponsored by garages and gas stations. They were high-powered but relatively light, no more than 850 pounds, which made them entertainingly dangerous. Hill had a close-up view as the cars skidded around dirt tracks in a movable scrum, thumping off each other and smacking the fence — all the while kicking dirt into the grandstands and belching cumulus clouds of blue smoke. The drivers sat upright, exposed to flying clumps of hard sod. They pulled into the pits with fractures, burns, busted noses, and cracked teeth.

Midget racing played to beery blue-collar crowds. It was a cross between demolition derby and NASCAR — an ugly distant cousin of the European road racing Hill revered. During the warm-up laps at Gilmore Stadium in West Hollywood, an 18,000-seat arena built specifically for midget racing, a designated bad guy named Dominic "Pee Wee" Distarce ("Mussolini's gift to midget racing") gave fans the finger. A jolly chorus of boos rained down. Vendors hawked beer and peanuts. The air was filled with exhaust plumes and a cinderous odor.

A rousing former pilot named Gib Lilly drove the Edwards midget. He raced twice a week, at the Rose Bowl on Tuesdays and the Orange Show Speedway on Thursdays, consistently finishing near the top. In the grimy midget demimonde, he was a hero. Hill was a junior mechanic, known as a "stooge," but he learned how to keep a car in winning form. He worked in the pits, a half-covered concrete command post stinking of Castrol oil and stocked with spare tires and tools laid out like an operating theater. When Lilly pulled in, Hill went to work — refueling, repairing, banging off worn tires and wrestling on fresh ones. "I was just a mechanic's helper, but I had an identity," he said. "I had a real label which I could hang onto at last."

Not long after Hill began working for Sumpter, Hearst asked him to pick up his new car. Hill drove down Wilshire Boulevard to the dealership and saw Hearst's MG-TC, a small, boxy British two-seat roadster, parked at the curb. The MG was a favorite of GIs stationed in England, and it touched off a sports car fad when they began bringing them home at the end of the war. The MG was flashy and fast — effortlessly reaching 70 mph on empty roads. It looked like a car Cary Grant might drive.

In the 1940s European sports cars were so rare that American owners honked and waved to one another. Hill had seen MGs in magazines, but this was his first intimate look at its round tachometer mounted on a curvy walnut-veneer dashboard, red leather upholstery, swoopy fenders, carpets, and wire wheels. "I could see so much classic beauty in that car," he said.

After inspecting the MG, Hill sold his Ford, borrowed money from his aunt and assorted friends, and bought his own MG for a little more than $2,000 from International Motors, a dealership next to Grauman's Chinese Theater on Sunset Boulevard. It was his first taste of European engineering, a revelation of handling and lively pickup. By comparison "the typical American car of the day was a wallowing pig. The sports car had — how should I put it? — an air of truth about it."

Hill was working at the midget tracks two nights a week, but he now added a day job as a mechanic and salesman at International Motors, which sold MGs, Jaguars, and Mercedes to business leaders and movie stars. Their customers included Humphrey Bogart, Clark Gable, and Gary Cooper. He shared the showroom with Bernard Cahier, the son of a French general and a member of the Resistance who had enrolled at UCLA and married a sorority girl. Cahier's gravelly French accent gave him a big advantage, particularly selling the two MG models, TCs and TDs, that were popular with American women. "You wanna Tissy or a Tiddy?" was his standard opening line.

Compared to the flamboyant Cahier, Hill was an unexceptional salesman, in part because of his unhinged enthusiasm for esoteric mechanical matters. "I'd stop to talk at length about cars and certain drivers and about the advantage of one kind of suspension over another with almost every customer who came in the place," he said.

His jittery, overkeen manner might have vexed the management if Hill had not soon distinguished himself as a driver. In January 1948 he drove his MG in his first real competition, a rally at Palos Verdes, where he finished just behind his boss, an established amateur driver named Louis Van Dyke.

In 1949 a mix of foreign cars — MGs, BMWs, Morris Minors, Simcas, Fiats, and Austins — began racing on a half-mile paved oval called the Carrell Speedway in Gardena. Hill cleaned up. "Attendance was heavy for a while," he said. "People came out for the comical aspect, to see those funny little wire-wheeled cars being stuffed into the fences. I avoided the fences and on a good night I could earn $400 to $500."

California sports car culture was evolving fast and Hill moved with it. He traded his MG for a newer model with rounder lines and a stiffer, sturdier suspension (the same model that James Dean bought a few years later after earning a part in *East of Eden*). He hopped it up with tricks learned in the dirty midget pits: He installed a supercharger and modified the powerplant, lowered the compression ratio and used larger inlet valves. He knew that worn tires got better traction with more air pressure, and he figured out how to adjust the leaf springs to keep pressure on the inside rear wheel. He finished it off with a red-and-black paint job with white stripes along the doors.

"Certain guys had the touch, and Phil was one of them," said John Lamm, a friend of Hill's and a columnist for *Road & Track*. "He knew how to get that something extra out of an engine. It's an instinct."

When there was no official race Hill and his friends organized their own illicit rallies. As the sun set over the Pacific, half a dozen would meet at Saugus, twenty miles north of the San Fernando Valley, and take off down dark canyon roads at one-minute intervals. They considered it safer at night because headlights alerted them to oncoming cars. They called their fifty-mile loop the Cento Miglia in imitation of the Mille Miglia, a thousand-mile road race in Italy. Afterwards they bragged and joked and drank beer at a roadhouse restaurant.

With the MG's windshield folded flat, the breeze whipped over the long hood, ruffling Hill's dark hair and tearing his eyes. He felt as if he shared a nervous system with the car. He knew its moods and how to spur it on by dancing lightly on clutch and brake.

Hill still considered himself a misfit, an incorrigible car wonk, but he was unknowingly in tune with a restless undercurrent. Like many Americans coming of age between the atomic bomb and the Beatles, he turned to acceleration as an antidote to restive estrangement. "I mean, man, whither goest thou?" Jack Kerouac would write in *On the Road* a few years later. "Whither goest thou, America, in thy shiny car in the night?" Like the Kerouac hero Dean Moriarty, Hill was alive to the road without much thought of where it might lead.

Hill began dating a receptionist from International Motors. After work they drove his MG to Hollywood or San Bernardino for the twilight midget races. She sat in the stands eating hot dogs and talking with friends while he repaired midgets down in the pits. "I loved those days," Hill later recalled. "I don't really know why except that it was such a simple life. I was totally devoted to it and totally interested in it."

The midget team was now racing seven nights a week. When a driver broke his leg, Sumpter asked Hill to replace him in a field of forty cars. He spun badly on the first lap of a qualifying race, then settled down as he got the hang of sliding around the dirt oval. The trick was to ride in what drivers called the groove, a line that cuts low on turns and wide on straightaways. He qualified for the finals "even though they told me I looked like a cow walking across an icy pond."

Hill drove well enough to earn a regular spot, though the assignment soured when he performed poorly in a stretch of races, finishing in the back of the pack at Gilmore Stadium and smacking the fence at San Bernardino. Hill blamed his washout on poor mechanics. Sumpter disagreed. Hill quit.

Midget racing was a uniquely American sport taken up by tough young men from blue-collar neighborhoods. The fastest advanced up the ranks to the Indianapolis 500, the pinnacle of American driving. Hill might have followed that path, but he found oval racing a deadening merry-go-round. California had not yet built an extensive network of roads. Its racing was consequently modeled on horse tracks. Cars skidded counterclockwise around the same quarter mile lap after lap, their wheels perpetually swung leftward. European races, by contrast, were run on a car's natural surroundings — long loops of closed-off public roads with a rich variety of rises and dips, twists and hairpins. As sports cars grew in popularity, the divide deepened. Hill's friends from the midget ranks dismissed European sports car drivers as effete "tea baggers." The tea baggers, in turn, mocked the midget drivers as "circle burners."

Hill was more connoisseur than combatant. He far preferred the continental aesthetics of speed — the contours of a tapered car body, a finely calibrated engine working its way up the gears like musical scales, a coupe braking at just the right moment as it swung through a curve shaded by overhanging trees.

From his greasy perch in the repair shop of International Motors, he could imagine no happier future than tuning and repairing European cars. With that ambition in mind, he persuaded Van Dyke to send him abroad to study mechanics with the great British carmakers. In the late fall of 1949 he traveled by freighter from Boston to Southampton, England, and then by train to Leamington Spa, a short drive from the Jaguar plant. Hill was met at the train station by a man with the implausible name of Lofty England, who as team manager would lead Jaguar to five victories at Le Mans.

Hill spent a cold winter in a series of boardinghouses while he performed month-long apprenticeships at Jaguar, SU Carburetors, Rolls-Royce, and MG. It was a harsh change from Santa Monica. In 1949 England was still scraping by on rations. Hill ate mutton and drank lukewarm beer with a coarse-talking crew of Cockney mechanics. "He found himself in this stunningly shabby and war-battered country where seagulls were coughing into the fog and people went about their business looking pale and broken," said Doug Nye, author of more than fifty books on motor racing. "It was as different from California as a place could be."

While training at Rolls-Royce, Hill stayed in a drafty Kew hostelry where guests deposited sixpence into an electric radiator for twenty minutes of heat. On his first night he noticed that one of the two heating coils was disconnected, so he screwed it back on. The next night he found that the landlady had disconnected it again. "Every day was this ritual of reattaching it before bed," he said, "and detaching it in the morning so [the landlady] wouldn't start augmenting my room rent."

His intimate encounters with sports car history made up for the rude accommodations. The monthlong training sessions were like a master class, and they allowed him to bask in greatness. He was photographed behind the wheel of "Old Number One," the first MG ever produced, and he met Goldie Gardner, an elaborately mustachioed old driver who held twenty-two international speed records. In May, toward the end of his stay, Hill rented a room on a farm in Billingshurst, south of London. Spring had come to West Sussex, and the countryside glowed emerald green. The fields carried the rich scent of springtime. That month may have been the only time that Hill enjoyed a peace of the spirit. "During that final month down there, before I headed home, I swore that I would never let myself get tense or nervous again," he said. "The area had an Old World calm that settled into your bones. I'd roam the hills, walking the country, which was really beautiful at that time of year — and nothing seemed important enough to worry over."

Hill broke from his respite long enough to attend the British Grand Prix held on a former World War II bomber base at Silverstone, Northamptonshire. It was a far grander event than he had ever seen, with 100,000 spectators in their Sunday best eating sandwiches in white canvas food tents and drinking pints served from forest-green beer trucks. It was the first race attended by a British monarch. King George VI and Queen Elizabeth shook hands with all twenty-six drivers, then retired to the royal box.

From his grandstand seat Hill could see the paddock, an enclosed area beside the racetrack where drivers, managers, reporters, and mechanics mingled among trailers and refreshment tents. The cigar-shaped single-seat Maseratis, Talbots, and Alfa Romeos rolled to the starting line and barked to life. They rumbled nose-to-tail around the flat 3.6-mile course marked by hay bales, flashing by the grandstand with a thumping vibration that Hill could feel in his sternum. He could not imagine that he would ever drive in such an event.

Seventy laps later the Italian anthem

43

played in honor of the winner, an impassive Italian named Nino Farina who sang as he raced. Like the drivers of the 1930s, he wore no helmet, only leather goggles pulled over a linen aviator's cap. He was among the first to strike a casual posture behind the wheel — arms outstretched at ten and two o'clock, head cocked to the side — that would be widely adopted by Hill's generation. Farina would go on to win the 1950 championship, the first held after the war and the first governed by a new set of specifications for cars and engines known as Formula 1. It was considered the fastest, most advanced class of racing.

Hill returned to the United States in June with a souvenir, a long-hooded black Jaguar XK120 with an open cockpit, red leather upholstery, and rakish windscreen — a gleaming trophy of postwar modernity. The efficient sweep of its lines captured what speed looked like in 1950. Hill made it even faster by drilling holes in the alloy chassis for lightness and replacing the heavy leather upholstery with airplane seats.

During the war Jaguar had been limited to production of military motorbikes and armored sidecars while quietly refining the XK120's engineering on paper. It was unable to produce the car until 1949. In May

1950, the roadster clocked 136 mph on a straight run along a Belgian highway, making it the fastest production car in existence. It was a sensation: Within a year it would be driven by Humphrey Bogart, Ingrid Bergman, Clark Gable, and Lauren Bacall. The MG roadster that had seemed so advanced a year earlier now looked outmoded.

Hill's Jaguar came with a plaque bolted to the dashboard certifying that it was a replica of the record-breaking model. It was packed in the hold when Hill arrived in New York on the *Queen Mary*. He disembarked on a West Side pier, drove over the George Washington Bridge, and motored 2,440 miles to California, stopping en route to see the Indianapolis 500. Before the construction of interstate highways, cross-country drives threaded through small towns. One can only imagine the reaction when the black Jaguar stormed by at 30 miles over the speed limit.

At twenty-three, Hill had no designs on greatness. "The limit of my ambition," he said, "was someday to become mechanic to a great racing driver." That would change soon enough.

On November 5, 1950, five months after returning from England, Hill waited in the fifth row of bulbous sports cars — Allards, MGs, a Frazer Nash — pushed into position at a makeshift starting line beside a horse corral. Earlier he had snuck into the woods to heave a hearty vomit, as he often did before racing. He inhaled deeply and rested his hands on the steering wheel. It was the biggest race of his life.

Hill saw plenty of familiar faces on the starting line. He had chased them in illicit drag races on the back streets of Santa Monica and on the dry lakebeds northeast of Los Angeles. They had converged from all over California — Altadena, Oakland, Beverly Hills — for the Pebble Beach Cup, one of the first open-road sports car races in America. In imitation of European races, the course ran clockwise on winding public roads for a total of 100 miles. The program listed Hill as "a driver to watch."

From the starting line Hill could see down the opening stretch of a tree-lined race course on closed-off roads, much of it gravel, that looped almost two miles around the rugged Monterey Peninsula with sly turns and clumps of spectators standing behind flimsy snow fencing. A cold wind rustled the cypress trees and fog drifted in from Carmel Bay, slicking the road.

Hill faced a dogged pack of Californians

at a distinct disadvantage. Earlier in the day he had broken his clutch by shifting through the gears without letting off the throttle, a hot-rodding trick known as speed shifting. Now, in the day's main event, he would have to make do by timing his gearshifts to the engine revs. Normally he would do so by watching the rev counter on the Jaguar's dashboard, but he was determined to time his shifts by listening to the engine revs so that he could keep his eyes on the road. A slip-up could be disastrous.

When the flag swung down, the cars leapt away in a swirl of dust and blue smoke. All but Hill. His Jaguar stalled. He jabbed the start button. Nothing. In a panic, he waved over the handful of friends who passed as his pit crew. Richie Ginther, a skinny, freckled kid from Hill's Santa Monica neighborhood, and his friend Hearst jogged over and pushed the black Jaguar into motion. The engine bucked to life, catapulting Hill forward.

Hill was last across the starting line by three hundred feet, but he caught up fast, passing two cars on the first lap. "I drove with a thrusting kind of fever," he said. "Winning was essential and I just more or less drove over anyone who got in my way."

The cars flicked by spectators at fifty,

sixty, seventy miles an hour, but for Hill time slowed. He could see every dodge and feint with uncanny clarity. He was in what athletes now call the zone — a lonely state of heightened awareness.

As Hill wove through the pack, the leader, a white Jaguar driven by Hill's friend Bill Breeze, came into view a quarter mile ahead. Hill gained steadily, but he fumbled the timing of his downshifts and repeatedly sent the Jaguar skidding to the shoulders. By lap 9 he was within striking distance of Breeze. He could tell that Breeze's brakes were failing because he was slowing earlier before turns. Two laps later he pushed by him. Breeze dropped out with smoking brake drums.

Halfway through the race, with Hill comfortably in front, Ginther held up a sign saying "Long Lead." He was trying to tell Hill that he could afford to slow down and spare his engine, but the protocol of road racing was so new to Hill that he misunderstood. He thought that somebody named Long was leading.

By now Hill's brakes were also failing. When his speed was too great to negotiate a turn, he slowed himself by tossing his rear wheels around in a sideways slide — a maneuver known as drifting. "The first Jags had notoriously bad brakes," Hill later said, "but I got so that I learned how to run without using the brakes much."

With shrouds of fog closing in and pursuers pressing the pace, Hill downshifted through hairpin turns and ripped down the dirt-packed backstretch. "He was driving the wheels off that car," said Bill Pollack, a friend who had dropped out of the race and watched from the sidelines.

By the final lap the Jaguar was brakeless and mud-covered. Its humped fenders were dented from clobbering protective hay bales along the roadside. Ginther thrust both hands in the air as Hill crossed the finish line to take first place. Minutes later he cradled a trophy, surrounded by grinning locals.

It was an auspicious performance. Word of Hill's last-to-first scamper spread among racing circles as far as New York. "That was my breakthrough race," he said. "With everything going wrong, I still won. It was there that people began to take notice." All his expectations now shifted. The son of abusive alcoholics, a childhood misfit and college dropout, he felt the stirring of possibility. He would devote himself to working his way back to Europe, this time as a driver.

His greatest obstacle would be his state of

mind. In the following months he seized up with anxiety before each race and grasped at any advantage he could find. It was not unusual for him to stay up all night refining his car, tweaking and tightening until minutes before the flag dropped. After each win, or near win, he slid into depression. He attributed his success to the mechanical edge he had fixed for himself, not his driving skill.

Hill had earned a reputation as a sensitive type prone to hand-wringing, but he was also capable of a cold detachment in the face of death. When his mother lay gravely ill in the winter of 1951 she asked him to be baptized. It was her dying wish. He refused.

A few days after she died in March, Hill, then twenty-four, stood over the casket studying her countenance. His only emotion was irritation at her makeup. "Those aren't my mother's lips," he told the undertaker. "That is not the way they were." Then, in precise detail, he described how his mother had made herself up so the undertaker could repaint her face. Hill's father died three weeks later, on Hill's twenty-fifth birthday, days after suffering a heart attack during a medical checkup conducted in preparation for a cruise with the naval reserves.

The deaths brought Hill more relief than grief. He had long since severed his emotional ties to his parents, if he ever had any. With his parents gone, he blithely used his inheritance to buy a Ferrari. It must have given him wry pleasure to plow the dividend of his unhappy family life into exquisite machinery. He was unaware that the car would draw him into another dysfunctional family struggle.

Enzo Ferrari in front of his Maranello factory: "I don't care if the door gaps are straight. When the driver steps on the gas I want him to shit his pants." (Getty Images)

2
A Song of Twelve Cylinders

Hill bought his Ferrari from Luigi Chinetti, an importer who acted as Enzo Ferrari's ambassador and talent scout in America. After the Pebble Beach race, Chinetti took notice of Hill's ability, however callow. In the following years he would become something of a godfather to Hill, as he was to other promising American drivers. "I look for the fighter," Chinetti said.

A moody man with a pronounced forehead, thick eyebrows, and an impenetrable Italian accent, Chinetti had a reputation as a tough long-distance driver, twice winning the 24-hour race at Le Mans before World War II. (He won in 1932 after plugging a leaky fuel tank with chewing gum.)

He came to the Indianapolis 500 as a Maserati manager and mechanic in May 1940, just weeks before Paris fell to Germany and Italy declared war on Britain and France. Chinetti was an ardent anti-Fascist and he chose to stay in New York as an enemy alien and work as a mechanic for a Jaguar dealership.

Chinetti returned to Europe in 1946 as a U.S. citizen, flying with his wife and four-year-old son on one of the early transatlantic flights to Paris. He drove from Paris down to Modena, Italy, home of Enzo Ferrari, in a borrowed front-wheel-drive Citroën with tires so worn that a friend sat on the hood for traction as they crossed the snowy Alps.

At 11 p.m. on Christmas Eve, Chinetti pulled up in front of 11 Viale Trento e Trieste, a two-story stone building with a pair of Shell gas tanks stationed out front like sentries. This was the old factory where Enzo Ferrari had started out. He still lived there, in a modest apartment above the workshop.

Chinetti was by now accustomed to the prosperity of New York. He was shocked when he stepped into Ferrari's first-floor office. Seated in a worn leather chair under a bare light bulb, Ferrari, then forty-eight, looked haggard and heavy-lidded. The war had aged him and laid waste to his operations. The workshop that once bustled with craftsmen sat silent. With fuel scarce, the hissing fire was the only source of heat. "The place seemed like a musty tomb reopened to a crack of light after centuries of isolation," Brock Yates wrote in his biography of Ferrari.

The two men had raced together on the Alfa Romeo team fifteen years earlier. They talked as old friends surrounded by dusty trophies and black-framed photos of drivers, many of them victims of crashes or combat.

Ferrari had built a small factory in the nearby town of Maranello, where he fabricated machine tools and other munitions for the German and Italian armies. An American bombing raid in November 1944 put an end to production. He spent three months digging out. The Allies pounded him again in February 1945.

All around him was death and destruction. A year earlier Mussolini had been shot and hung by his ankles from the roof of a Milan gas station. On the same day Ugo Gobbato, an Alfa Romeo director and an advocate of Fascist-style efficiency, was shot dead as he left the Alfa factory. Advancing and retreating armies had blown up bridges, hampering even the simplest travel. Fighting between Fascists and the Resistance ravaged the countryside. Villagers settled old scores with seizures and executions.

Ferrari's personal life was no better. He

had fathered a son out of wedlock with a fair-haired girl who worked in his factory during the war. The baby arrived as Ferrari's thirteen-year-old son, his only child with his wife, Laura, fell ill with muscular dystrophy.

Before the war Ferrari had directed Alfa Romeo's almost unbeatable racing team. By 1946 he was in the early stages of building sports cars under his own name, but in his weary condition he told Chinetti that he could not imagine much demand for them anytime soon. He might concentrate instead on making machine tools.

Chinetti responded that as a tool fabricator Ferrari would amount to no more than a cog in northern Italy's industrial machinery, but as a carmaker he could be triumphant. Chinetti promised that he could find plenty of buyers in America, an acquisitive country that had emerged from the war with half the world's wealth. Within a few years it would own 60 percent of the world's cars. In the early hours of Christmas morning Chinetti made Ferrari a promise: If you make them, he said, I will sell them.

Three months later Ferrari, dressed in his customary dark suit, white shirt, and tie, seated himself behind the wheel of a Tipo 125, the first car to bear the Ferrari name. It was still unfinished. Bodywork was missing and wires dangled from the dashboard. But it was complete enough for a test drive. With mechanics and engineers standing by in coats and overalls, Ferrari nosed across the cobblestone forecourt of the Maranello factory and out onto the Abetone Road for a ten-mile shakedown.

Six weeks later two Ferraris debuted at a street race in Piacenza, seventy miles from Maranello. Ferrari did not attend. He stayed home and waited for a report by phone, as he would throughout his life. Neither car finished, but Ferrari declared it "a promising failure." The Italian press was not convinced. One newspaper called the cars "small, red and ugly."

Ugly or not, they had a mighty asset beneath the hood: a lovingly assembled V12 engine with two banks of six cylinders. Ferrari called it "an ambitious dream" to build the complex twelve-cylinder engine, though it was hardly a first. Packard had built them as early as 1916. (Ferrari claimed to have fallen in love with "the song of the twelve cylinders" when he heard U.S. Army officers driving Packards across Italy during World War I.)

It may not have been new, but the V12 nonetheless made a statement: Ferraris would be built on power. The engine came first. Everything else was secondary. Winning, Ferrari believed, was 80 percent engine strength. "I build an engine," he told *Der Spiegel* years later, "and attach wheels to it."

To build the first V12 Ferrari had recruited Gioacchino Colombo, his former assistant, who was on leave from Alfa Romeo while a trade union committee investigated his role in the Fascist Party. During Ferragosto, a mid-August feast day, Colombo slipped away from his sister's dinner table. Seated under a tree in her garden, he sketched a V12 engine with pistons shorter than the diameter of the cylinder bore, allowing the engine unusually high revs. It would have the quickened heartbeat of an adrenalized animal. Ferrari built three cars with Colombo's engine in 1947, and nine more in 1948. Meanwhile, Chinetti opened a Ferrari dealership on the Avenue d'léna in Paris, and he elevated the new Ferrari brand by easily winning a 12-hour race in Paris in a 166 Spyder, an open two-seater with a grille like a gaping beetle. All unnecessary hardware had been removed. The result was a rounded red aluminum torpedo. The Italian press nicknamed it the *barchetta,* or "little boat."

The Paris race was the first long-distance

victory for a Ferrari outside Italy and a boost to its growing reputation. After the race Chinetti shipped the car to America and sold it to Briggs Cunningham, the son of a Cincinnati financier. Cunningham in turn drove it to a second-place finish at Watkins Glen, in upstate New York, which helped introduce the Ferrari name to America.

Le Mans, known simply as the 24 Hours, was one of the few European races that Americans noted. Chinetti won it for the third time in 1949 — its first running after the war — in a Ferrari *barchetta.* It is a race of withering duration, lasting from 4 p.m. Saturday to 4 p.m. Sunday. Normally a pair of drivers trade shifts at the wheel. Peter Mitchell-Thomson, the second Baron Selsdon, Chinetti's co-driver, was ill (reportedly with a hangover), so at the advanced age of forty-seven, Chinetti drove for all but thirty minutes of the 24-hour race, a demonstration of grit that added to his stature when he met customers in Manhattan.

Ferrari could not have hoped for a more masterful point man. Chinetti romanced the brand as an electrifying alternative to Jaguars, Lincoln Continentals, and Cadillacs. With racecar handling and a speedometer that swung thrillingly up to 180 mph, it was not a car for ferrying the family to country clubs. Ferraris contained almost no luggage room. They were concerned only with horsepower. "I don't care if the door gaps are straight," Ferrari reportedly said. "When the driver steps on the gas I want him to shit his pants." Chinetti's customers, affluent young lawyers and account executives, could imagine how that rumbling horsepower might affect a girlfriend.

Max Hoffman, an Austrian-born dealer, sold Porsches from a Park Avenue showroom with a circular ramp designed by Frank Lloyd Wright. Chinetti took the opposite tack. His customers had to venture to the far West Side of Manhattan, in those days still a gritty industrial backwater. His first two locations, on West 55th Street and West 19th Street, hardly even qualified as showrooms. They were more like ordinary garages identified only by a discreet decal of a prancing horse. The setting was a powerfully understated sales pitch: Ferrari was only about the car, and the car was only about speed.

With the manner of an imperious maître d', Chinetti acted as if he were doing customers a favor by allowing them in for a look. "He used his position as purveyor of new Ferraris much as ancient popes once granted indulgences for rich noblemen," Mike Covello wrote in a catalog of Ferrari models. If a prospective customer seemed worthy, Chinetti granted a test drive. If they handled the car reasonably well he might consent to an actual sale. Even then it could take as much as a year for the car to arrive from Italy. Sometimes it never came. The Ferrari factory kept scant inventory, and customer service was not a priority. Most carmakers raced in order to sell. Ferrari sold only to pay for the racing.

The Carrera Panamericana was a 1,933-mile survival test. Drivers raced the length of Mexico in the fastest sports cars made, dodging armadillos and burros along the way. (The Collier Collection)

3

THIS RACE WILL KILL US ALL

Chinetti sold Hill a *barchetta* painted blue, the French racing color, for $6,000, or about half what he would have charged other customers. He slashed the price because it benefited Ferrari to get cars into the hands of young racing talent like Hill, and because the car had a history. Earlier that year a French driver named Jean Larivière had failed to make a 90-degree turn at Le Mans and landed in a garden. The car took a beating and a strand of fence wire neatly sliced Larivière's head off. Hill found a hole in the floor drilled to drain Larivière's blood. Damaged goods or not, the car came to Hill with the graceful Ferrari fender lines and a small badge with the company's logo, the black stallion rearing against a yellow background.

All the cars Hill had driven made variations on the same sound: a mild *blat-blat-blat,* the rhythmic hum of a lamb. The

Ferrari had the vocal cords of a lion. With its short stroke and twelve cylinders it roared out a commanding song as it came up through the gears. "It sounded like a factory," said Tim Considine, an automotive historian. "At 8,000 rpm it is just the sweetest sound. It's smooth, but a big sound. Like an orchestra, like thunder."

The *barchetta* had some foibles, including a side-to-side roll, which made it hard to steer. Hill corrected that, and he reworked the shock absorbers. "The 12-inch finned aluminum brakes were fantastically good though, and showed no signs of fade, so I knew I could really punish them . . . if I had to," he said. "No car I had driven had pleased me as much in this regard."

Hill now drove with extravagant horsepower under his toe. "With Ferrari you not have to worry," Chinetti told him. "You get in. You drive. You win." He was right. Three months after buying the *barchetta* Hill finished first at Torrey Pines, a makeshift racetrack on a 2.7-mile loop of blacktop service road on a disused army base north of San Diego. Spectators could hear him coming like a wall of sound, a high-pitched whine amplifying to a full-throated scream as he hove into view. They glimpsed him in the leather cockpit as he passed at 112 mph, his head cocked to one side as he down-shifted into turns.

Hill belonged to Chinetti's coast-to-coast network of drivers, mechanics, patrons, and friends. At regional racetracks in places like Elkhart Lake, Wisconsin, and Madera, California, he drove cars provided by wealthy backers, or by Chinetti himself. In return, he helped place the Ferrari name before prospective buyers. In one town after another he appeared in local newspapers cradling a trophy and wearing windbreakers, biking shoes, and polo shirts dark with sweat. His face was slack with exhaustion, his hair tousled. In every case he had just sustained terrible road poundings with lungfuls of fumes and pebbles bouncing off his goggles. The camera caught him depleted and half-smiling, as if winning provided only the tiniest respite.

In 1952, a year after they met, Chinetti invited Hill to drive a Ferrari in his first international race, a weeklong odyssey that jounced 1,933 miles over the jagged spine of Mexico. The racing calendar was sprinkled with long-distance sports car events, known as "endurance races," lasting twelve hours or more. The Carrera Panamericana was the longest by far, unfolding in nine legs over five days. The course

65

stretched all the way from the Guatemala border to Texas. The drivers took off each morning at one-minute intervals with the shortest cumulative time determining the winner. The fastest cars in the world tore through backcountry where some locals had never before seen a car. Mexican newspapers called it "the race of death."

The Carrera was started in 1950 to mark the completion of the Mexican portion of the Pan-American Highway (nicknamed "Langley Turnpike" by CIA operatives), which extends from the southern tip of South America to Prudhoe Bay, Alaska. Mexican officials hoped the race would persuade American business leaders and tourists that Mexico was no longer a backwater of burros and shanties. Captain Eddie Rickenbacker, the World War I flying ace, donated a trophy.

The inaugural race was mostly an amateur escapade. The Carrera's 132 entries included Mexican taxi drivers and a British actress named Jacqueline Evans who had married a Mexican bullfighter. A bra manufacturer sponsored Mrs. H. R. Lammons of Jacksonville, Texas; illustrations of their products festooned the side of her Buick.

In following years some of the big European carmakers — Lancia, Mercedes, Ferrari — signed up. The Carrera lacked the prestige of endurance races like Le Mans or the Mille Miglia, but it offered carmakers a chance to prove their durability on the world's roughest road and promote themselves to the insatiable American market.

The Carrera started as a showdown between American and European car brands, or marques, both of which advanced rapidly in the postwar years but rarely faced each other. The strapping Chryslers and Studebakers were expected to muscle their way to the fore, but they maneuvered sluggishly on the mountain roads while the lighter European sports cars scurried through the climbs and turns as adroitly as cutting horses. Before the 1952 Carrera, the Americans lobbied for, and received, a split between the two-seat sports cars sent from Europe and the big production sedans from Detroit. They would share the same dusty roads, but the box score would no longer compare them. The race was a face-off no longer, but it was still an important proving ground.

In November 1952, Hill flew south with Arnold Stubbs, a fellow Californian who would act as navigator and help with repairs. They stayed a few days in Mexico City, practicing on a twisty canyon road just outside the city. "One day we were chasing this idiot Pontiac station wagon that was all arms and elbows," Hill said. "It was sliding all around the road." The two idiots, it turned out, were Alberto Ascari and Luigi Villoresi, two of Europe's most revered drivers.

A few days later Hill and Stubbs arrived at the starting point, the mud-street jungle town of Tuxtla Gutiérrez, where mariachi bands played and banners flew in the central square. Mongrels barked. Peasants stared silently as the foreigners outfitted gleaming cars as if for war. They tore out backseats to make room for auxiliary fuel tanks and spare tires. Shock absorbers were upgraded and earsplitting horns wired up. Drivers taped headlights to protect them from flying rocks.

"This race will kill us all," the Ferrari driver Giovanni Bracco had said after the 1951 Carrera. "The Italians will not race in Mexico again." He was wrong. Hill found the Ferrari crew encamped in a rented garage on the edge of town. Inside sat half a dozen long-hooded cars as red as nail polish with their hoods agape. Drivers and mechanics conferred in clusters, like surgeons in an operating room. Bracco was there, despite his reservations. He had prepared by driving all 1,933 miles in advance, stashing Pirelli tires along the way and marking bumps, blind turns, and other hazards in a cryptic code of yellow circles and arrows painted on the road surface.

Chinetti had arranged for Hill to drive a well-worn black-and-silver Ferrari coupe owned by Allen Guiberson, a Texan who had amassed a fortune manufacturing oil-field equipment. Hill was a private entrant — a "privateer," as they were called — but it was in Ferrari's interest to assist him, since Hill's results would reflect on the company's reputation. So team managers welcomed Hill into the garage, and they would supply him with parts, lodging, and other help as the Carrera made its way north over the next five days.

Hill felt scarcely qualified to join Ferrari, which had three of the world's top road racers — the formidable Italian trio of Bracco, Ascari, and Villoresi — driving a new model, the 340 Mexico Berlinetta, shipped from Genoa. The Berlinettas looked devilishly fast, and they were: They went from 0 to 60 in under six seconds, topping out at 174 mph. The mighty V12 engine sat in a light-weight chassis skinned with sleek and sinister bodywork.

The Ferraris faced a Mercedes team that had resumed racing that year with the experimental 300 SL coupe, a low-slung silver roadster nicknamed the Gullwing because its doors hinged upwards like wings. It gleamed with the impeccable metallic beauty of German engineering. (In a case of inspired casting, Grace Kelly drove a Gullwing in the 1956 film *High Society*.) The Mercedes factories in Stuttgart had suffered severe bombing during the war and had yet to resume full production. Drawing on existing parts, the engineers created a car with exceptional acceleration and low aerodynamic drag. Earlier in the year the Gullwing had won at Le Mans and placed second in the tortuous Mille Miglia, the 1,000-mile race over narrow Italian roads.

Mercedes prepared for Mexico with Teutonic thoroughness. A team of two dozen drivers and specialized mechanics arrived weeks in advance armed with rainfall charts, road temperature gauges, and three diesel trucks that distributed mountains of spare tires along the route. (Oddly enough, the Mercedes drivers included John Fitch, a former Nazi prisoner of war and one of the first American pilots to down a Messerschmitt.) Impressive as it might be, the German show of force left Hill flat. He preferred the Italian artistry of Ferrari, even if it looked outmatched.

Hill's unheralded arrival in Tuxtla Gutiér-rez marked his debut in international competition, an advancement earned with thousands of gut-thumping miles on ovals and back roads. He would now face his gravest test yet. A poor showing would demote him to provincial races, possibly forever. Worse, it would confirm Hill's gnawing self-doubt. He feared that he wasn't good enough to race at this level and would end up trapped in a life like his father's, a 1950s organization man with a suburban home and loveless marriage.

So Hill stepped up to the big leagues scared of failure, and equally afraid of persevering. Cars had once been an escape from an unhappy household and a path to self-esteem. Now, for the first time, he confronted a frightening reality: Sports cars were lovely, but cruel. On the eve of his international debut he suffered the first onset of a debilitating anxiety. "It came home to me that I was in a sport in which people were getting killed," he said. His apprehension was heightened by internal conflict: The closer he moved to elite competition, the more he anguished over whether he could qualify as a legitimate career racer. The more he won, the more unworthy he felt.

His anguish expressed itself as a debilitating sinus condition, muscle spasms, heart palpitations, and an ulcerous inability to digest solid food. In the company of daredevils he was reduced to eating jars of baby food. "Most of this stemmed from my basic uncertainty about life," he said. "I just didn't feel that I belonged down there in Mexico racing against all these professionals. My system rebelled, and I recall almost blacking out a couple of times before the race was over."

At 6:30 a.m. on the morning of November 19, the cars lined up single file at the edge of town and took off into a foggy dawn at one-minute intervals. Hill bent over for his customary pre-race vomit, then took off at his appointed time. A movable city of support staff followed in cars and planes.

The Carrera Panamericana was modeled after the Mille Miglia and other town-to-town road races held in Europe, but it was more like a survival test. Cars splashed through rivers and flew off humps on half-paved roads. It was a murderous marathon plagued by washouts and brake failure. Tires cooked on the baking concrete and popped like firecrackers. Between deathly heat and diarrhea, some drivers lost fifteen pounds over the course of the race.

On the first day the pack drove north to the mountains. Hill and Stubbs struggled to see through the dust and dead bugs caked on the windshield. When Stubbs spotted an upcoming bend he would shout a warning and Hill would downshift three or four gears. It was so noisy that they often resorted to hand signals.

Some stretches of road were no more than unevenly paved cart tracks connected by narrow bridges with planks set down for tires. It was not uncommon for drivers moving at 120 mph to spy an armadillo crossing the road, followed by a thump and crunch as it went under the wheels. Farm animals were a bigger problem. "How do you factor in a burro in the middle of the road in a corner just over the brow of a hill?" Hill wondered.

Hill was accustomed to short circular racetracks, where, over the course of several laps, drivers gradually figure out the advantageous line into curves and where best to brake. By comparison, each Mexican mile brought a lurid surprise. Shortly after the start, Ascari, the world champion, crested a hill and found a left-hand turn where he had expected to go right. He rolled his Ferrari coupe at 90 mph and skidded a hundred yards on its roof, thereby eliminating Ferrari's biggest threat to Mercedes.

"We saw Ascari's mechanic rushing toward us down the highway waving excitedly," Hill said. "The road disappeared into a sharp cut and as we slowed going through we saw this battered Ferrari rolled on its side, with Ascari standing calmly beside it. This shook our confidence, but then we saw two of the Mercedes undergoing tire changes by the edge of the highway, and this really cheered us up."

One hundred and ninety miles into the race, a blistering hot stretch winding through sand dunes, a vulture angling for a freshly flattened armadillo smashed through the windshield of a Gullwing driven by Karl Kling, who had started as a reception clerk at the Mercedes office in the 1930s. The vulture knocked Kling's navigator, a former Luftwaffe pilot named Hans Klenk, unconscious (he was not wearing a helmet) and showered the car with bloody chunks of bird flesh and broken glass. Klenk awoke within minutes and urged Kling to keep driving. The next morning all three Mercedes appeared at the starting line with protective vertical bars soldered over the windshields and megaphones to help the navigators shout warnings to the drivers.

Seventeen of the ninety-two starters failed

to finish the first leg. A Lancia rolled and ignited after its tire blew. Two Mexican drivers were hospitalized after steering their Oldsmobile off a mountainside. Philip Gow of Fond du Lac, Wisconsin, fell out the side of his Lincoln while trying to extinguish an electrical fire.

Hill fared slightly better. Mexico's southernmost roads were made with crushed volcanic rock that wore on tires. Hill cut a hole in the front fenders so that he and Stubbs could check the wear as they drove, but it was hard to see the lacerations at 120 mph. After 330 miles, he crossed the first day's finish line in the Indian town of Oaxaca in ninth place. His tires were worn to bare canvas.

At beery evening gatherings the drivers shared gallows humor in a chatter of French, English, Italian, and German. As a matter of survival they shared information about upcoming hazards and arcane mechanical issues, such as high-altitude carburetion. "They were a band of brothers," said Doug Nye. "They all knew that tonight could be their last. There was a good chance the next bed they slept in would be a hospital bed, or a sleep for eternity."

Armed guards watched the cars at night. The locals had a taste for violent mischief perpetrated more out of boredom than animosity, as Hill learned the next day in the hamlet of Acatlán. A handful of *policía* stood on the outskirts of town enthusiastically waving the cars down a narrow main street shaded by four-story buildings. It was a trick. A waiting crowd of men wearing straw cowboy hats and women in long braids laughed and clapped as the drivers abruptly entered a rectangular plaza and frantically tried to make a series of 90-degree turns. Hill skidded on the wet clay and clouted the central fountain. He and Stubbs stepped out into the blasting midday heat and squandered ten minutes hauling the car off the plaza and replacing the left front wheel. They limped through the afternoon with the front end out of alignment.

Jean Behra, a stocky former motorcycle champion driving a French-made Gordini, led the race on the second day as the course climbed 7,000 feet in the Sierra Nevada. This was the wildest stretch of the race, with steep climbs and roller-coaster curves marked only by white-painted stones strewn along the shoulder. There were no guardrails. Drivers flew around corners and skated to the edge of the roughened asphalt with nothing between them and sheer dropoffs. In some places rock faces fell away a thousand feet on both shoulders.

Thirty miles from the town of Puebla the road plunged into a gorge and made a series of switchback turns. Hill saw tire marks running straight off the road just before a bridge. Behra, still leading, had overshot the turn and vaulted over the edge at 120 mph. He would have plunged into a boulder-strewn river had his car not lodged between two rocks after a tumble of about thirty feet. The spare tires piled in the backseat may have saved his life by acting as a roll bar. He staggered from the car with a severe concussion and seven broken ribs.

After a half-hour stop in Puebla, the surviving drivers flew along a road lined with old eucalyptus trees and passed over the Río Frío Pass, the highest point in the race. On the far side they descended 10,000 feet through a series of switchbacks into Mexico City where 500,000 waving, singing peasants filled the streets for the anniversary of the 1910 Revolution, the Mexican equivalent of the Fourth of July. The crowd surged and seethed even after news that their countryman, Santos Letona Díaz, had died after driving his Jaguar XK120 into a bridge parapet. Nor did they heed the urgings of soldiers standing by with fixed bayonets.

The throng parted reluctantly as the cars inched forward, escorted by motorcycle police. Young men ran alongside drumming on the hoods. Hill spent the night pounding dents out of the car body and fixing its leaking radiator.

The pace quickened with the mountains behind them. Over the next four days the drivers crossed broad parched plains as they pushed on to León, Durango, Parral, and Chihuahua. Hill had by now found the right tire pressure and fuel load, and he managed to stay just behind the lead pack where Ferraris and Mercedes fought. On the second to last day it looked as if he might move up a notch by overtaking Jack Mc-Afee of Manhattan Beach, California, who was slowing as he struggled to see through a cracked windshield. Just as Hill caught up, McAfee's windshield shattered. His sight restored, McAfee pulled away.

Meanwhile Kling, in a Mercedes Gull-wing, went all out to catch Bracco, who led the race in a Ferrari. The final run was treacherous with sand blowing across the road, but Kling managed to erase an eight-minute deficit with a blistering desert sprint to win the Carrera. A crowd of Mexicans and Americans watched him nose ahead at a finish line set up at the Ciudad Juárez airport, across the Rio Grande from El Paso.

Mercedes had toppled the indomitable Ferrari team with obsessive planning and the renewed muscle of German engineering. Over the five-day race Kling averaged more than 100 mph. "We were so fast on some of the stages that even in a chartered DC-3 our director of motorsport, Alfred Neubauer, couldn't keep up," Kling said after the race.

Neubauer stood at the finish line in a suit and trench coat, smoking cigarettes and bear hugging his drivers. The Carrera was Mercedes' first win in the Western Hemisphere and an important step for a company fighting its way back to the top after the devastation of war.

With his suspension nearly gone, Hill thudded his way to a sixth-place finish, earning $581. It was a striking rookie showing, particularly for a driver too unnerved to eat solid foods. His Ferrari was pockmarked from flying stones. Patches of paint were sandblasted off, leaving bare metal shining through. Bits of animal stuck out from the radiator grille. Hill stepped from the car, wind-beaten and dust-covered. Snowflakes had fallen on the high desert earlier that morning. A handful of drivers drank whiskey with Mexican blankets draped over their shoulders. They posed for pictures with a woman bullfighter. Strangers pounded them on the back. Photographers pressed in for portraits.

Hill had reason to smile as he shivered in the desert chill. For promising young drivers, a show of toughness counted as much as a win. Hill had proven his resilience with a gutty five-day run over some of the worst roads in the world. "If ever there was a racing event in which I felt I had countless times been close to wiping myself out, it was the Carrera," he said.

He had shown that he was capable of exceptional mettle. If he could conquer his nerves, or at least control them, he might drive his way into the foreign circles that had enchanted him from childhood — and that he had glimpsed firsthand in Mexico.

When the 1953 season got under way a few months later, Hill went back to campaigning in regional circuits — Carrell Gardens and Pebble Beach in California, Sebring in Florida, the Phoenix Raceway in Arizona. He still saw himself as a misfit, and his tour did nothing to dissuade him. Americans viewed sports car drivers as suspect athletes engaged in a bastard sport, like surfers or bull riders. He celebrated his wins with lukewarm beers sipped by motel swimming pools, or with nothing at all. His disparaged standing seemed to corroborate his father's view that racing was a waste of time, a dropout's last resort. So, as much as anything, Hill raced for credibility. If he could go fast enough, he thought, he might earn respect.

It was a revelation to see the comparative stature of European drivers when Hill served as an alternate for an American team at Le Mans, the storied 24-hour race held 113 miles southwest of Paris. The drivers came from Europe's most prominent families. They attended galas and cocktail parties thrown in their honor and lounged in hotel bars pealing with the sound of laughing women. Strangers bowed to them on the streets.

At Le Mans the drivers operated in teams of two, switching off in 2.5-hour shifts. Hill co-drove a little Italian-made Osca *barchetta* with Fred Wacker, a veteran of the American sports car circuit. They led their class after eight hours, but withdrew when their axle broke. The crew blamed Hill, saying he had ignored their orders to avoid first gear. "That might be and I remember feeling guilty about it," he later said, "but I was at a time in my career when getting me to go slow was a difficult thing to do."

During a particularly misty dawn, Tom Cole, an American driver sharing a 340 MM Ferrari with Luigi Chinetti, overturned and was killed at a tricky curve known as Maison Blanche. As much as anything Hill had seen, Cole's death made vivid the perils he would face. "I began to brood over the whole business," he said. "Cole's death intensified my feelings in this regard, and while I could appreciate the new attitude I had found in Europe it did not cancel out the extreme tension and anxiety which was building up within me."

He would find nothing to reassure him in the following weeks. Bill Spear, a thirty-six-year-old driver from Connecticut, had invited Hill to co-drive a Ferrari with him in a 12-hour race in Reims, France. They picked the car up in Italy and drove over the Alps with Spear and his mechanic, a Frenchman named Maurice, leading the way in a Bentley. Hill followed in the Ferrari.

The sun rose before 4 a.m. as they crested one of the highest Alpine passes and coasted down the far side. On the long descent Spear somehow lost control and the Bentley slid off the road and rolled down an escarpment. "It looked like a toy tumbling in front of me," Hill said. He parked the

Ferrari and clambered down the mountain-side to find Spear and his mechanic pinned in wreckage. "Maurice had blood coming out of his ears and nose and he was moaning," Hill said. "I couldn't handle it. I went around to Spear and told him I'd be back with help. I went back up the road and talked to myself the whole way to prevent myself from flying off the road. I was so frantic about what to do."

Within five miles Hill came to a village of stone cottages called La Grave, appropriately enough. It was now 4:30 a.m. He banged on random doors until he found a doctor who loaded a stretcher into the back of his Renault. They managed to remove Maurice from the wreck, but he died during the hour drive to Grenoble. Later that day Maurice's wife arrived from Paris and demanded to know if anybody had prayed for her husband or administered last rites.

Spear survived, but he was unfit to race in Reims. Hill entered the 12-hour race with Chinetti instead. The brakes were erratic and the windscreen was puny. Chinetti's helmet blew off on the second lap and they found themselves squinting into the wind at 150 mph. They lasted four hours.

Whatever his reservations, Hill returned to Mexico later that year for the 1953 Carrera Panamericana, again driving a Ferrari provided by Allan Guiberson. Richie Ginther, who had recently been discharged from his duties as an army helicopter mechanic, joined him as navigator.

Hill and Ginther flew to Mexico City and drove south to Tuxtla Gutiérrez. As they traveled the race route in reverse they notated blind turns and other danger spots in a logbook. Meanwhile, Jean Behra, the French driver who had crashed into a gorge a year earlier, was supposed to be making his own scouting trip. Instead he spent his team's reconnaissance money at one of Mexico City's best brothels, an establishment favored by high-ranking politicians.

Debauches were common among the sport's European stars, but it was not Hill's style. He and Ginther had started as mechanics. They were clean-cut American gear heads, not carousers. In the heat of Tuxtla Gutiérrez they focused only on preparations — pumping the right fuel for the altitude, loading spare tires, welding a broken shock absorber.

They rose at 4 a.m. on the morning of the start, after an hour's sleep, to adjust the gas level in the carburetor and make final refinements. In the darkness they drove the Ferrari to the starting line, a mile from town, where Hill made a last-minute check under the hood and noticed that their battery was unfastened. The bolts had jarred loose on the drive south. Ginther ran the full mile back into town to look for a battery box and returned empty-handed. Now in a panic, Hill sent Ginther on a second run to town while he tried to strap the battery down with fencing scavenged from a cow pasture. When that failed he found a parked car and tore out the needed parts with seconds to spare before the 6 a.m. start. "Richie comes staggering in all out of breath from his run into town," Hill said. "I drag him into the cockpit just as the flag falls."

They were off, sliding around corners and kicking up a thirty-foot tail of dust. Within minutes they had caught up to the front pack. Hill blasted by them in a single surge.

Now he was in the lead, running through patches of fog, with Ginther looking out for abrupt turns. "He'd yell 'LEFT!' or 'RIGHT!' at the last second and I'd get all over the brakes and scramble down three or four gears and we'd just by the grace of God make it around the turn."

They held their position until popping two tires. While they replaced them and pounded out a damaged fender, a twenty-five-year-old Italian driver with soft, handsome features named Umberto Maglioli blew by in a powerful new 4.5-liter Ferrari. They overtook him in turn when bumps dislodged Maglioli's radiator hose. In his rearview mirror Hill could see that Maglioli had painted the name of Quintus Fabius Maximus, a Roman general known for wearing down enemies, on the upper portion of his windshield.

The bloodshed began less than two hours after the start when a Ferrari driven by Antonio Stagnoli blew a tire at 165 mph and flew 180 feet off the side of the road. The car landed hard, flipped, and burst into flames. The navigator, Giuseppe Scotuzzi, was thrown from the car and died instantly. Stagnoli was taken to an Oaxaca hospital for burn treatment. He died the next morning. Nine more drivers would die before the race ended.

The death toll at the 1953 Carrera was not confined to the drivers. An hour after Stagnoli crashed, a Ford rolled off the road and landed in a riverbank without injury to its drivers. Spectators gathered for a look, spilling onto the road. Another Ford swerved to avoid a little girl and ran into a roadside banking, where it killed six spectators.

Hill had by now driven roughly 3,000 miles in Mexico over the course of two years without serious mishap, but his luck would run out the next day when he crested a hill on the mountainous leg to Mexico City and began a mean downhill turn to the right. Sliding to the edge, he realized that he did not have enough brake power to stay on the road. "I was mentally considering how far down we'd fall because at our speed we were sure as hell going over," he said. "Some drops are sheer, down hundreds of feet, and you don't stand a prayer — and we didn't know about this one."

Hill and Ginther spun perpendicular to the road and slid off the edge backwards, bouncing end-over-end for a hundred feet before coming to a hard stop against a tree with the roof caved in. Hill's first thought was of how Stagnoli had burned to death in his car the previous day. After checking that Ginther was safe, he got out fast — so fast that he cut his shoulder on a sheath of torn metal. The two men scrambled up onto the road, where they found that a group of locals had removed the turn sign so approaching cars would have no warning. The culprits were standing in a hidden spot where they could watch the cars go over the edge. As Hill confronted them a Cadillac flew off the road and came to a stop near the same tree.

"We knew how deadly this spot was, so Richie and I shook off the guards who were trying to drag us into a first aid tent and went up on the road to flag down the approaching cars," Hill said. "I had my bright red coveralls on and they could see us clearly; we'd wave as the guys came in, and we must have saved at least a dozen from going over the edge." The crowd booed and hissed and shook their fists, but Hill and Ginther stayed on the shoulder for seventeen hours. When the last car had passed they hitched a ride to Mexico City.

The next day Felice Bonetto, a fearless Italian driver nicknamed Il Pirata (the Pirate), told the press that he would "be driving until I die." He was leading the race an hour later when he failed to slow for a deep drainage ditch traversing the road in the farming town of Silao. The front wheels of his Lancia hit the ditch at full speed, flinging his car sideways into a lamppost. When Bonetto's friend Piero Taruffi stopped to help he found that the impact had broken Bonetto's neck. He was the third Italian killed in the first three days of the race.

Taruffi knew that he had to drive on, but it took him twenty minutes to compose himself and leave his friend's body in the wreck. A short time later Bonetto was removed to a hospital where a wooden cross was placed in his hands and local women gathered to pray for the stranger who had died 6,000 miles from home.

Hill was long gone by the time Juan Manuel Fangio of Argentina won the Carrera in a Lancia D24. After their crash Hill and Ginther went to Acapulco where Guiberson had docked a yacht converted from a tugboat. They swam in the harbor and fished for sailfish. There were girls about. But even in that tropical setting Hill could not let go. The crash could easily have killed them. And there were nothing but curves in his future.

One late afternoon Hill sat on deck with a beer and watched a parade of rats trying to come aboard. One by one the rats crawled along the slip lines, only to fall in the water when they encountered a metal cone guard. But that didn't stop them; they swam back to the dock and tried again. That night in his bunk Hill dreamed the rats were attacking him.

At twenty-six, Hill was on the brink of leaving the regional races behind. The faith placed in him by Chinetti and Guiberson had paid off as he racked up solid showings in races near the top of his sport. Success now depended more on his state of mind than his skills: The more he mixed with established racers like Alberto Ascari and Juan Manuel Fangio, the clearer it became that he lacked their coolness toward mishap and death. His hands and feet were willing, but his head faltered.

At home in Santa Monica for the off-season he tried to soothe his nerves by listening to Chopin and Rachmaninoff. In January he packed his goggles and gloves for the first event of the 1954 season, a 1,000-kilometer race in a Buenos Aires *autódromo* built by Juan Perón. A bad clutch forced him to leave his Ferrari by the roadside after thirteen laps. He rode to the pits on the back of a policeman's motor scooter. As they neared the grandstand they saw an Aston Martin DB3 driven by Eric Forrest-Greene, a fifty-year-old Argentine raised in England who now sold Bentleys and Rolls-Royces in Buenos Aires. They could see Forrest-Greene heading into a spin as he exited the *autódromo* and continued onto a highway used as an extension of the track. It was not a grave mishap — drivers spun out all the time. But Forrest-Greene's car hit a curb and rolled, landing upside down in a ditch. Hill slapped the policeman's side, urging him to speed up so they could pull Forrest-Greene from the car. Frustrated with the policeman's pace, he jumped off and ran the last fifteen yards.

"As I got towards the car, there was this tremendous 'Whump!' and it just exploded," Hill later said. "There was burning fuel everywhere, including in the ditch. And somehow Forrest-Greene got himself out of the cockpit, crawled out of the ditch, climbed the bank, and emerged on the road, staggering towards me. He was burning from head to foot."

A series of photographs, published two weeks later in *Life* magazine, showed Forrest-Greene lurching forward for help, his clothes wrapped in flames, while a handful of bystanders backed away. Moments later two policemen came forward to smother the flames with a blanket and a uniform coat. Forrest-Greene was rushed to a hospital, where he died the next day. "It was hopeless of course," Hill said. "I've never forgotten it. There is just nothing like fire."

The specter of Forrest-Greene stayed with Hill. Two months after leaving Buenos Aires he was leading a twelve-hour race in Sebring, Florida, but dropped out with a faulty differential. Beforehand he had suf-

91

fered from heart flutters and stomach spasms. Once again he could not eat solid foods. He wanted to keep racing but his psyche rebelled. Back in Santa Monica Hill consulted a family doctor who diagnosed an ulcer. If Hill did not remove himself from the stress of racing, the doctor said, he could hemorrhage. At the moment that he was poised to start winning on the big stage, Hill had finally lost control of his nerves.

At the 1955 running of Le Mans, Pierre Levegh's Mercedes spun into the grandstand, killing eighty-three spectators. For Phil Hill, it was a barbarous introduction to the European circuit. (Getty Images)

4
THE ROAD TO MODENA

In the spring of 1954 Hill heeded his doctor's warning and quit racing. For the first time in five years he was spared the gnawing pressure of competition. With both parents dead he lived in his aunt Helen's house and worked as a part-time mechanic at Brentwood Motors, a foreign car dealership in Santa Monica.

His temperament was not suited to idleness. After tuning and restoring the family piano he gravitated to a more demanding project. Inside Helen's garage sat her blue 1931 Pierce-Arrow convertible, the lustrous object of childhood admiration. Its aura had hardly dimmed, though it sat in disrepair. Hill and his brother Jerry had talked about reconditioning it for years.

Hill could not do anything about his unhappy childhood, but he could restore this bright remnant. As spring turned to summer he redirected his obsessive, tightly coiled energy from racing to automotive forensics. Day after day for ten full months he stood in the garage and diagramed each coil and spring's place in the intricate greasy puzzle and taped his notes on the rafters. He labeled the parts, hundreds of them, and stored them in neatly stacked boxes. He bought a similar model to cannibalize for parts, and with help from specialists he rewired and restored the wood-lined cabin and restitched its leather seats. After months of cleaning, sanding, and rechroming, layers of blue lacquer went on and a detailer applied white piping.

The restoration was the toil of a fastidious mind, a labor few drivers would consider. It must have cheered Hill. He felt sufficiently recovered from his ulcer, in any case, to race a boxy British Triumph TR-2 at Torrey Pines over Fourth of July weekend, winning his class but staying clear of the main event. A few weeks later he went to work on the set of *The Racers,* a Kirk Douglas movie based on a novel about a bus driver who enters the Grand Prix. Darryl Zanuck made it as a vehicle for his mistress, Bella Darvi, who later dumped him, racked up prodigious gambling debts at Cannes and Monte Carlo, and killed herself by sticking her head in an oven.

European racing was still relatively unknown to Americans. To show its full spectacle, Zanuck shot a wealth of widescreen CinemaScope footage during the 1954 season, including aerial views captured from an airplane trailing Juan Manuel Fangio, Alberto Ascari, and other standouts as they raced through the streets of Monaco and the Rhineland hills. Zanuck built exact replicas of the pits on the back lot at Twentieth Century Fox.

The world Hill abandoned had returned to him through the odd prism of Hollywood. His job was to maintain the three Maseratis and two Ferraris imported for the shoots, and to show Douglas and other actors how to drive them in and out of the mock pits without stalling or stripping the gears.

He also did stunt driving for the film. On a canyon road north of San Diego he and Dave Sykes, an old racing friend, were driving side by side behind a camera car when they locked wheels and spun off the road. Neither driver was hurt, but for Hill it was like a Stanislavski exercise, as if he were acting out his worst fear for the camera. (The crash footage was not used because it didn't fit the script.)

In the fall of 1954, with the Pierce-Arrow restored and *The Racers* wrapped, Hill suffered what he called "the strain of inactivity." He was twenty-six, and for the first time in his life he had nowhere to go. In October, after six idle months, he received an envelope postmarked Dallas. It contained a photo of a white Ferrari 375 MM with a shark tailfin and pronounced air vents added to the feline bodywork. Stapled to the photo was a note from Allen Guiberson: "Guaranteed not to cause ulcers." In fact, Hill's ulcer had improved. Becalmed and unsure what to do with himself, he accepted Guiberson's invitation. "So despite my qualms and X-rays," he said, "Guiberson's temptation tipped me back over the edge."

Years later Hill would say that he had no choice. Racing was irresistible because he excelled at it. He could not turn away from it any more than Picasso could lay down his brush. "It was so dangerous back then," he said, "you'd have had to be crazy to do it unless it was something you had to do."

His retirement ended at March Field, a military airport in Riverside, California, converted for racing, where Hill placed second in a crowd of Ferraris, Jaguars, and Allards. Encouraged to find his skills intact, he agreed to drive Guiberson's Ferrari in the Carrera Panamericana in December 1954, in what would be the last staging of the race. This time he stood a better chance of a top finish. For one thing, he would not have to compete with Mercedes. The company skipped the Carrera because the Gullwing's sequel was not ready.

His main competition would be Maglioli, the rare Italian driver who was both determined and disciplined. "He is not wild," a friend said. "He does not eat much; he drinks less than he eats. He is not crazy over women. The head rules him. For a young Italian that is odd. For an Italian race driver it is nearly impossible."

Maglioli would drive the fastest car in Mexico, a new Ferrari 375 Plus with a 4.9-liter engine. It was a full 20 mph faster than Guiberson's three-year-old car. With elevated speeds, the race would be even more dangerous than in previous years. "A car which goes off the road," Maglioli said, "goes to death."

The Carrera was the usual clash of car cultures. Maglioli and the other Europeans lined up alongside oddball entrants like Akton Miller, a Californian who had assembled a rattletrap roadster, nicknamed El Caballo de Hierro (Iron Horse), from a hodgepodge of parts. El Caballo had earned a folksy following among Mexican locals, who enjoyed seeing a homegrown car go up against contenders like Porfiro Rubirosa, a well-tanned dandy who wore a scarf, polo sweater, and kid gloves behind the wheel of his privately owned Ferrari. When the Mexican press mischievously invited him to pose for a photo in El Caballo, Rubirosa sniffed and waved them off. "Rubirosa wouldn't even sit in El Caballo," Miller said, "let alone have his picture taken."

Ten miles into the first leg, Miller saw Rubirosa's Ferrari pulled to the shoulder with a steaming radiator. As he shot past, he repaid Rubirosa's hauteur by flipping him the finger.

Within an hour another Ferrari fell out of the race. Jack McAfee steered into a tricky right-hand turn at 120 mph and slid sideways off the road, tumbled off a thirty-foot embankment, and rolled twice in the sagebrush. He suffered no more than a few bruises, but his navigator and close friend, Ford Robinson, broke his neck and died instantly. "No blood," a Mexican bystander told a reporter. "A clean break of the neck." McAfee swore he would never race again, but of course he did.

Meanwhile, Hill, again joined by Ginther, thundered to the lead in the mountainous first leg from Tuxtla Gutiérrez to Oaxaca with an average speed of 94 mph — a record for the stage — with Maglioli riding his tail the whole way.

By 10:40 the next morning a crowd had gathered in the hamlet of Atlixco to watch the first cars come in. The central square buzzed with anticipation: Would Hill or Maglioli appear first? A loudspeaker crackled to life: *Carro a la vista, señores* (car in sight, gentlemen). Moments later the whine of a Ferrari revved to 7,000 rpm echoed off the adobe walls. Maglioli's red car flashed down the main street, pirouetted through two 90-degree turns in the central square, and vanished in a swirl of dust. Three minutes later Hill appeared, his tailfin covered in soot. For reasons Hill could not understand, the crowd threw rocks at him as he slowed for the turns and sped off.

Maglioli won the 252-mile run to Puebla by more than four minutes that morning, but Hill gained it back in the afternoon by driving like a madman down the short, down-plunging run to Mexico City. Hill knew his cumulative 45-second lead would not hold up when they left the mountains. Maglioli's newer Ferrari would outmuscle him on the featureless straights where forty miles could pass without a turn. Hill's only hope was to stay close and hope for mishap.

Sure enough, Maglioli ended the duel by

gunning his Ferrari to 160 mph through the wide-open desert. He gained more than a three-minute advantage on the run to León, leaving Hill to follow his taillights in the fog. Maglioli padded his lead on the next day's leg to Durango where the drivers stopped for a party on the set of a western called *Robber's Roost.* Maglioli led by ten minutes after booming his way to Parral and Chihuahua over the next two days. Hill stood securely in second place, but his three-year-old Ferrari was running rough. "I'll settle for second place," he said in the high-walled enclosure where Ferrari bivouacked on the eve of the finish.

The Juárez desert glowed with campfires that night. Hundreds camped out and five thousand more parked along the race's final mile the next morning. The *policía* guarded the road, shooing cattle and spectators to the shoulder. A dozen private planes flew over the desert looking for the finishers. By 11:40 a.m. a tiny dust cloud gathered on the southern horizon. The two cars appeared as distant specks, followed by a loudening howl. Maglioli took the checkered flag at 134 mph, three seconds ahead of Hill. Both finishes were concealed in clouds of dust.

"Road racers are like roulette players,"

Maglioli told the press a few minutes later. "We who race know that it is dangerous, but once we get the fever, we are satisfied with nothing else."

Hill lost the 1954 Carrera by twenty-four cumulative minutes, but winning three of nine legs and pressing Maglioli in an outdated Ferrari counted as a win of sorts. The Mexican press called him El Batallador, the battler.

Hill headed north with a sense of resolution and relief. For years he had agonized over what career to pursue — mechanic, driver, or something more conventional? "I was finally able to come to terms with myself and admit that racing was the profession I wanted to follow," he said. It was a turning point. Now the question was how far could he go, and would he survive long enough to get there?

Ambitious young drivers hoping to advance up the amateur ranks had one thing working in their favor: attrition by death. The racing squads run by European carmakers, known as works teams, needed a supply of fresh blood to replace the drivers who burned to death, snapped their necks, or catapulted into trees. All of which happened with alarming frequency in the days before

103

seat belts, fireproof coveralls, and other safety concessions.

Drivers talked about many things while they drank burgundy in cafés or waited in airport lounges — where to eat, practical jokes played on teammates, and, of course, the long-legged girls who followed them from race to race. They rarely talked about death. Whether they discussed it or not, they were acutely aware that roughly half of them would die in the coming seasons. The odds were grimmer than those their older brothers had faced in the war.

The death rate was so high that the great Italian driver Alberto Ascari distanced himself from his two children so that they would not miss him when he died. "I don't want them to get too fond of me," he said. "One of these days I may not come back and they will suffer less if I have kept them a bit at arm's length." His only defense against death was the set of superstitions he faithfully followed.

Ascari was a self-possessed Milanese with ample cheeks and hazel-blue eyes who came to the racetrack each morning in a coat and tie, as if preparing for a day of desk work. He first sat behind the wheel at age five, on the lap of his father, Antonio Ascari, who led the Alfa Romeo team when Enzo Ferrari broke into racing in the 1920s. Like his father, Alberto became a national hero, twice winning the Grand Prix championship for Ferrari. Italians followed his career the way Americans followed Joe DiMaggio. They affectionately called him Ciccio, or Chubby.

The evening before the 1955 Monaco Grand Prix, Ascari watched a movie with Fangio and a few other drivers. Afterwards they walked a part of the circuit that zigzagged down the hilly principality overlooking the Mediterranean. When they came to a swerve leading onto the long harborfront straight, somebody said, "Whoever falters here, goes into the water." Ascari touched wood. The next afternoon Ascari clipped a curb at that very spot, brushed an iron mooring bitt, and plunged into the harbor with a geyser of spray. Rescue divers stationed nearby dove in after him. After twenty agonizing seconds Ascari bobbed to the surface ringed by oily bubbles. When he found that he had come up without his pale blue helmet he sent a diver back down to retrieve it. The helmet was his good luck charm. He never raced without it. He was taken to the hospital with lacerations to the head, but he was otherwise unhurt.

Four days later Ascari turned up at the

track in Monza, where his friend and pro-
tégé Eugenio Castellotti had completed
twenty-five test laps in a new Ferrari sports
car they were to share in a 1,000-kilometer
race. Most of what Castellotti knew about
racing he had learned from Ascari. "Be
calm," Ascari had told him on practice runs.
"Slip into the car like you were going for a
normal drive, instead of at 120 mph. Put
your wheels where I put mine." Ascari
became not just a tutor, but a loved men-
tor. Castellotti bought the same string-
backed driving gloves as Ascari, the same
blue polo shirt, the same goggles.

Ascari had not planned on driving that
day in Monza, but when Castellotti took a
break he impulsively decided to take a few
laps before going home for lunch with his
wife. "You have to get straight back into the
saddle after an accident," he told a friend,
"otherwise doubt sets in."

He slipped behind the wheel in his street
clothes and peeled out of the pits with his
tie flapping over his shoulder. The chinstrap
of his lucky blue helmet was being repaired,
so Ascari uncharacteristically borrowed
Castellotti's white helmet. After a warm-up
lap he waved, as if to confirm that he was
okay. He slid his hands around on the
wheel, gripping and ungripping as he always

did. On the third lap Castellotti could hear Ascari change gears out of sight on the far side of the track, then the engine fell silent. Castellotti ran across and found the car upside down in a patch of bushes. Ascari had been thrown from the cockpit and landed on a stretch of grass. He was gasping faintly when Castellotti reached him. Blood trickled from a nostril. "His eyes seemed to stare at me with their usual kindness," Castellotti said. "I knelt down next to him as if to help him, but by then my best friend had left me."

Castellotti was inconsolable. "When I close my eyes," he later said, "I can hear Alberto giving me advice."

The exact cause of the crash was never determined. Two days later a horse-drawn wagon carried his black coffin through the somber streets of Milan with his blue helmet resting on top. He was buried next to his father, who had died in a similar crash while leading the French Grand Prix at Montlhéry, outside Paris, thirty years earlier. They were the same age almost to the day.

While Ascari was laid to rest at the end of May 1955, Hill and Ginther were headed to Genoa on a freighter with Allen Guiberson's Ferrari 750 Monza in the hold for a series of races in France, Italy, and Germany. They were nearing Gibraltar when the captain told them in broken English that a famous driver had died. He had heard a bulletin on the ship's radio, but missed the name. Hill and Ginther stood on deck, the freighter rolling and lifting beneath them, trying to guess whom the driver might be.

The next day they received a shipboard wire from Chinetti: Get off at Barcelona and go directly to Modena. Ginther slept on the all-night train up the coast of Spain and France while Hill looked out the window at the passing towns. At dawn they pulled into Modena where a rosy morning light shone on the ancient stone campanile and a piazza cluttered with market stalls. Modena was a provincial center one hundred miles southeast of Milan known for balsamic vinegar and a sweet, fizzy wine called Lambrusco. Most crucially to Hill, it was the engine capital of northern Italy — home to Ferrari, Maserati, and a supporting cast of parts manufacturers, transmission shops, body fabricators, car journalists, assorted flunkies, and a healthy population of whores.

Hill dropped his bags at a hotel and went directly to the Ferrari factory, a tidy fortress nine miles up the road in the village of Maranello. A guard opened the gate and Hill walked through an archway beneath the Ferrari name spelled out in its distinctive early modern lettering to wait bleary-eyed in a dingy cubicle. The door opened and there was Enzo Ferrari, age fifty-seven, standing over Hill in a dark suit and tie, his receding silver hair swept back and his rheumy hooded eyes hidden behind thick sunglasses. Ascari was dead, he explained, and he needed an understudy.

Ferrari led Hill to the factory floor where mechanics were readying the Ferrari 121 LM that Ascari was to have driven at Le Mans. It had a long sinuous body suggesting coiled energy, like a cat waiting to pounce. Ferrari created it to counter the experimental Mercedes 300 SLR, which had rolled out of the Stuttgart factory earlier in the year with an early version of fuel injection and magnesium alloy bodywork. Ferrari asked Hill what he thought of it. Beautiful, Hill said.

"Then how would you like to drive it at Le Mans," Ferrari said, "with your great antagonist from Mexico, Umberto Maglioli?"

The 24 Hours of Le Mans were among the most prestigious in the world of racing, and crucial to carmakers' fortunes. The entrants were modified showroom models or prototypes that would soon be put into commercial production. The event acted as a measure of their relative durability and the marques' progress in developing new engine and brake technologies. Everyone wanted to know if the British, Germans, or Italians were winning the engineering race, and Le Mans gauged their relative standing. To put it another way, Le Mans was an arduous form of consumer testing. The eight-mile loop on closed country roads was an agony of acceleration and braking repeated over the length of a full day.

Among other things, Le Mans was an extreme driving test wrapped in a Gallic carnival. Every June, 300,000 revelers arrived in caravans of dented Deux Chevaux and Peugeots packed with *poulet,* baguettes, and wine. They came for the spectacle, and for the ghoulish prospect of witnessing a crash. They were rarely disappointed.

The racing fans, *les fans de courses à voiture,* rode the Ferris wheel, cheered professional wrestlers, packed into all-night dance halls, and whistled at girls in the burlesque tent. On Sunday, mass was held every few hours in an outdoor chapel. The cars whizzed by hour after hour as French carnival music blared. The drivers could tell when dawn was near by the smell of bacon.

"I hate Le Mans," said Stirling Moss, the golden boy of British racing who had recently joined the Mercedes team. "It's not a race but a circus."

It was a circus, to be sure, and more dangerous than ever with the bigger, more powerful Mercedes, Ferraris, and Jaguars sharing the roads with swarms of puny MGs and Gordinis. Alfred Neubauer, the Mercedes team manager, complained to French officials that the road was too narrow, particularly around the pits where drivers slowed and veered before they pulled in. The new Mercedes SLR, which could reach 185 mph, would jostle wheel to wheel with little MGs on a track no wider than a two-lane road. "Just imagine, a driver realizes a fraction of a second too late that he's been told to slow down," Neubauer said. "He tends to brake suddenly. On a narrow track like this it could have disastrous consequences." We have been organizing the race since 1923, sniffed French officials. Nothing like that has ever happened.

During practice, Pierre Bouillin, a twenty-year veteran who raced under the name Pierre Levegh, coasted into the pits in his Mercedes after a close brush with a little 2-liter Gordini. "We have to get some sort of signal system working," Levegh said.

"Our cars go too fast."

Levegh was a short, solemn man. Friends called him "the bishop" behind his back. He was hell-bent on winning Le Mans as a matter of national pride, for *la gloire*. Still downtrodden from the war, France clamored for a hero to stand up against the foreigners — particularly the Germans. Levegh was consumed by a dark, bullheaded determination that it would be him.

Levegh did not compete at Le Mans until 1951 when, at the advanced age of forty-five, he finished fourth in a Talbot Lago, a car made in the suburbs of Paris. Talbot offered Levegh a team car for the next Le Mans, but he felt that mechanical failure had prevented him from winning in 1951. So he turned them down and spent an enormous sum — nearly three times the first-place prize money — preparing his own Talbot.

At first it looked as if his plan might work. He stayed with the lead pack into the night hours of the 1952 race. By 3 a.m. many of the top contenders had broken down. Levegh took the lead. The two drivers who shared a car normally switched places every two and a half hours, but Levegh was so obsessed with winning, and winning alone, that he waved off his co-driver every time he pulled in for refueling. By dawn he hardly knew whom he was talking to. He looked ashen and his head teetered with sleeplessness and road fatigue. He sucked on an orange and refused to relinquish the wheel.

With every stop he appeared more dazed, but the tingling possibility of winning sustained him. By dawn he suffered stomach cramps and struggled to focus his eyes. His lap times were slowing, but he nursed a three-lap lead on the more powerful Mercedes. The public address announcer's voice cracked with emotion. Spectators streamed over from the dance halls and shooting booths. Could this one man hold back the hated Germans single-handedly?

With an hour and a half to go, exhaustion caught up to him. He fumbled a gearshift, causing the crankshaft to whirl and blow the engine. His car clanked to a halt. Two Mercedes passed him to claim the top two finishes, a result so repulsive to French spectators that race officials chose not to play the German anthem for fear it would incite a riot. The French press blamed Levegh for the German win, accusing him of vanity and foolishness.

Levegh was inconsolable. He had trouble breathing after he was pulled from the car.

He vomited and gagged for an hour, then wept in his wife's arms. If his car had lasted another hour or so he would have become a French folk hero and the only man to win Le Mans alone. It was bad enough to lose, but to lose to the Germans, occupiers of France, was more than he could bear.

For its part, Mercedes was in the delicate position of trying to win, and win with overwhelming force, without raising the specter of German machinery crushing its neighbors. If nothing else, the company wanted to engender goodwill so it could sell plenty of cars in France. Neubauer saw a public relations opportunity in Levegh's defeat. After the race he told Levegh that he would hold a place for him at Le Mans if he wanted to join them.

By the time Hill arrived in Le Mans three years later, Levegh had agreed to race a Mercedes. In doing so he had placed himself in the middle of what the press called "World War II on the track," a confrontation between the British and Germans on ground once occupied by German soldiers. The Luftwaffe had used Le Mans as an airstrip, and two miles away the Nazis set up an internment camp for captured members of the French Resistance. Many of Levegh's countrymen disapproved of his alliance with the German company, but Levegh knew that it offered the best chance of winning. The new Mercedes 300 SLR was so advanced it bordered on science fiction: It had a space-frame chassis and hydraulic flip-up air brakes, similar to those used in airplanes, designed to take pressure off the disc brakes. With an engine capable of 185 mph, the drivers would need all the brakes they could get as they slowed at sharp corners, most crucially the hairpin turn at the end of the long Mulsanne Straight.

At age forty-nine, Levegh knew that this was likely his last chance for redemption. He was a somber presence at the otherwise lighthearted meals the Mercedes team shared at their hotel. "He was torn between his fear and his ambition," said Artur Keser, the company's public relations director.

A few minutes after 3 p.m. on a hot and windless afternoon, gendarmes began herding people from the start area. One of the unique aspects of Le Mans was that it began with a short footrace. In keeping with this custom, sixty cars were lined up at a 60-degree angle to the track, their hoods pointed to the runway. The drivers waited directly across the road beside a flimsy white fence where a crush of spectators stood thirty deep.

As the starting clock ticked down to 4 p.m. all chatting and rustling hushed. For a moment it was so quiet the drivers could hear birds singing. The grandstand crowd stood on their chairs for a better view. The Italian count Aymo Maggi, one of racing's elder statesmen, stepped from a cluster of race officials and swung the French tricolor. The drivers sprinted across the road, jumped into their cockpits, and hit the start buttons. Fangio was among the last to pull away, having caught his pant leg on the gearshift. Eugenio Castellotti shot to a quick lead in a big 4.4-liter Ferrari, followed by a Jaguar D-Type driven by Mike Hawthorn, a British driver with whitish-blond hair and the generous cheeks of a well-fed English schoolboy. The French called him Papillon because he always wore a bow tie in the car. In third place was Maglioli in the Ferrari he would share with Hill.

The pack whipped under a pedestrian bridge shaped like a Dunlop tire and into the sharp Tertre Rouge turn, flooded down a four-mile tree-lined straightaway to the 300-degree Mulsanne turn, and on around past a swerve called Maison Blanche before the long straight back to the grandstands.

Castellotti was clocked at 181 mph, but

he fell off the pace after the first hour, leaving Hawthorn to fight it out with Fangio, the five-time world champion driving a Mercedes. In his memoir Hawthorn admitted that he was "momentarily mesmerized by the legend of the Mercedes superiority. . . . Then I came to my senses and thought, 'Damn it, why should a German car beat a British car?' "

Hawthorn and Fangio passed and repassed each other a dozen times, setting lap records ten times in the first two hours. They drove side by side much of the time, stealing looks at each other. Fangio drove in a relaxed posture, as he always did. Hawthorn slouched forward with his mouth agape, as if urging his car on. The public address announcer shrieked *les voilà!* — here they come! — as the pair passed in streaks of silver and green. "At this stage I was driving flat out all the way and had absolutely nothing in reserve," Hawthorn later wrote.

Hill watched from the half-covered Ferrari pits, one of more than a dozen lined up directly across from the grandstand. The Ferrari 121 was the most powerful machine he had ever driven. "I was pumped," he said, "ready to take on just about anything." Beside him the team manager barked orders and the mechanics carefully arranged their gear — wrench sets, cases of oil, air canisters, and jackstands — in preparation for their own long struggle. As drivers began pulling in at the end of the first two-and-a-half-hour shift, the pit crews jacked up cars, knocked off hub nuts, yanked away worn tires, and shoved gas nozzles into empty tanks. The incoming drivers shared a few words with their substitutes. *Don't let her overheat. Watch for the oil spill just beyond the hairpin.* Then the car was gone with a shattering bellow.

By 6:20 p.m., with the early summer sun still high, Hill was preparing to spell Maglioli, then in fifth place. He was standing on a counter behind the pits with his helmet and goggles under his arm when a mechanic tugged on his pant leg and pointed across the track. Somebody in the grandstand was trying to get his attention. It was Tom McGeachen, a neighbor from Santa Monica. He was holding a 16mm movie camera and waving. The track was so narrow that the two could shout across to each other in the lulls between passing cars.

As they talked Mike Hawthorn neared the pits in his long-nosed Jaguar. With its rounded flanks and single tailfin, it looked like a sea creature moving at 160 mph. He had gone twenty-eight laps in less than 120 minutes. His pit crew signaled him to pull in for refueling. They may have been late holding the sign up, or perhaps Hawthorn was slow to respond. Either way, he abruptly braked his Jaguar and swerved to the right toward the pits. In doing so he cut off Lance Macklin, a British driver in an Austin-Healey who was running four laps behind Hawthorn. In his split-second desperation to avoid hitting Hawthorn, Macklin jammed on the brakes and swung left into the path of Levegh, who was coming up behind at 150 mph — too fast to steer clear. Levegh's Mercedes hit the rear of Macklin's Austin-Healey and bounded end-over-end for eighty-five yards. It flew over spectators, its white underbelly flashing overhead, and landed on a dirt barrier. The Mercedes bounced and rammed hard against a concrete stanchion, spraying its parts into the tightly packed grandstand. "The crushing sound of its landing is unforgettable," said J. D. R. McDonnell, a reporter sitting at the start line.

The hood spun loose and sliced through the crowd like a giant scythe, decapitating a row of spectators. The engine, suspension, and brakes followed in a hundred parts. A fireball of burning gasoline sprayed through the scene. Entire families died in a second. A woman awoke from unconsciousness to find herself lying under a pile of bodies. Fifty yards from the grandstand a girl screamed when a severed foot hit her.

Meanwhile, Macklin's Austin-Healey spun along the pit wall to the right and rebounded across the track, where it came to rest on the embankment. Macklin was barely hurt, and he ran back across the road to the pits.

There was a moment of silence, followed by police whistles and the insistent two-note siren of French ambulances. Black smoke hung over the scene. Body parts and pieces of cars lay scattered. Many of the uninjured spectators surged forward for a closer look, pushing through the recoiling throng. The loudspeaker called for doctors and blood donors. Priests in long black robes administered last rites to the gravely wounded. They pulled back sheets covering the dead and whispered prayers as they made the sign of the cross. Neubauer stepped out from the pits and waved cars through the smoke and debris. Through it all the French carnival music droned in the background.

"The scene on other side of the road was indescribable," recalled Duncan Hamilton, a British driver. "The dead and dying were everywhere; the cries of pain, anguish, and despair screamed catastrophe. I stood as if in a dream, too horrified to even think."

Eighty-three people died and more than a hundred were seriously injured. Hill's friend Tom McGeachen was not hurt, though blood splattered his camera case. The hulk of Levegh's car was crumpled against the stanchion, its magnesium alloy frame burning like a white-hot furnace. Levegh's body, singed to a black crisp, lay on the pavement in full view of his wife. "He is dead," she said over and over. "Pierre is dead." A gendarme ripped down a banner and laid it across the body. Levegh's helmet was later found with bits of his brain in it.

The moment before hitting Macklin, Levegh had raised his arm in warning to his teammate Fangio, who was a hundred yards behind him. It was the last gesture Levegh would ever make, and it likely saved Fangio's life. With that tiny bit of notice, he veered to the right and slipped untouched through the smoke and wreckage. "It was by pure chance, by destiny if you like," Fangio said, "and after I had passed through the crashing cars, without touching anything or anyone, I started to tremble and shake, for at that moment I had been holding strongly to the steering wheel, to wait for the blow. Instead the way had opened and I passed through."

Hill had a front-row view of it all. "I could see a body up on the burning hay bales," he said, "and there was smoke and lots of commotion." He moved forward for a closer look, but the Ferrari pit manager held him back. Better for a young driver not to see the carnage up close, particularly one as sensitive as Hill.

The Ferrari team always locked the door at the back of their pit area to prevent curious passersby from entering. "Now the lock meant we couldn't get out," Hill said, "and everyone scrambled over each other." In their panic they knocked over Joan Cahier, wife of Bernard Cahier, Hill's friend from International Motors, who was now working as a correspondent for *Road & Track* and other publications.

As ambulances carted off the casualties, Maglioli pulled into the pits. The last thing Hill saw before taking his first laps was a gendarme with his leg neatly severed. On his first lap he encountered wreckage all along the track from unrelated crashes. As Hill rounded the Maison Blanche turn he saw a plume of smoke where an MG had overturned and caught fire.

"At this point I was numbed by it all,

shocked that all this could be happening at once and on my first-ever Ferrari racing lap of Le Mans," Hill said. "But then Stirling Moss went by me like a streak in his Mercedes 300 SLR, and that woke me up. That was a lesson I never forgot, which was that when something happens, get on the gas."

By several accounts Hawthorn stumbled around behind the pits weeping and hysterically declaring that he would never race again. (He would absolve himself of blame in a memoir published three years later.)

On every lap Hill passed a yellow flag, the warning signal waved after crashes. He passed the amusement park and dance hall and the endless flash of headlights as the sun set and the race bore on into the night. Officials decided against canceling the race because they didn't want departing crowds to block the ambulances and other rescue vehicles. *Et la course continue,* said Charles Faroux, a veteran journalist who served as race director. So the race went on with a persistent rain adding to the gloom. Hill and Maglioli moved up as high as third place before a rock pierced their radiator, forcing them to withdraw.

That night John Fitch, who had been Levegh's co-driver, urged his Mercedes handlers to quit the race out of respect for the dead. They might win the race, he said, but they would surely lose the public relations battle. The headlines in European newspapers, he predicted, would be "Germans Trample 80 Frenchmen on Their Way to Victory," or some such.

Stirling Moss, who shared a Mercedes with Fangio, argued against pulling out, saying it was a "theatrical gesture" that appeared to accept blame.

After some debate the company directors in Stuttgart sent orders to withdraw the two remaining cars, one of which was in first place. They were flagged in a few minutes after 2 a.m. "It's finished," Neubauer told the press. "There are too many dead." The Mercedes team was already gone when the church bells rang from the Catholic chapel early the next morning, summoning the faithful to mass. Four months later Mercedes stopped racing altogether. Its factory team would not compete again for more than fifty years.

Mercedes invited Jaguar to withdraw from Le Mans with them, but Lofty England, the Jaguar team manager, refused. There was a smattering of applause when Mike Hawthorn crossed the finish line the next afternoon to win in record-breaking time. He smiled on the podium and swigged from a bottle of champagne. A French newspaper ran a photograph of him with the sarcastic headline, "Here's to You, Mr. Hawthorn!"

Hill had planned to barnstorm Europe in Guiberson's Ferrari, but so many races were canceled after Le Mans — Spain, Mexico, and Switzerland banned racing altogether — that he returned home instead. Away from the endless rehashing and recriminations he could more "easily build a case inside my head for racing," he said. "It's pretty amazing what the mind can do for us. It allows a young race driver faced with death and his own mortality to write his own story reconciling racing with his continuing existence."

Hill was stunned when Phil Walters, one of the drivers he most admired, decided to quit racing after Le Mans. Walters was an aggressive, sharp-elbowed New Yorker who grew up racing hot rods and midgets under the pseudonym Ted Tappett so his family would not know. He flew gliders during the war, until he was shot down and severely wounded during the invasion of Holland. By coincidence the German surgeon who saved his life by removing a lung and kidney had seen Walters win a midget race in Philadelphia five years earlier.

After the war, Walters thrived on the European sports car circuit with a smooth, nuanced driving style. He was so respected that Ferrari waived the customary test drive when he came to Maranello to discuss a job. "Why test? I'm sure he can do it," said Nello Ugolini, the Ferrari team manager.

After witnessing the full horror of Le Mans, Walters called up the Maranello office and, using a secretary as a translator, told Ferrari that he could no longer race. "So many women and children were killed there," he later said. "I just couldn't justify having anything to do with even the possibility of something like that happening." He never raced again.

Walters' retirement should not have shocked Hill, given his own ulcerous history. But Hill had by now learned to protect his enthusiasm for the sport by hardening his mind to its harsher realities. He could no longer imagine abandoning his quest for a life on the European circuit. "I spent a great deal of time pondering why this driver for whom I had so much respect walked away from the sport I held in such esteem," he said.

In the months after Le Mans, Hill raced in Beverly, Massachusetts; Elkhart Lake, Wisconsin; Torrey Pines, California; and the

Bahamas. It must have seemed as if he were one step ahead of a curse. On September 30 the actor James Dean was driving his Porsche 550 Spyder to a sports car race in Salinas, California — the kind of regional race Hill might easily have entered — when he collided with an oncoming Ford coupe at the intersection of Highways 46 and 41, about a mile from the town of Cholame. Dean was taken to a local hospital where he was pronounced dead on arrival.

In January 1956, Hill returned to Buenos Aires, where he had seen Eric Forrest-Greene burn to death two years earlier. This time he shared a Ferrari with Olivier Gendebien, an aristocratic Belgian who had distinguished himself as a Resistance fighter during the war and now lived in a grand manor house in the Fontainebleau Forest. In a field that included the biggest names of the day — Juan Manuel Fangio, Eugenio Castellotti, Stirling Moss, and Jean Behra — they came in second.

After the race Hill sat gasping in the pits with exhaust stains smudged across his cheeks and two pairs of goggles dangling from his neck. Eraldo Sculati, the Ferrari manager, walked over and casually asked if he would like to join the Ferrari team for the rest of the season. Hill was beside himself with joy, and he showed it. Any competent driver could drive a privately owned Ferrari, but the company team — the works team, as they called it — was reserved for an elite. This was the invitation he had dreamed of since his hot-rodding days but had never fully believed he would earn. No American had ever raced on the Ferrari team.

A few weeks later Hill traveled to Modena and checked into the Albergo Reale, a hotel across from 11 Viale Trento e Trieste, the old company workshop where Enzo Ferrari lived in a modest upstairs apartment. The hotel was a de facto Ferrari dormitory run by a bustling red-haired woman, a former brothel madam, or so it was said. The drivers met in the lobby over grappa, Campari, and Lambrusco, and they ate as a group at a long table in the simple dining room. In a city where the cathedral and other landmarks dated back eight hundred years, the drivers discussed how to shave lap times by tenths of a second. Six thousand miles from California, Hill had found a place that felt like home.

It would not be an easy home. As he would soon discover, Modena was a Shakespearian court, full of friendships cut short

— and lorded over by the implacable Enzo Ferrari.

Enzo Ferrari as an Alfa Romeo driver in 1921. "One must keep working continuously. Otherwise, one thinks of death." (Associated Press)

5
POPE OF THE NORTH

For all the glamour of the Ferrari name, its founder lived a circumspect life of Old World persuasion. Enzo Ferrari parked his considerable heft in the same barber chair — the first one on the left — at 8:30 every morning for a shave. He ate lunch, *salsicce cotto* or *tortellini alla panna,* with the same consiglieri in a private room at Il Cavallino, a restaurant he set up in a farm building directly across from the factory gate in Maranello. He and his cronies talked about the blunders of Il Canarini, the local soccer team, the evening card game, and the whores who joined them for grappa.

Ferrari was a tall, bulky man with a sweep of receding white hair and a prominent Roman nose. He was rarely seen without sunglasses and his trademark baggy suit. His pants rode high on his tub-shaped midsection, hoisted by suspenders.

There were many women in Enzo Ferrari's

life, but none held a central place. He once said that the greatest love a man could know was the love between father and son. If so, Ferrari was doubly blessed. He had two sons: Dino by his wife, Laura, and Piero by his mistress Lina Lardi. He had dozens more, if you count the drivers.

Dino was a tall, dark-haired boy whom Ferrari hoped would succeed him as head of the Ferrari marque. It was an unrealistic ambition. Dino was born with a rare form of muscular dystrophy and doctors warned that he would not see adulthood. To complicate matters, his congenital ailment afflicted only men. Ferrari's wife, Laura, had been the carrier, which stirred the simmering mix of resentment and guilt in the Ferrari marriage. (In his 1991 biography of Ferrari, Brock Yates suggests that Laura may have been a prostitute when she met Ferrari, and Dino's illness could have been syphilis transmitted in the womb.)

Dino's disease was easily thrust from their minds as long as he was active and strong. As a teenager he happily rode a bike from the Ferrari apartment in Modena to the factory nine miles up the road in Maranello, where he was a bright-eyed apprentice. He spent long days hunched over the drafting board as an engineering student in Modena and Switzerland, but he tired easily and returned home before completing his studies.

"The symptoms of his illness were now perceptible," Ferrari wrote in his memoir, "erupting dramatically" for the first time at a dinner with drivers and mechanics when Dino was nineteen. They had gathered to celebrate a win at the Mille Miglia, but Ferrari cut the dinner short when Dino was too weak to eat.

When he wasn't caring for Dino or meeting with engineers at the factory, Ferrari visited Lina Lardi, the mistress who lived with their son Piero in the village of Castelvitro, nine miles south of Modena. She was by all accounts a sweet-natured woman who made few demands. Her red-brick farmhouse surrounded by cherry trees was a sanctuary from the trials of Ferrari's office and the enmity of his marriage. Like many aspects of his life, this alternate household lived in the half shadows.

By the fall of 1955 Dino was bedridden with kidney failure. His parents hovered, attending to blankets and meals. "I had always deluded myself — a father always deludes himself — that we should be able to restore him to health," Ferrari wrote. "I was convinced that he was like one of my cars, one of my engines."

Ferrari drew up daily charts to track Dino's calories and urea in his blood, and he noted them in a log. One night, with the end in sight, he wrote, "the race is lost," and put the log down for good. Dino died on June 30, 1956, seven months short of his twenty-fifth birthday. A troupe of factory engineers in overalls carried his coffin to a tomb in the San Cataldo cemetery on the edge of Modena.

Ferrari did what he could to keep Dino's memory alive. His son's little Fiat sedan sat under a tarp outside the Modena workshop where Dino last parked it. Ferrari would not allow it to be moved. He hung a black-framed portrait of Dino in his Maranello office with votive candles burning beneath it, and embossed Dino's name in script on the valve covers of a line of engines. Every morning, after visiting the barber, he pushed through the iron cemetery gates and perched on a bench, speaking aloud to his son about the week's events — driver gossip, engineering advances, race results — as if they were seated at lunch.

Without an heir, Ferrari lived only with the constancy of death. Dino's passing shadowed him, and he relived it with the death of each successive driver. Only one thing kept the darkness at bay: the affirmative force of winning races. For Ferrari, it was an endless, insatiable need.

Ferrari was born on the northern outskirts of Modena on February 18, 1898, the son of a blacksmith who fabricated sheds and gangways for the railroads spreading like tendrils through the Italian countryside. The household clanged with hammering in the adjacent ironworks as the old metal craftsmen tried to keep pace with the demands of industrialization.

When Ferrari was ten his father took him and his older brother, Alfredo Jr., to see the great Italian driver Felice Nazzaro win on a 30-mile circuit of dusty public roads winding through the Bologna countryside. "It was watching races like that, being up close to those cars and those heroes, being part of the yelling crowd, that whole environment that aroused my first flicker of interest in cars," he wrote.

His ambition to drive race cars himself was put off when his father died of pneumonia in 1916. Alfredo Jr. died the same year of an undiagnosed illness while serving in the ground crew of a World War I air force squadron. Within a year of their deaths the Italian army drafted Ferrari and sent him to shoe mules used to pull artillery for a squadron on the mountainous Austrian front north of Bergamo. He nearly died after contracting pleurisy during the 1918 flu pandemic. He lay among other incurables relegated to a compound of wooden huts. According to Richard Williams, a Ferrari biographer, he woke each morning to the hammering of coffin makers.

Despite all expectations, Ferrari gradually recovered. After his discharge he returned to Modena with no money or prospects. It is easy to trace the brooding, melancholy presence of the older Ferrari to this period of sorrow, guilt, and apprehension. "I was alone," he wrote. "My father and my brother were no more. Overcome by loneliness and despair, I wept." He considered himself an orphan, despite his mother's presence.

He parlayed his modest metalworking skills into a job with an outfit that turned surplus army trucks into passenger cars. His duties included driving the trucks ninety miles from Turin to Milan. In 1919, he entered the Targa Florio, a road race run annually through the Sicilian mountains. In those days getting to the race was often more demanding than the race itself. En route to Sicily he crossed the Abruzzi Mountains, where he claimed to have driven through a blizzard and chased off wolves with an army handgun that he kept under his seat cushion. As with many episodes in Ferrari's life, it is hard to distinguish fact from the legends he invented for himself.

By 1923 Ferrari had joined the Alfa Romeo team. Photographs show him sitting in the high cockpit of the period, wearing a long coat and operating gear levers as long as golf clubs. He recorded his first win by holding off a snarling pack of pursuers in a 225-mile road race through pine forests fringing Ravenna. It was one of the few stirring performances of his middling driving career. The crowd carried him on their shoulders after he crossed the finish line at the steps of the local basilica. Before returning to Modena he was introduced to Count Enrico Baracca, father of Francesco Baracca, a World War I pilot who shot down thirty-four planes before crashing to his death at the front. His squadron emblem was a prancing horse, a *cavallino rampante,* painted on the side of his biplane. At a later meeting with Count Baracca's wife, the Countess Paolina, she purportedly urged Ferrari to adopt the emblem. She promised that it would bring him luck.

What happened next is a mystery of the soul. In the summer of 1924 Ferrari had a shot at joining the top ranks of drivers. He won three races in a row when he arrived in Lyon for the French Grand Prix. He took practice laps on a muddy road in his cigar-shaped Alfa Romeo, then abruptly lost his nerve. He left the track without explanation and boarded a train for Modena. His inner resolve had crumbled, leaving him unable to face the heightened expectations. Unsteady nerve was a failing he would never forgive drivers in later years.

Ferrari entered a few more races, but by the time Dino was born, in January 1932, he had found a new calling as the shrewd and exacting manager of Scuderia Ferrari (*scuderia* is an Italian term for horse stable), a racing arm of Alfa Romeo that competed with the adopted emblem of the black stallion that Ferrari brought with him. Scuderia Ferrari was hugely successful, but success did not guarantee longevity. In January 1938 Alfa Romeo ran low on funds and scaled back its racing program. An Alfa Romeo truck pulled up to 11 Viale Trento e Trieste, Ferrari's Modena workshop, and began hauling away spare parts and machine tools. Ferrari was absorbed into the main workings of the company, but he left in November to operate the *scuderia* independently. When Ferrari beat an Alfa Romeo for the first time, in 1951, he said, "I have killed my mother."

By the time Phil Hill came to Maranello in 1956, Ferrari was a national hero for producing cars that consistently beat the hated foreign marques. The low, powerful machines with distinctive Ferrari engines and long voluptuous lines had won hundreds of races on four continents. They won in the mountains of Mexico and the forests of France, on roads cut through the sands of Africa and the winding streets of Monaco. In doing so Ferrari restored a measure of pride to a country humiliated by war. When Ferrari won, Italy won.

Ferrari came to be known as the Pope of the North. The more his cars won, the more actors, business leaders, and politicians gravitated to Maranello, as if making a pilgrimage. His clients — he always called them clients, not customers — included Nelson Rockefeller, Jimmy Stewart, Prince Bernhard of the Netherlands, and King Leopold III of Belgium. "There is no finer thrill in the world than driving a Ferrari flat out," said Roberto Rossellini, the film director and avid client who occasionally came for lunch with his girlfriend Ingrid Bergman.

Appointments to see Ferrari were as

coveted as a papal audience. The *clienti* entered through an archway in the low brick factory compound and sat waiting — and waiting — in a bare blue chamber outside Ferrari's office. The delay was his passive-aggressive way of showing disdain for clients who tried to reward themselves for financial success or retrieve part of their youth. Rudeness was a way of expressing, however obliquely, that humble Italian workmen, like his father, were the equals of his moneyed customers, who in his opinion rarely deserved such exquisite cars. Ferrari was not handsome or well bred, nor did he pretend to be. But he possessed something almost incalculably desirable. In a mid-1950s culture enthralled by jets, rockets, and the prospect of space travel, he held the keys to the most glamorous expression of speed — and he was not shy about lording it over his supplicants, however well known they might be.

"In later years I saw many instances of Ferrari's mastery in putting even the most important visitors off balance with long heel-coolings in those dim chambers," Hill said. After making his point, Ferrari received them in a dark, bare office dominated by the shrinelike photograph of Dino with candles lit beneath it. The most important callers got a tour of the Ferrari plant, which was considered one of the wonders of Italian industry. Ferrari walked them around a factory floor as tidy as a laboratory and bustling with craftsmen from small towns tucked in the Apennine foothills. The visitors were "nearly always accompanied by breathtaking women," Ferrari wrote in his memoir, "who exercise a magnetic effect on every mechanic in the workshop."

There was an Old World aspect to the workers, with their brown coveralls and roughened hands. Somebody once observed that Ferrari seemed to like his mechanics and craftsmen more than his drivers. "I don't think he liked anyone," Luigi Chinetti replied.

One day a young woman introduced herself to Hill as a friend of Enzo Ferrari. After she left Hill said to an acquaintance, "What a ridiculous thing to say. Nobody is a friend of Enzo Ferrari."

Maybe so, but the blacksmith's son knew how to bond with his workers. He won their loyalty by playing up his *paisano* roots, patting them on the back and telling uncouth jokes in local dialect. The Modena region of northern Italy was a Communist stronghold, but Ferrari never endured a serious strike, despite his earlier membership in the

Fascist Party. During the Mussolini regime Ferrari was named a Commendatore of the Kingdom of Italy. The title was rescinded after Mussolini's death, but his staff continued to address him as Il Commendatore.

The factory was more like an atelier than a production plant. While the Fiat factory in Turin manufactured hundreds of cars a day, Ferrari produced only five hundred or so road cars a year, each lovingly made by hand. "I am not an industrialist," he said. "I am a *costruttore* — a constructor."

Mechanics spent more than a week machining a single crankshaft from a solid billet of steel, and they cast cylinder blocks and gearboxes from aluminum alloy produced in their own foundry. They hand-tooled every facet, right down to tiny screws and wing nuts. The precisely assembled engines were tested in special rooms that replicated the exact temperature and atmospheric pressure of racetracks around the world, from the mountains of Mexico to the deserts of North Africa. Ferrari gave his cars power, but he relied on outside coachbuilders to give them character. There was something unmistakably masculine about the hard-pounding Ferrari engine, but it was clothed in a body as unmistakably feminine as Gina Lollobrigida, Sophia

Loren, and other buxom Italian actresses.

As a young man Ferrari aspired to sing opera, and he handled company affairs with a prima donna's high-flown repertoire of belittling, sulks, browbeating, threats, castigations, walkouts, curses, lawsuits, and reconciliations. Somehow it worked. The Ferrari team was in a constant state of hysteria and chaos — and consistently won through it all.

Scuderia Ferrari dominated in part because the founder was an impossibly hard-driving boss who rarely spent a day away from the factory. He worked seven days a week, even in August, when Italian industry shut down. He claimed to have never vacationed. "One must keep working continuously," he wrote, "otherwise, one thinks of death."

Ferrari intimidated his drivers with extreme outbursts of temper and gratuitous displays of bullying. The first time Hill visited Modena, Ferrari took him to lunch at Oreste, a restaurant in the old district. The owner brought out a special reserve of Lambrusco and made an elaborate presentation of its uncorking. "Ferrari took a little mouthful, thoughtfully testing, and then, with a grimace, spat it on the floor," Hill said. "He made no attempt at not making a

143

mess of it, and said it was the worst stuff he'd ever tasted." Then he laughed to show that it was a sardonic joke.

When drivers died, Ferrari put on florid demonstrations of mourning. For days he skulked about in a bathrobe, unshaven and inconsolable. "The violins would come out," said Denise McCluggage, one of the first woman drivers and a correspondent for the *Herald Tribune.* "He was a tenor, for God's sake." He wept with the widows and intimated that he was too heartbroken to continue racing. For a man capable of cyclonic fits of rage he could speak in a surprisingly soft register. "Will God forgive me for fabricating such fast cars?" he asked. His mourning was a one-act opera. Ferrari never went to the funerals. He sent his wife Laura in his place while he resumed brooding over engineering details.

Ferrari never became a great driver. Nor was he an engineer or industrialist. Instead, he called himself *un agitatore di uomini.* An agitator of men.

Oddly enough, Ferrari rarely saw his cars in action. He stopped attending races in the 1930s because, he said, it was too painful to see the inert material he had brought to life brutalized on the track. He preferred to listen to radio coverage (in later years he

144

watched on a small black-and-white television) in the gloom of his office with his consiglieri. Occasionally he would telephone instructions to his team manager in the pits. His absence only amplified his authority. Automotive historian Doug Nye compared Ferrari to "a Dr. No character sitting at the center of his web with tinted glasses."

Ferrari was a menacing figure, but magnetic. It was natural that Hill, who felt no warmth for his father, would gravitate to Ferrari as a surrogate. Ferrari was a "man I respected, from whom I wanted more than anything affection and for him to be a good daddy to me," Hill said.

Winning Ferrari's affection would prove more difficult than winning the races. For one thing, Ferrari had more sentiment for the cars than the drivers. When Robert Daley, a *New York Times* correspondent, asked Ferrari why he never went to the track, he said, "Because when a man has taken something, some material and, with his own two hands, transformed it into something else, has made not a machine out of it, but a soul, a living breathing soul. Well, then, he goes to a race and he hears this soul which he has created, hears it being mistreated, hears that it is not going right . . ." Ferrari placed his hand over his heart. "It makes a man suffer here. A man cannot bear such things."

"You mean you suffer too much for the car, not the driver?" Daley asked.

"Oh, the driver too, of course," he added.

Hill arranged the interview for Daley and sat in during the discussion. Afterwards he said, "I never thought [Ferrari] would say such a thing in front of a driver. I guess we like to think he loves us because we are all so brave and drive so fast. But deep down I suppose all of us knew he cares more about his cars than he does about us."

The drivers were naturally more concerned with their own welfare. They talked constantly among themselves about how fast they could go without losing control. They believed that every curve had a theoretical maximum speed, known as the limit, beyond which a car's four wheels lost adhesion to the road and the car would spin or flip. "If you go into a 100 mph corner at 101, that's too fast and 99 is too slow," said Stirling Moss. "You'd better be able to feel the difference in the seat of your pants." Depending on the car, course, and conditions, the limit could lie anywhere from 65 to 180 mph. The trick was to identify it and stay close for as many laps as possible —

146

but not too close. Moss said that he and the other drivers spent so much time in intimate contact with the limit that they had a "nodding acquaintance with death."

As much as any driver, Hill knew how to respect the limit. He was shrewd enough to recognize it and disciplined enough to stay within its confines. Not that self-control curried any favor with his boss. On the contrary, Ferrari discouraged drivers from letting lifesaving calculations deter them from speed's mystic calling. "Racing is a great mania," he said, "to which one must sacrifice everything, without reticence, without hesitation. No reasoning is valid. For no matter how logical the argument, when the race begins it is less than useless."

There was a rookie Ferrari driver who captured this spirit of abandon, but it wasn't Hill. It was a handsome young German, Count Wolfgang von Trips. Shortly after Hill joined Ferrari, von Trips had shown up in Modena with a playful smile and a driving style that bordered on a death wish.

Burg Hemmersbach, a forty-five-room stronghold sur-rounded by a moat and prodigious farmlands—a vestige of feudal Germany. It would pass to the young count someday, or so his parents hoped. (Gräflich Berghe von Trips'sche Sportstiftung zu Burg Hemmersbach)

6
COUNT VON CRASH

Count Wolfgang von Trips was heir to a seven-hundred-year-old dynasty of German knights and the only child of Eduard Reichsgraf Berghe von Trips and his wife, Thessa, the daughter of a Bonn city official. In the early part of the twentieth century, German society still clung to a feudal code. Marrying below one's station was considered scandalous; Eduard's family spurned him for sullying the bloodline. When his father died, Eduard received no money or inheritance, only the family castle and land granted by law to the oldest son.

In 1932, when Wolfgang was four, his parents moved into Burg Hemmersbach, a moated compound eleven miles west of Cologne that his family had owned for nearly two hundred years. At its center stood a forty-five-room Georgian manor house built incongruously on the remains of a Gothic stronghold burned by Austrian soldiers in 1793. The result was a layer cake of historical styles, with symmetrical Georgian windows and cornices capped by a mansard roof and a domed turret overlooking a grassy U-shaped forecourt enclosed by redbrick farm buildings. The high-ceilinged rooms contained ancestral portraits and antlers of animals collected on family hunting trips. Lest anyone forget the von Trips pedigree, a family tree was painted on a parlor wall dating back to the feudal robber barons who tyrannized the Rhineland with taxes and tolls. Beyond the compound lay hundreds of acres of farmland — a vestige of feudal Germany. It was an imposing layout, but charmingly attuned to its wooded setting with stone walls, rustic studded doors, and the sound of gurgling water.

Wölfchen (Little Wolf), as his parents called him, bridled against the formalities of his highborn home — the ceremonious greetings to guests, the Old World table manners, the leggings and ruffled shirts forced on him for social outings. "The days of my youth when I had to go to those parties and was not allowed to get dirty, those are dark memories," he later wrote in his diary.

Left to himself, von Trips ran wild through

the apple orchard and paddled a johnboat along the moats that wound among the grounds. He walked the fields with plow horses and rode harvest wagons. When his parents found his secret treehouse, the little count sat defiantly on a high branch ignoring their pleas for him to come down.

It was a rambunctious childhood, but rarefied and isolated by privilege. He had little contact with other children until he went to a local elementary school where he mixed with the sons of farm laborers and coal workers. "The village boys were rather rude to me at first," he said. "I got many a beating because of the way I dressed. At first I didn't know how to protect myself."

When his new school friends came to the castle he led them in pranks. "My friends and I did the cruelest things to stir up the grown-ups," he later wrote in his diary. "We pushed again and again, and sometimes went a bit too far." One early summer day they capsized his canoe in the moat and hid beneath it to scare his grandmother and nanny.

Von Trips' first car crush was the family Opel Super 6, a boxy German sedan polished and cared for by a chauffeur named Arnold. At age eight von Trips was too short to reach the pedals, so he directed a friend to sit on the floorboards and push the clutch while he steered around the cobbled driveway inside the courtyard. His father allowed them to muck about with the car as long as they stayed under Arnold's watchful eye.

When von Trips was ten he snuck the car out when his parents and Arnold were gone. His friends sat on the hood and stood on the running boards. "We drove the car through the gates, careful that nobody saw, and out into the park," he said. "Then we raged around like savages. Branches whistled past. The Opel got its first scratch. A few tumbled down and sprained ankles, and whatever else you can sprain. Then we put the car back in the garage. Of course, everything was found out. There was a murderous row. I couldn't touch the car for weeks."

Von Trips was also a horseman, a fast one, galloping across potato fields and through oak forests on his stallion Rialto. He often rode the castle grounds with his father, who had raced horses and fought with the Düsseldorfer Cavalry in World War I.

Despite his own intrepid history, Eduard urged his son to curb his wild streak. As if to dramatize his warning, Eduard took a harrowing fall one Sunday when Bianca, his beautiful giant mare, bucked him over its head. Eduard landed head first on the cobblestones. He crawled to the curb with blood streaming down his face and asked his son to fetch the car.

In 1939, when von Trips was eleven, he joined his father on holiday trips to the family hunting lodge in the Eifel, a low mountain range with rushing trout streams and steep valleys wreathed in mist. For weeks they chased boar, red deer, and rabbits accompanied by Breitschwert, a quiet gamekeeper and guide who patiently answered the young count's questions about the mysteries of the natural world: Where do the forces of nature come from? How do trees know where to grow? How far away are the stars?

A distant engine drone sometimes broke the silence of the woods as von Trips walked with Breitschwert beneath beech and spruce. The hunting grounds lay within a few miles of the Nürburgring, a racetrack built in the 1920s and refurbished to showcase the Silver Arrows, the thunderously powerful cars produced by Mercedes-Benz and its German rival, the Auto Union, with generous Nazi subsidies. They shot through the wooded hills like silver projectiles.

In 1936 Wolfgang persuaded his parents to take him to the Nürburgring to see the

German drivers Bernd Rosemeyer and Rudolf Caracciola duel in the German Grand Prix. Nazi troops accompanied the cars to the starting line, and at the race's end Rosemeyer hoisted a trophy donated by Hitler. A portrait of Hitler was printed on the cover of the race program, as if the Führer himself were responsible for the strength of the Silver Arrows.

In the summer of 1936, as Hitler presided over the Berlin Olympics, Wolfgang told his governess that he wanted to be a great German driver like the ones he had seen at the Nürburgring. Not surprisingly, Rosemeyer was Wolfgang's particular hero. He was tall and blond with buoyant charm. He was married to the tomboy aviatrix Elly Beinhorn — Germany's answer to Amelia Earhart — who had flown solo to Africa and South America. They were darlings of the German press. Hundreds of thousands of Germans came to see Rosemeyer race. Millions more listened on the radio.

On January 28, 1938, Caracciola broke the land speed record by rocketing down a stretch of Autobahn at 268.9 mph. Rosemeyer stood by, prepared to better Caracciola's time. He was clocked at 267 mph — less than 2 mph slower than Caracciola — when a gust of crosswind blew his car onto the grassy median where it hit a stone marker and broke apart in a series of cataclysmic rolls. His body was found in a grove of trees a hundred yards away. In the Nazi depiction, Rosemeyer was a Wagnerian hero slain in the dark German forest. Goering, Himmler, and Hitler sent condolences. SS troopers flanked Rosemeyer's coffin during a Berlin funeral styled and stage managed by Nazi officials.

Three months after Rosemeyer died, German schoolchildren, including von Trips, received a handout printed with a poem about Rosemeyer written by Ernst Hornickel, the editor of a car journal:

Let the weakling, fearful, dither;
Who fights for higher things must dare,
He must choose 'twixt life and death.
Let the roaring breakers thunder,
Should you safely land or founder,
Always hold the wheel yourself!

In September 1940, as the Luftwaffe bombed British ports and factories, von Trips suffered the first in a series of illnesses that would afflict him during the war years, starting with an ear infection that required surgery and kept him home from school for a month. A second sickness, probably

155

meningitis, caused intolerance to light. He spent six months recovering in a darkened room. By the summer of 1942 he was well enough to vacation with family friends on the Walchensee, an Alpine lake, when he lost feeling in his face. He was sent to a Munich hospital where doctors diagnosed polio. Within days he had lost all sensation in his lips and cheeks. He could no longer blink. Nurses refreshed his eyes with drops of saline solution.

By the time von Trips returned to the castle the alarm of war had intruded on the fairytale setting. The neighboring village of Horrem lay on a strategic rail line connecting Cologne and Düren, a manufacturing center. Night after night the air raid sirens sounded and the family scurried to a bomb shelter.

It is not known how the von Trips family felt about Hitler. There is no indication that they supported the Führer, but the German aristocracy tended to back him, however reluctantly, in hopes that he would strengthen the fatherland and hold off the Bolsheviks. Whatever the case, the count and countess sent their son for paramilitary training with the Hitler Youth. Wearing the Hitlerjugend uniform of black shorts and khaki shirts, he hiked, drilled with air guns, and sang songs glorifying Nazi martyrdom. After suffering three serious illnesses in as many years, he left for winter defense training at Ordensburg Sonthofen, a military school in the Bavarian Alps, where he took an eight-week course in mountaineering and igloo building. He was recalled to Sonthofen later that year, but he missed several weeks when, with his propensity for mishap, he broke his foot skiing down the Nebelhorn, a 7,300-foot peak. "Nobody had seen me fall," he said. "I poked my way down to the valley in horrible pain."

By late 1944 the Rhineland had become a crumbling front. As the Allies swept east from France and Belgium, bombers spared the seven-hundred-year-old cathedral in central Cologne. But beneath its Gothic spires lay a city in flames and ruins. Virtually every building was damaged or destroyed. Rubble and broken glass choked the streets, starving families camped in basements, and corpses floated down the Rhine.

At age sixteen, Wolfgang was drafted to search through air raid debris. Working alongside other teenage boys, he sifted among the shattered remains of apartment buildings, schools, offices, theaters, and stores. "I can't remember how many corpses we carried out of cellars and picked off streets," he said. "I saw the whole of human suffering firsthand."

The horrors glimpsed in the rubble would stay with him — families killed in an instant, bodies of children charred beyond recognition, men weeping, women who had lost their minds, the elderly expending last breaths asking after loved ones. "I experienced hell for the first time," he said.

In October 1944, as Allied forces attacked the nearby town of Aachen, von Trips rode his bike into Horrem and climbed a mountainous coal stockpile for an unobstructed view of the air raids. "From there you can follow the battle," a friend had told him, "like Blücher on the general's hill." It wasn't long before he scrambled down and ran for shelter. "The planes were literally flying around my ears," he said. "It was wide-open there, up on a hill. I got such a fright. . . . From then on I was always first in the cellar when the sirens wailed."

In the final desperate months of the war the Hitler Youth deployed von Trips to the Belgian front for combat training. After learning to handle machine guns and shoulder-mounted antitank rockets he suffered what was called a nervous breakdown. It would be understandable if he collapsed at his impressionable age after his nightmarish air raid duties. It might also be excusable if he exaggerated his condition to escape an odious mission in a failed cause. Either way he was dismissed — only to be recruited along with his father by a citizen militia, the Volkssturm, to dig foxholes as Horrem braced for a last-ditch defense against American battalions fighting their way east from the Roer River.

With the outcome no longer in doubt, von Trips, now seventeen, and his father decided to skip out on the digging and evacuate their home. They packed von Trips' mother and grandmother into the Opel and went into hiding. As the U.S. troops closed on Horrem, the family drove southwest, crossing the Old Rhine Bridge at Bonn minutes before German troops dynamited it to slow the American advance.

A farmer agreed to hide them at his home near the village of Rederscheid. Even there, tucked among the forested hills, they were not safe from the oncoming storm. Shortly after arriving they heard the drone of Allied aircraft, followed by dozens of bombs exploding with concussive blasts of light on the surrounding fields. Their host led them through the darkness to a damp cave entered from a hillside. They crouched inside with the Opel camouflaged under a layer of leaves until the bombing subsided.

U.S. First Army tanks and infantry entered the cobbled streets of Horrem on the morning of March 1, 1945, after killing or capturing groups of German soldiers firing down on them from quarries and low hills east of the village. The Americans paused at Burg Hemmersbach before the final push into Cologne. Any bivouac with running water and flushing toilets was a luxury. Before moving out, the GIs burned and looted art and heirlooms, and they jimmied open a private compartment in the count's desk filled with souvenirs — Nazi propaganda and leaflets dropped by Allied aircraft showing broad fields filled with German graves. One soldier plundered the countess's boudoir, then left a sarcastic note promising to repay her after the German surrender.

The von Trips returned in May to find a second wave of Americans camped in their parlors. These troops had fought their way from Normandy and overcome a stiff German counteroffensive at the Battle of the Bulge during Christmas 1944. They were in no mood for charity to German nobles. The soldiers gave the family half an hour to collect what was left of their belongings, and allowed them to stay in one of the brick courtyard buildings used for farm work.

The family reclaimed silver utensils stashed in the castle and rounded up horse and cattle. "We were really down, had nothing left, had nothing to eat," von Trips said. "Everything was destroyed. We had just enough not to starve. Even so — it was one of the best times I can remember with my family. Our fear of death was gone. We were able to stay warm. We had a place to sleep. We were back on our own land."

The von Trips family still owned the castle and property, but they had lost practically everything else. They were forced to sell some parcels of land to survive. Wolfgang scrounged pocket money as the operator of his own miniature black market. If the British soldiers encamped nearby wanted whiskey or cigarettes, he bought them from the Americans and marked them up, or vice versa, traversing between camps in the battered Opel.

Within a few weeks the initial occupiers were replaced by a black unit, which acted more sympathetically. We were the black slaves in our country, they said. Now you are white slaves in your own home.

Like Jim, the British boy in J. G. Ballard's novel *Empire of the Sun,* von Trips came to identify with the enemy. He tagged along

Wolfgang von Trips around 1945, after his family returned from hiding to find Burg Hemmersbach occupied by American soldiers. (Gräflich Berghe von Trips'sche Sportstiftung zu Burg Hemmersbach)

with the black soldiers, listening to jazz on the radio and learning their slang. He went about the castle grounds in lederhosen, cast-off U.S. fatigues, and army boots. For the rest of his life he would speak nearly flawless Americanized English with the slight singsongy uptilt of German cadence.

The soldiers whooped when they saw his jury-rigged repairs to the claptrap Opel, which had been converted to run on charcoal and wood. The carburetor was attached to the side with an inner tube and the accelerator operated with a wire strung through the window. The radiator was connected to the engine with an American gas mask instead of a water hose. The soldiers gave von Trips his first lessons in car handling, and they donated oil, gas, and spare parts.

A British regiment, the Scots Guards, eventually replaced the black American unit. On the transfer day the incoming major pulled up to the castle forecourt in an officer's jeep and formally introduced himself to the Count and Countess von Trips. While the major inspected the house, a pair of departing Americans struggled to start a coughing, backfiring jeep. Von Trips jumped into the major's jeep and pushed them down the lengthy driveway. The major returned from the castle tour to find his jeep missing. "In a magnificent cloud of dust I rushed back," von Trips said. "At full tilt I shot through the gate, and right outside the castle I slid to a quick stop with full brakes." He stepped from the jeep and greeted the major in English with a slangy black accent. "May we present our son," his parents said.

Stealing a jeep from an occupying officer was no small offense, and the major might have jailed von Trips. In the end, he judged it not worth the trouble.

It was not von Trips' last brush with martial law. A Scots Guard sergeant gave him an old set of British tires for the Opel. When a military patrol spotted them, they pulled von Trips over and arrested him for possession of stolen property. A tribunal sentenced him to house arrest and confiscated the tires. The sergeant could not testify on von Trips' behalf because he had fallen out of a window and died during a drinking bout.

When his sentence was over, von Trips sold the Opel and bought a British prewar JAP motorcycle with no lights, muffler, or starter. "She stood out and made a spectacle of herself," he said. "I dreamed of my JAP. I wish I could have taken her to bed."

Von Trips was driving the JAP to school in Bad Godesberg, outside Bonn, when the motorcycle slipped out from under him on wet tram tracks. He fell and broke his hand.

The pain was excruciating, but he tried to hide the injury from his parents. Inevitably they found out and traded the JAP for a jeep so that he could travel in comparative safety. They knew their son was in some ways ill-equipped for messing with motor-cycles and cars. He was too dream-headed, too tender. They knew him as a gentle child with an almost girlish weakness for the natural world. He rescued swallows from nests perched precariously on high window ledges and lovingly cultivated carnations and tulips. He listened rapt when his mother played Chopin and Liszt. Throughout his life von Trips' sensitive, ingenuous disposition would add to his appeal, particularly to women. At Bad Godesberg he fell in love for the first time. He had met "a girl who lit me on fire, made both of my ears red." He walked with her beside the Rhine talking of his future like any lovesick teen.

When Wolfgang left for agricultural school at Walsrode, in Lower Saxony, his parents agreed to pay for a light 125cc Maico motorcycle from their modest budget. He was stopped at a railroad crossing one day when a classic twelve-year-old BMW 500 motorcycle with a black gas tank pulled up beside him. "She was like a princess in a fairy tale," he said.

"Holy buckets," he told the rider. "This is a beautiful thing. Where did you get it?"

"From my brother," the rider said. "He was killed in the war. During the war it was under a blanket in the hayloft."

Von Trips memorized the license number before the gate lifted and the BMW took off. He tracked down the driver, who offered to sell it for 1,750 deutsche marks. "Seventeen hundred fifty deutsche mark isn't much for a princess," von Trips said. He sold his radio, wristwatch, and, finally, the Maico. He was still short.

Von Trips had a tendency to swoon when he went without eating. He likely suffered from diabetes, though it was never diagnosed. To ensure that their son ate properly away from home, his parents made a deal with a hotel near his school: They would pay a generous monthly fee. In return von Trips could show up at any time for a complete meal.

The count and countess were unaware that their son revised the terms in order to complete his motorcycle purchase. He went to the hotelier and struck a deal: Von Trips would take 90 percent of the payments; the hotelier could keep 10 percent without providing any meals. With his parents' money now rerouted to his own pocket, von

Trips financed the BMW.

By 1950 von Trips had finished his agricultural studies and returned home. He was on a break before attending business classes — typing, bookkeeping, and shorthand — in preparation for managing the farmlands. At age twenty-two he could look forward to a life spent raising flowers, apples, and potatoes on the family grounds. Like his ancestors he would be an aristocrat farmer. A good marriage might even restore the family name.

At a local motorcycle rally he met a plumber and locksmith in his early thirties named Hans-Rolf Clasen. Clasen's workshop, along with the neighboring restaurant that his family operated, became a second home for von Trips and the center of a roughneck motorcycle life hidden from his parents. The two joined up with a young cheesemaker named Helmut Beyl to form a racing team. They called themselves the Wild Pigs. They wore leather jackets, slicked their hair back, and painted boars' heads on their fenders. They spent weekends tearing down country roads and skidding into hay bales.

Whenever he could, von Trips snuck over to Clasen's to tune his motorcycle and talk about racing at the family restaurant. Clas-

167

en's wife packed their rucksacks with butter sandwiches and saw the Wild Pigs off to motocross rallies all over Germany. Afterwards Frau Clasen washed von Trips' mud-splattered clothes so they would not raise suspicions at home. For the first time he was earning something on his own merits, without a count's entitlements.

Von Trips belonged to the impoverished nobility, and it amused his new friends when he borrowed money for gas and motorcycle parts. Clasen could afford to help. He earned a good living selling stolen and scavenged radiator components on the black market.

Beneath his leather jacket von Trips was still sickly and physically unsuited to long racing excursions. "He sleeps easily," Clasen said, "and if he stays awake, mistakes creep in or he loses focus." Clasen nicknamed von Trips "Tripsy Butterbread" because he weakened without food. He could lose as much as four pounds over the course of a race. "Man, Trips, now eat something," Clasen said, and von Trips obeyed.

The young count struck his new friends as too soft for life outside the castle. "The count was a chicken," said Clasen's nephew Helmut, who was then a teenager. "He had no courage. The question about him from a young age was why does he have a boy's body but a girl's mind? When he got a little older he realized he was afraid of just about everything, and he forced himself to prove that he was indeed a man. All his life he would try to prove that — not to the world but to himself."

In his urgency to prove his ruggedness, von Trips developed a bent for mishap and accidents. "We often went together to the Cologne skating rink," Helmut Clasen said. "In the summertime there was a go-kart track set up there. One day we were out there having fun, and all of a sudden the count was on fire. His wool sweater, which was hanging loose around his shoulders, had dangled a sleeve over the exhaust and caught fire. Suddenly there was the count, jumping off and rolling himself on the infield to get the flames out."

Clasen added, "He always had accidents. Things never worked out, but he would try again and again to get it right."

Even as he fumbled the go-kart, von Trips was thinking ahead to his next step. Motorcycle racing was the lowest rung of motor sports. If von Trips was to become the next Bernd Rosemeyer he would have to graduate to cars. A school friend named Friedrich-Victor Rolff raced a Porsche, and he urged von Trips to join him. He introduced von Trips to Hans-Willi Bernartz, president of the Cologne Porsche club, and a circle of amateur drivers. "At the moment my dreams are haunted by Porsches," von Trips wrote in his diary.

His Porsche came sooner than he dared hope. Bernartz, who was a lawyer, had a client who was repairing a 1.3-liter Porsche damaged in an accident. He was willing to sell it for 4,500 deutsche marks. Von Trips sped over on his motorcycle to inspect it. He did not have the money, but Bernartz wrote a letter of guarantee. Von Trips then sold his motorcycle and used the proceeds to prepare his Porsche for racing.

On March 5, 1954, von Trips entered his first car race, a rally in the Rhineland town of Bad Dürkheim. With no money for lodging, he slept in his car the night before the race. Rolff won. Von Trips finished third. "I've become a different person since I got the Porsche," he wrote in his diary, adding that he had "forgotten just about everything else: writing letters, working, whatever."

He was so debt strapped that prize money and modest sponsorship deals became a necessity. He helped pay off his Porsche with long-distance races for Tornax, a German motorcycle manufacturer. "Every gold medal meant 75 smackers," he said.

Bernartz tried to help von Trips solidify his racing career by referring him to Alfred Neubauer, who had directed the stirring Silver Arrow Mercedes teams of the 1930s and managed the company's return to racing in 1952. Neubauer rebuffed von Trips, saying he had no use for well-born dilettantes. "What we need, and now possess, are drivers that will be successful at the Grand Prix," he wrote back. "We also need world-class champions, and we can't accomplish it if we try out every gentleman who wants the possibility of training themselves to be a champion on our watch."

Von Trips was unsure that he could even race his own Porsche after he broke a piston by revving the aging engine too high. It was beyond his ability to fix, and he lacked money for a new one. He went to the Porsche factory in Stuttgart, hoping that they might give him a used one. In the company's headquarters he met Huschke von Hanstein, a former SS member and head of Porsche's racing program. Like von Trips, he belonged to the extended family of German gentry. In driving circles he was known as "the racing baron." He replaced the piston and made a surprise offer: He asked von Trips if he would like to race a

Porsche in the Mille Miglia.

"I said, 'The Mille Miglia? What's that?' "

Von Hanstein explained that it was a 1,000-mile race around Italy, one of the most dangerous and prestigious in the world. "I had never driven a car over 85 miles per hour in my life at that time," von Trips said, "but I said to them, 'Of course I'd like to drive in the race.' "

He may not have known what he was getting into. Every spring six hundred drivers blasted out of Brescia before dawn and scorched down the Adriatic coast on narrow Italian roads, the blue sea shimmering below. After crossing the mountains to Rome, the cars headed north through Siena, Florence, and Bologna to finish back at Brescia. It was racing's longest day.

Seasoned drivers hated the Mille Miglia because they maneuvered among packs of erratic amateurs. Plus, it was impossible to remember the nearly 7,000 turns. They rounded them at 140 mph without knowing what lay on the far side. Curbs, trees, and other deadly obstacles waited a few feet away.

If von Trips was daunted, he didn't show it. He kept his plans a secret from his parents. On the eve of the race he drove his Porsche down the Autobahn. "I was at a crossroads," he later said. "From now on I belonged to the car with body and soul."

He stopped at Stuttgart to pick up his co-driver, Walter Hampel. Von Trips was surprised to find that a car accident had left Hampel's arm in a sling. Hampel, in turn, was disappointed to learn that his co-driver had only driven in two real races.

Nobody in Brescia gave them much notice when they rolled down the starting ramp in Viale Venezia, Brescia's central square, at 2:28 a.m. For a thousand miles they flew over hummocks and slid around cobblestone corners slick with oil, leaving skids the size of hallway runners. They powered past clumps of Renaults, Fiats, and Gordinis on the coastal straights, pausing only to refuel and wipe dead flies from the windshield.

Hampel found von Trips to be a feckless companion. First he fell asleep during one of Hampel's shifts at the wheel. Then he wandered off to urinate behind a tree during a refueling stop. "I was half a minute late getting to the car," von Trips said. "Hampel was behind the wheel, trying to shout louder than he could honk."

Von Trips redeemed himself with a series of lightning turns at the wheel. "I had never seen the roads before, nor driven the car before," he said, "but I didn't make one single mistake." He saved his best performance for the final 100 kilometers. "There were masses of people on the side of the road, left and right," he said. "And finally there was the finish line."

Von Trips and Hampel came in first in the 1300cc class, and thirty-third overall. "The experts looked at us," von Trips said, "and shook their heads as if to say: how is that possible?"

That evening the count and countess stepped into the dining room of the Bayerischer Hof, a hotel in Munich. The maître d' asked if they were related to the von Trips who had posted a class win at the Mille Miglia. "I'm sorry, no," the count said. "My son is studying agronomy in West Germany." Or so they believed until they read the next day's newspaper.

Von Trips' parents could not understand why he would endanger himself after suffering so much childhood illness and narrowly surviving the war. They did not grasp his need to assert his toughness. "I always had the ambition to keep up with the others," he said. "I could never tolerate special treatment."

After the Mille Miglia, von Trips tried to hide his racing from his parents by registering under the pseudonym Axel Linther, a name he borrowed from a dead-end branch of the family tree. He was standing on the podium after a second-place finish at the Nürburgring when a friend pointed to the distant edge of the crowd. There was his mother watching him through a pair of binoculars. He waved. She waved back. He came down from the podium and went to her.

With his secret revealed, von Trips felt the need to resolve racing's place in his future. He had made an identity for himself as a driver, but it conflicted with the future he and his parents had always imagined. Was racing a youthful diversion, or would it replace the agronomy career that he had diligently prepared for? He found himself in limbo, unwilling for the moment to commit either way.

"I have no idea yet how to justify [racing] at home," he wrote in his diary earlier that year. "But that's no excuse to justify dropping out, either, because I've put time and money into this. Sometimes I see myself as the heir of a noble family that in his youth runs races and later in life has no idea about anything and has no money. I won't do that. I must learn something else. But I can't leave driving behind: I've put too much into it."

The uncertainty surrounding his future came to a head on September 19 when an important season-ending race in Berlin coincided with his agronomy exams. Von Trips persuaded his professors to let him sit for the exams on Monday so that he could race on Sunday.

He might have regretted the arrangement, considering the frustrations that followed. First he broke a fan belt and had to scavenge a replacement from a Volkswagen. Then his oil temperature soared to 275 degrees Fahrenheit, obliging him to slow down. "That was the hardest," he said. "I twirled comfortably around and around, and came in howling with rage."

Von Trips finished fifth, high enough to earn him the German championship in the 1500cc class. "I thought I was struck by lightning," he said. "I made the call home: 'Put the champagne on ice.'" But his parents were more concerned with his exams, which he managed to pass the next day. In April he was back at the Mille Miglia, soloing in a Porsche. Shortly after the start he rolled onto the shoulder with a loose fuel pump. A dozen strangers appeared from the darkness to help fix it and send him on his way. By the time he reached

Rome he led his class by six minutes.

On the northward run to Brescia a piece connecting the gas pedal to the carburetor broke, so he used a wire to pull the carburetor wide open. Then, with one hand on the wheel, he adjusted his speed by turning the ignition key on and off. "I was strained to the breaking point," he said, but he managed to finish second in his class.

Von Trips worked as an intern in a Munich bank that spring until his boss concluded that his mind was elsewhere and gave him the summer off to race. In early August he received a telegram from Stuttgart. His hands shook as he read the words: "I request you call immediately. Daimler Benz. Neubauer." The Mercedes manager who had earlier rejected von Trips as a dilettante summoned him to a racetrack in Hockenheim for a tryout the next day, then sent him to a series of races in Sweden, Norway, England, and Ireland.

Whatever strategies and skills von Trips developed in those apprentice years he learned from Neubauer, a rotund figure standing astride the pits like a walrus in a flannel suit. He leaned his bulk on a black umbrella while reading from three or four stopwatches slung about his fleshy neck. A chest of iced beer sat at his feet. Von Trips and his teammates called him the Fat Man.

By day Neubauer was a Prussian taskmaster, threatening encroaching reporters with a stick and drilling drivers in blackboard sessions. In the evenings he became a garrulous dinner host performing uncanny impersonations of Hitler and Marilyn Monroe. He could tell jokes in four languages.

"He was an amazing character who could have anybody snapping to attention if necessary, but also show great thought and understanding," said Stirling Moss, who spent two seasons on the Mercedes team. "In relaxed moments he could have us all rolling about with laughter."

Neubauer believed that a driver behind the wheel was the "world's loneliest human being." He offered encouragement and coaching by devising a system of hand signals and handwritten placards. In truth, he may have created the system to control drivers more than support them. When a driver ignored his sign to slow down he stood shaking his fist in the middle of the road. By one account he even waved a pistol at the driver.

Neubauer is said to have concocted a racing restorative made of black coffee, egg yolk, sugar, and wine, mixed with spices. If so, he may have helped von Trips stave off the diabetic spells that caused him to wilt in the cockpit.

In the summer of 1954, in Bern, Switzerland, the West German soccer team, in its return to international competition, beat the strongly favored Hungarians in the World Cup finals. It was the first time since the war that the German national anthem was played in public, and among the first successes enjoyed by a crushed country. Throughout Germany it was called *Das wunder von Bern,* the Miracle of Bern.

Neubauer was working on his own miracle. In 1946 the Mercedes plant in Stuttgart was 70 percent ruined. Six years later the company was racing with overwhelming force, as they had in the 1930s. In doing so Mercedes faced a delicate proposition. Could it restore German pride without stirring up bitter memories? They were, after all, trying to sell cars to the same foreigners they had strafed and bombed a decade earlier. Von Trips might have provided part of the solution: He was a fearless driver with the friendly, handsome face of a new Germany.

Hill and von Trips would have raced against each other for the first time at the 1955 Le Mans, but Neubauer chose Levegh, the more experienced endurance driver, instead of von Trips, with tragic results. Von Trips was sitting in the grandstand when Levegh hurtled off the road, sending the deadly spray of parts and burning gas through the crowd, ending the Mercedes revival just as von Trips was solidifying his place on the team.

At Burg Hemmersbach, von Trips' parents pressured him to quit racing and assume more responsibility for the farmlands. He was their only child, they argued, and the seven-century family tree would end with him if he died on the racetrack. Von Trips did not dismiss their pleas out of hand. If anything, the quiet of the castle grounds, enveloped by a thick shroud of trees, had grown more enchanting after the travel and stress of competition. "I notice how the big races stay with you. They carve a little out of you," he said. "Inwardly, I'm at a pretty low ebb. No close friends, no girlfriend."

The castle had almost no modern comforts. The family lived in conditions that Americans would consider semipoverty, with a handful of rooms heated by fireplaces. Von Trips spent a lot of time staring into the embers that winter, as if studying a crystal ball. In the end, he resolved to continue racing, though he had no immediate prospects since Mercedes had quit the circuit. Throughout December and January he sat at the big oak desk in his top-floor study writing a ream of polite queries. "It would be very kind of you," he wrote to Stirling Moss, "to let me know if you hear of anywhere I might have a chance to race."

In February of 1956 he drove to Munich through a snowfall to meet with Huschke von Hanstein of Porsche, who had given him his big break two years earlier. "Can you do anything for me?" von Trips asked, sounding a little desperate.

"Let's see," von Hanstein said as they strolled the Theatinerstrasse, one of Germany's most fashionable avenues. "Maybe you can come practice with us across the pond."

A month later von Trips was in Sebring, a track laid out on a disused bomber base in a drowsy central Florida town. Von Hanstein paired him with Hans Hermann, a driver so boyish that he was nicknamed Sonny Boy Hans, in a 12-hour sports car race. They finished sixth — twelve places ahead of Phil Hill. Von Trips returned home to find that Neubauer had scrounged a Mercedes 300SL for him to race at the 1956 Mille Miglia.

Von Trips cut a smart figure wherever he appeared on the circuit, even by the glamorous standards of European racing. At a press event in Brescia before the Mille Miglia he posed in his car with a relaxed smile. He had a thick head of dark blond hair to go with expressive blue eyes and a hawk nose. His resemblance to the young Robert Redford has been noted more than once.

The next day he flew down the slippery roads along the Adriatic in a persistent downpour, dueling for the lead with Eugenio Castellotti before going off the road in the coastal town of Pescara. He was unhurt, but unable to continue. In May he and Umberto Maglioli co-drove a Porsche to a fourth-place finish in a 1,000-kilometer race at the Nürburgring, almost within sight of the woods where he had walked with Breitschwert. In June he was back at Le Mans, finishing fifth in a Porsche.

Von Trips had made the most of these freelance outings, grinding out a string of finishes that showed him to be determined and unafraid of edging up to, and over, the limit. "The race leaders directed their gaze at Wolfgang like butterfly collectors observing a particularly rare specimen," wrote Hermann Harster, a German newspaper reporter who later collaborated with von Trips on a biography. "Unknown drivers are more commonly treated like aphids."

Aggressive drivers inevitably caught Enzo Ferrari's eye. In August he teamed von Trips with Peter Collins, a British driver, for a 621-mile race in the Swedish city of Kristianstad where they finished second, less than a minute behind Hill. That night the Ferrari drivers stole a crate of whiskey from the hotel bar. Luigi Musso deliberately knocked over a table, and in the confusion Hawthorn passed the crate back to teammates who smuggled it down a hallway to a sitting room. At 4 a.m. they each dropped a contribution into the empty crate and returned it to the bar.

In September Ferrari offered von Trips a car for the 1956 Italian Grand Prix at Monza, Italy's premier racetrack. It was an important audition for a rookie who had barely proved himself in the lower ranks. For the first time he would race a Formula 1 car, a stripped-down single-seat racing machine built to specifications set by the sport's governing body specifically for a series of races known as Grand Prix — racing's highest tier. "To climb into the cockpit of a Formula 1 car," Harster wrote, "takes more effort than to climb the steps to a royal throne."

Unlike sports cars, which were modified

showroom models, Formula 1 vehicles were made exclusively for racing. They looked like wicked ground-hugging torpedoes with open cockpits, wraparound windscreens, and outrigger wheels. Stripped of nonessential hardware, they were lighter, faster, and far less forgiving than anything von Trips had previously driven. The smallest error could remove a driver from a race, or kill him. A Formula 1 car, von Trips said, "was a fencing foil, a sports car a heavier saber."

The first thing von Trips noticed was the piercing high-pitched whine. "When the engine began to howl for the first time," he said, "I thought my eardrums would break." Next came the sickening G-force of acceleration, pulling and distorting his cheeks as he rounded turns.

Formula 1 cars were gorgeous, but tricky. The gas pedal sat between the clutch and brake, obliging drivers to downshift with a little dancing maneuver known as "heel and toe." The steering wheel was so sensitive that von Trips found himself swerving all over the track in his first day of practice. "My arms were completely stiff," he said, "so tensely had I been holding the steering wheel."

He was coming out of a curve at 125 mph

when he saw "the right front wheel flutter, as if it were drunk," he said. "There was no control over the wheel." His car careened off the track like a skipping stone and veered into a forest, heading for a group of stout trees. Every driver feared these few seconds of helplessness. There was nothing to do but wait for the impact.

"I saw the tree coming at me and I said to myself: 'you're dead, Trips.'" Wham. The tree unpeeled paneling from one side of the Ferrari. Whack. A second tree scraped away the other side. Stripped of wheels and body, the naked chassis dug nose first into the soil. It flipped end over end eight times and landed in a bush. Along the way von Trips flew from the cockpit. "I lay on the ground," he said, "and then I realized I was smelling the dirt, and I said to myself: 'Trips, you're not dead.'" He limped back to the pits with a badly injured arm and a leg placed in a splint by the track doctor. Castellotti went pale when he saw him. "He looked at me like I was a ghost," von Trips said.

Castellotti was troubled less by von Trips' narrow escape than by what it would provoke: Ferrari was enraged, as he always was at news of a car trucked away in pieces. Von Trips insisted that he had made no mistake. In any case, the injury prevented him from racing. "The next day I could barely move," he said. "Dressing was an ordeal." He was vindicated two days later when Luigi Musso, driving the same model in the lead of the Grand Prix race, also lost control. Forensics revealed that the cars shared a metallurgical defect: Both steering arms had snapped under stress.

As if to redeem himself, von Trips won a pair of races in Berlin two weeks later in a Porsche and a Mercedes, in spite of his injuries. "I wanted to prove that my double somersault in Monza left no lasting shock," he said. He nearly blacked out from the pain of shifting gears with his right hand, so he somehow reached across his body and shifted with his left hand. "Ferrari decided that if I wanted to drive that badly," he said, "I could drive for him."

Von Trips could not stay in Ferrari's bad graces for long. He had what Ferrari called "a noble spirit."

"He was very fast," Ferrari wrote in his memoirs, "and capable of the most daring feats, always with that slightly melancholic little smile on his aristocratic face."

A week after the Italian Grand Prix, Ferrari wrote von Trips a conciliatory note saying that he was holding his prize money from the Swedish race for him, and that a guard had retrieved his helmet after the Monza crash. Ferrari followed these niceties with a bombshell: He offered von Trips a contract for the 1957 season.

When Ferrari offered Hill a position eight months earlier, he practically jitterbugged in the pits, and understandably so. A Ferrari contract was an invitation to join racing's most exalted circle. But von Trips at first demurred. Racing for a German marque had always been central to his ambitions. He had dreamed of inheriting the mantle of the smiling, warmhearted German hero from his childhood idol Bernd Rosemeyer. His assertive driving reflected his urgent desire to restore honor to a country disgraced by Nazism and split by Cold War borders. Germany needed a hero. He was determined that it would be him. Besides, von Hanstein of Porsche had been a supportive, avuncular figure. Von Trips knew that he could not expect the same from Ferrari. He asked for time to consider the offer.

In the end he could not resist the siren call of the Ferrari engine. The prospect of winning, and winning big, outweighed his allegiance to Porsche. Just before Christmas von Trips signed on. He would go to Modena as the first German to race for

Ferrari. The unforgiving V12, in all its power, could either propel him to a championship or feed his propensity for mishap.

Von Trips gave off none of the grandiosity or self-regard you might expect from a handsome count. "He conducted himself as an ordinary guy," said Stirling Moss. "He was an aristocrat without being haughty." For example, when a reporter came to Burg Hemmersbach to interview von Trips, he was directed to a group of farmhands laboring in a field. "The dirtiest one there," an employee said. "That's the count."

On the race circuit, he was unfailingly cordial, even a little shy. As he laughed a trace of sadness showed in his soft eyes. "His voice did not sound as if it were coming from the hatch of a tank, as it so often does with seemingly tough guys," Hermann Harster wrote. "He was a different kind of man with quick eyes, lips and hands, a man who loved stillness, despite all the victories."

As junior members of the Ferrari team, Hill and von Trips naturally fell into friendship. Both were single men living in the quiet provincial town of Modena in the years before handlers and flacks isolated drivers from one another. They spent a great deal of time together — testing, talking, traveling, eating, and drinking. Von Trips teasingly Italianized Hill's name, calling him "Philee Hillee." Hill called von Trips "Taffy," a Welsh nickname he had acquired for reasons nobody could recall.

But their temperaments and backgrounds could not have differed more. Put in the starkest terms, Hill drove with his head and von Trips drove with his nerves.

Hill was sensitive to every flaw and frailty of the machine. It was as if he could train his musician's ear on the engine song, listening for telltale pings, clunks, or grinding that signaled a weak part or balky transmission. He fussed to the point of obsession over the springs, shocks, and camber changes. It was not uncommon for him to slow down to preserve an ailing engine, even if it meant dropping back a few spots. In the pits he was known as "Professor Piston."

Von Trips, by contrast, had an unquestioning Germanic faith in machinery. He drove the car as it was prepared for him, just as his father rode a stallion brought by his groom. "Anyone as intense as I was at that time," Hill said, "was a bit skeptical of those like von Trips who seemed, at least on the surface, a bit lackadaisical." His habit of wrecking within the first lap or so earned him the nickname Count von Crash, a joke he accepted with customary good humor.

Von Trips may not have grasped the engineering subtleties, as Hill did, but he had something arguably more valuable: an instinctive mastery of speed and cat-quick reflexes. He was brilliant at the sheer physical aspect of racing — the coordination of hand and feet, the smooth procession of gearshifts, the long pause before breaking in a turn. "You don't need a mechanical knowledge," Stirling Moss said. "What you need most is a certain feel. Von Trips had that feel."

He also had a talent that lived in his guts. He was capable of driving with a fury that verged on desperation. More than most, he was willing to hang it all out. "He is the type who does not gingerly taste the limit, but goes straight after it," said Richard von Frankenberg, a German driver and journalist. "If he goes slightly over the frontier, well, he has such fast reactions that he can catch the car again with almost absolute certainty."

For all their differences, Hill and von Trips shared something fundamental: Each came to racing from traumatic upbringings. Each was trying to make the world right.

"Most racers I know had unhappy childhoods," Hill said. "They try to put order into their lives by taking something dangerous, potentially chaotic, and imposing their order on it. It gives them worth. A racer believes he can make his deadly machine safe. He is playing God."

By 1957, Phil Hill (at center) and Wolfgang von Trips (to Hill's left, in a polo shirt) had joined the Grand Prix, an international fraternity with a grisly mortality rate. (Klemantaski Collection)

7
GARIBALDINI

Ferrari drivers led an itinerant life — a movable feast by way of *la dolce vita.* They traveled among four continents in roguish packs, picking up girls in hotel bars and biding time in airport lounges, as rock stars would a decade later. They laughed easily and often, but they were deadly serious on the topic of driving. "They live in their own country," wrote Ken Purdy, a journalist who covered the circuit for *Playboy,* "and only the natives understand their language."

The drivers spent their days negotiating the limit, their evenings in laughter with wives and girlfriends jangling bracelets and calling for Campari and soda or vermouth cassis. They sat around long group tables in Milan trattorias and Buenos Aires dives, tossing wisecracks in Italian, French, and English. Their one mealtime rule: The first to mention cars paid for the wine.

Phil Hill and Wolfgang von Trips took

their places at these gatherings alongside their new teammates, a cast of international all-stars signed by Enzo Ferrari for the 1957 season: Mike Hawthorn and Peter Collins of England, Eugenio Castellotti and Luigi Musso of Italy, the Marquis Alfonso de Portago of Spain, Olivier Gendebien of Belgium, and Maurice Trintignant of France. The Italian press called them *la squadra primavera,* the spring team.

Von Trips had spent part of his adolescence dodging bombs and pulling bodies from rubble. For all his gentlemanly reserve, he was not about to miss out on life's recompenses. When it came to boozy nights with women wearing pale pink lipstick and tossing blonde curls, he was all in.

Hill, on the other hand, was just as happy to retire to his hotel room after dinner and soothe his nerves with Bartók's string quartets or Shostakovich's Fifth Symphony played on a Concertone reel-to-reel stereo that he traveled with. He also used the Concertone to record long audio letters that he mailed to his brother and sister in Santa Monica. He was friendly enough, but removed. He seemed content with the company of machinery and music. As he traveled through Europe he collected vintage music players and more than four thousand player piano rolls. More than anything he liked to drive his Volkswagen into Milan to sit in the *loggione* of La Scala, the gingerbread opera house. Surrounded by clapping, whistling Milanese, he heard Maria Callas sing arias of jealousy, treachery, and martyrdom. She could easily have been singing about Ferrari. More than any other marque, it roiled with intrigue and death.

On December 13, 1956, von Trips lugged a suitcase through the crowded Genoa dockyards and walked up a gangplank to the *Conte Grande,* a midsized passenger ship bound for Buenos Aires with a fleet of Ferraris stowed in the hold. He was joined onboard by a handful of mechanics and his English teammate Peter Collins, the lean twenty-six-year-old son of a wealthy car dealer in the Worcestershire town of Kidderminster. With his blue eyes and radiant smile, Collins had the classic well-scrubbed looks of a British public school boy. He had a habit of brushing back a sandy-blond forelock. "Peter was remarkably good looking, but somehow he had a vulnerable quality that made you fear for him," said Sir Peter Ustinov, the actor and filmmaker, who was friendly with the British drivers. "One somehow knew he wasn't going to survive."

195

Von Trips could not have hoped for a better guide to his new way of life than Collins. "Peter was a fantastic companion," von Trips wrote in an account of the trip. "We sat on deck for hours, with the equator approaching, weather getting warmer. Peter told stories about the legendary cars, the perils of the track and the intrigues, struggles, all going on behind the scenes."

After the two-week Atlantic crossing their ship stopped in Montevideo for two days. Collins vanished into the city with a young Brazilian woman he had met on shipboard. They had not returned when the steamer prepared to disembark. "The ship's horn sounded," von Trips wrote in his diary. "We looked everywhere onboard. . . . It was horrible. Would he be left behind? How would he make it with no luggage and no money?"

Von Trips pleaded in vain with the captain to wait, then stationed himself at the railing. As the ship edged away from its berth Collins appeared on the quay, running among piles of freight and pulling his girlfriend behind. "There he stood, wondering what to do next," von Trips wrote in his diary. "He had a shock when he saw all the water separating him from the ship."

Collins and his companion jumped into an old skiff and inveigled the crew to cast off. "So began a wild chase," von Trips wrote in his diary. "We were already picking up speed. All the people who were off-duty, the cooks with their tall white hats and passengers of all classes were on deck. They were desperately trying to catch us. Sailors lowered a rope ladder, but in vain. With two others I went back to the captain. 'Slow speed ahead' came the order, and with sweet and sour smiles both our refugees came on board. A raucous and enchanting evening followed."

The next morning they went ashore in Buenos Aires and prepared for the Temporada, a trio of races run in the heat of the Argentine summer. Von Trips' education in Formula 1, interrupted by his crash at Monza five months earlier, now resumed in the gray asphalt expanse of the *autódromo*. This was his chance to prove that the crash was an anomaly, and that he could compete at racing's highest level. It was no sure thing.

Collins watched from a viewing platform while von Trips fumbled through practice laps, trying to find the swiftest line into turns and hit the right braking spots. With the car in a four-wheel drift, he pressed the gas to increase the angle of slide; or, conversely, he reduced the speed to straighten the car out. "Every time I tried it I either

197

wound up on the lawn or spinning around like a carousel," von Trips wrote. "There was a very sharp corner driving me to despair, and I began to wonder about the infinite patience of Peter Collins, who came around each time to tell me what I was doing wrong."

Again and again von Trips sped too fast into turns and had to brake hard to prevent a spin. The trick, Collins explained, was to glide smoothly on the way in and accelerate on the way out while thinking ahead to the next turn. It required a fluid dancelike flow of shifting and braking with a lightfooted dab on the brake. The task was complicated by the heat and head-splitting racket of the unmuffled engine and the need to study engine revs on the tachometer while watching traffic in two rearview mirrors. The car shuddered whenever he braked and a blister festered on his right hand from the constant gear work. All the while he could feel the sickening centrifugal pull as he strained to go ever faster. "It took only a few laps for me to learn about the draining of strength and concentration out there," he wrote.

When he was not driving von Trips practiced the turning techniques in his mind. "I laid my head back, closed my eyes, thought about an extreme curve and put everything there in my mind's eye that I'd been trying to learn," he wrote. "Run into the curve, hit the brakes, slide, not too much, hit the gas. How often did I repeat this, talking under my breath, lost in my imagination? I don't know. At some point Mike Hawthorn poked me in the ribs: 'What's with you? Are you nuts?' "

Von Trips served as Collins' backup in the Argentine Grand Prix on January 13, the first of the Temporada. He did not expect to drive, but halfway through the race Collins pulled into the pits and turned the car over to him. " 'Go on, scram,' Collins said to me as he got out of the cockpit," von Trips wrote. "And I jumped into the Formula 1 as I had always hoped and dreamed. And off I zipped."

The Grand Prix went for the fourth time to the hometown hero, Juan Manuel Fangio, a stocky, balding former bus mechanic and son of an Argentine potato farmer. He was an empyrean figure, despite his humble bearing. At age forty-six, he was the sport's elder statesman and the Grand Prix champion in four of the previous five years. The drivers called him El Maestro. They stood up when he entered a room, as if greeting a head of state.

The day after winning the Grand Prix,

Fangio took von Trips and Joakim Bonnier, a tall, goateed Maserati driver from a wealthy Swedish publishing family, to Mar del Plata, a beach resort south of Buenos Aires, where passersby stopped and shouted "bravo!" as Fangio passed. In a hotel bar a guest jumped onstage with a guitar and played a song he had written about Fangio.

That kind of adulation was hard earned, as von Trips would learn thirteen days later at the 1,000-kilometer Buenos Aires, a sports car race run on one of the hottest days in memory. "When we came out of our air-conditioned hotel," von Trips wrote, "the heat hit us like a wall." The temperature exceeded 100 degrees in the city, and it reached 131 degrees on the track. Heat shimmered in woozy waves off the asphalt, clouding the drivers' view.

After forty minutes von Trips peered into the pits on successive laps to see if anybody had quit. He felt lightheaded, but he hated to be the first to withdraw. "You must not give up," he recalled in his diary. "Hell with it! You simply keep driving! One more round! God, I can't take any more! I'm getting the heatstroke! I wish I'd never come to Argentina!"

He eventually succumbed, pulling over just before fainting. "Sheer self-preservation led me into the pits," he wrote. "Once there, I collapsed in the car and the mechanics had to pull me from the seat." They laid him on a bed of wet towels in a corner and rubbed his body with ice. "It was a blissful feeling," he recalled. "After 10 or 15 minutes I came back to myself." Meanwhile Collins took over von Trips' car and finished ninth.

The Buenos Aires endurance race was a doubleheader. After an hour's respite, the drivers set off in the twilight for a second round of thirty laps. This time von Trips had arranged for an Argentine-German acquaintance to stand beside a hairpin turn and pour buckets of cold water on him as he passed at 40 mph or so.

Von Trips sought out every bit of adventure and fun his new life afforded. While most drivers flew directly back to Europe or accompanied the cars by freighter, he and Bonnier went on a grand tour of Latin countries. They hunted and rode horseback as guests on an Argentine ranch, then flew to Rio de Janeiro. Fangio had telegrammed ahead on their behalf, arranging for a Brazilian racer and other friends to entertain them for three days before they left for Caracas. Along their route they drank unfamiliar Latin drinks and recounted their racing deeds for the benefit of the señoritas.

Meanwhile, Peter Collins could not evacuate Buenos Aires fast enough. He had met Eleanora Herrera, a twenty-one-year-old insurance heiress, at a pool party before the Temporada. "It was love at first sight for me and I thought Peter felt the same way," she said. They went out frequently the week before the first race and she visited him in the pits on practice days. By her account, Collins proposed to her a week after they met. He gave her a platinum ring with a pearl set in diamonds, she said, and her family marked the engagement by inviting Buenos Aires society to a celebratory banquet. But as the racing wound down, she said, Collins withdrew. "He began to rejoin his racing friends in their exploits about town," she told the *Daily Mirror,* a British tabloid. By her account, he left without a goodbye. Collins denied that they were ever formally engaged.

After detaching himself from Herrera, Collins flew to Miami. He had three weeks to kill before the Gran Premio, a 300-mile sports car race along the curving waterfront esplanade in Havana, Cuba. He planned to spend a few days in Florida, then visit a square-jawed American driver with thick eyeglasses named Masten Gregory at his home in Kansas City. He never made that trip. Stirling Moss had given him the phone number of a slender American actress with a broad incandescent smile named Louise King, who was performing in *The Seven Year Itch* at a theater in the Coconut Grove neighborhood of Miami. King resembled Ingrid Bergman, but with freckles and the hearty laugh of a fun-loving American girl. She had owned a British Austin-Healey sports car, one of the first in America, until crashing it in a road rally outside Baltimore. In 1955 she bought a new one in London and drove it to Paris and Monte Carlo, where she mixed with the racing crowd. She had met Collins at a party Bernard Cahier threw at his Riviera home before the Monte Carlo Grand Prix, but they apparently made no impression on each other. Neither could remember meeting.

Collins called her on February 4 and arranged to join her for a drink at a bar off the theater lobby at 11 p.m., after the final curtain. Though they had met before, it was essentially a blind date. "He just sparkled," King said. "For me it was very close to love at first sight. He must have felt the same way."

Two days later, King was sunbathing between Gregory and Collins at the pool outside Collins' motel. He leaned over and, whispering so Gregory would not hear, asked King to marry him. She whispered back, "Yes!"

King's father, who was executive assistant to Secretary-General Dag Hammarskjöld of the United Nations, flew down from New York that Friday to talk her out of it. By the time King's father left on Sunday he had given his blessing. The couple married the next day — exactly a week after their first date — at an old stone church in Coconut Grove. Four hours later she was back on-stage.

In late February Collins and the other Ferrari drivers converged on Havana for the Gran Premio. Enzo Ferrari did not supply them with team cars. Instead he tele-grammed his permission to drive whatever privately owned cars they could find — as long as it was a Ferrari.

The government of Fulgencio Batista staged the annual Grand Premio to help fill the splendid hotels and casinos with free-spending Americans. This year there was a snag: A two-week longshoreman's strike in New York prevented a dozen sports cars from loading onto ships bound for Cuba. As a result, Havana was long on drivers and short on cars. Landing a ride for the Gran

Premio became its own competition. Von Trips partied deep into the nights, chasing tips and rumors in brocaded nightclubs and cheap rum dives tucked in Havana's dark corners. He and Bonnier promoted their cause by returning to the airport and reenacting their arrival for newspaper photographers. The resulting coverage helped him connect with an American who had flown down with an ancient Ferrari Testa Rossa. Its gearbox sprayed hot oil over von Trips' gloves and goggles until he wrapped the transmission in cardboard.

Even in 1957 there were signs of the seismic changes to come in Cuba. Twenty-seven spectators were injured when a temporary wooden footbridge collapsed during practice runs. It was suspected that Fidel Castro's guerrillas, who were fighting government troops in the mountains, had sabotaged the structure. In the days before the race, flyers had circulated in Havana reading, "Don't go to automobile races. Avoid accidents. (signed) Revolutionary Movement of Twenty-sixth of July."

On the first practice day von Trips met up with Hill, who was driving a war-weary Ferrari owned by the head of a New Jersey metal stamping company. Standing in the tropical heat, the two men compared notes on the waterfront road, known as the Malecón, which was buckled and undulated from years of tropical heat. During a warm-up run Hill chased Masten Gregory, whose heedless driving manner had earned him the nickname the Kansas City Flash. "Phil came in and said, 'Masten has no idea what he's doing. He's out there going like hell on that damn road,' " said Denise McCluggage.

"How do you know?" she said.

"Because I was right there behind him the whole time," Hill said.

"I started laughing," she said, "and then he started laughing too."

A month later, Hill and von Trips shared a year-old 3.5-liter Ferrari at a 12-hour race in Sebring, Florida. Belches of exhaust fused with Everglades humidity as von Trips stepped hard on the accelerator at the start of a practice run. The mechanics and team manager watched with concern. When von Trips pulled into the pits the Ferrari crew huddled around the cockpit to review the car's performance. "It runs fine unless I do this," von Trips told them. He leaned across the dashboard and flipped a switch on the far right side.

Hill, who was listening in, expressed

astonishment. "That's the fuel pump!" he said.

"Oh," von Trips answered with his easy, self-effacing laugh.

The car's brakes were so anemic that Hill did deep-knee bends with a hundred-pound weight on his back for weeks beforehand to build leg strength. In the end, a faulty battery proved their undoing. After they traded the wheel off and on for six and a half hours the car coughed and went cold. They were forced to withdraw.

After Florida, von Trips swung through New York, with long evenings at El Morocco and the Copacabana. He also made the obligatory visits to Sardi's and Le Chanteclair, customary Midtown gathering spots for the racing crowd. He had by now exhausted his travel budget. His one gray suit was wrinkled and wrung out from too many parties. "With Argentine saddles, Cuban drums and American cowboy hats, I was laden with four months of the gypsy life," he wrote. "I had a dollar in my pocket. It's going to take my poor mother a long time to — as she puts it — make a proper gentleman out of me again."

The news of Collins' marriage did not sit well with Enzo Ferrari. He encouraged his drivers to take up with the tanned women in tight cashmere sweaters and oversize sunglasses who hung around the pits, and he was delighted to hear about their sexual escapades. He took these things as signs of manliness. But he discouraged serious relationships for a simple reason: He saw love as the enemy of speed.

"Ferrari didn't like his drivers to marry," King said, "because it sounded like they were settling down, which means slowing down."

Ferrari had warned Eugenio Castellotti about this. "Men are creatures of their passions," Ferrari told him, "and this makes them victims of women." Like Collins, Castellotti ignored him.

Castellotti was an extravagantly wealthy young gentleman from Lodi who lounged in the pits with his white helmet pushed back over ink-black hair and a blue jacket pulled tight over sinewy shoulders. A cigarette dangled from lips so shapely they looked cartoonish. The Italian women called him Il Bello, the beautiful one.

When Alberto Ascari died in May 1955, Castellotti became Italy's last great hope to overcome the British virtuoso Stirling Moss and the Argentinean maestro Juan Manuel Fangio. He lived up to their hopes, winning a string of races. Most impressive of all, he took the 1956 Mille Miglia in a persistent downpour. Robert Daley, the *New York Times* correspondent, wrote that Castellotti "would pass other cars on the verge in a shower of stones, grinning like a fiend." He had shown himself to be a true *garibaldino,* a slang term for drivers who, in Ferrari's words, "put courage and verve before cool calculation."

Italy might once again have a great champion, Ferrari thought, if Castellotti could stay focused and avoid female entanglements. When the Ferrari team boarded an Alitalia flight from Milan to Argentina in January 1957, Castellotti was the only driver to sit out the poker game. His girlfriend had given him a bundle of letters at the airport with instructions to open one every hour. Castellotti had thrown himself into a blazing romance with Delia Scala, a classically trained ballerina with a flourishing career in movies and television. The couple was a gossip column staple.

Ferrari disapproved. So did Castellotti's mother. When Signora Castellotti met Scala she said, "You look like a waitress. The kitchen is this way."

Despite the objections, the couple became engaged in early March 1957, though they

209

bickered often, and publicly, over whether he should quit his career to spend time with her, or vice versa.

On March 13 Castellotti was in Florence where Scala was performing in *Good Night Bettina,* a play about a husband who finds that his wife has an unexpected literary talent. The phone rang in their hotel bedroom. It was Ferrari angrily summoning Castellotti. Jean Behra had been circling the rectangular *autodromo* on the edge of Modena at terrific speeds. He threatened to break the record for fastest lap held by Ferrari for years. What galled Ferrari most was that Behra was driving a Maserati, Ferrari's crosstown rival.

Modena was a city divided. An ancient Roman road, the Via Emilia, ran down its center. Ferrari and Maserati were encamped on opposing sides, less than a mile apart, like an automotive version of the Montagues and Capulets. Ferrari could not tolerate the prospect of Maserati stealing the local record. He considered it an affront to the natural order. Castellotti must return immediately to defend it.

Castellotti roused himself from Scala's warm bed before 5 a.m. the next morning and drove over the Apennine Mountains to Modena. Waiting for him behind the *auto-*

210

dromo's redbrick walls with peeling posters was a team manager, mechanics, and an untested Formula 1 Ferrari. He climbed in and blasted down a damp track at more than 100 mph. On the third lap the crew signaled to accelerate.

It would not happen today, but in the 1950s a driver going more than 115 mph could be easily jostled and lose footing on the pedals. Whether this happened to Castellotti is not known. For whatever reason, he bungled a crucial downshift coming out of a curve. The car lost traction and began to slide. After a few desperate swerves his car flipped and rolled into a concrete wall beneath a small grandstand. The *autodromo* rang with the sound of screeching brakes and crumpling metal.

Castellotti was thrown out and landed on the tarmac. Don Sergio Mantovani, a local parish priest who was a fixture in the pits, ran through the debris and knelt beside Castellotti. His left eye was open, but he was fading. Mantovani raised his hand and blessed him. He and Scala were to have been married twenty-five days later.

When Ferrari heard the news, he said, "What a pity. What about the car?" He later said Castellotti was probably thinking too much about Scala and not enough about driving. It was an implicit warning to the other Ferrari drivers: By all means court the coquettes, but never let love interfere with the proper handling of cars at the limit.

Ferrari skipped Castellotti's funeral, as usual. He had no use for the Catholic rituals of mourning. He did his own communing with death. He could feel its presence in the black-and-white photographs of drivers hanging on the walls of his gloomy office and in his morning cemetery visits to speak with his son.

Ferrari accepted that death was the inevitable result of his campaign for speed. His ambition was to win "even with the sacrifice of the most noble human lives." To be fair, he wasn't the only one. On every factory team managers bullied and prodded drivers to the limit, and beyond; at every juncture they watched for signs that drivers were losing their nerve — particularly those recently married or recovering from a crash. "The owners see us drivers as a bunch of funny little psychopaths who sooner or later get too chicken to stick their shoe in it," Hill said. "They want to know when this happens so that they can get someone else. So they pressure drivers in a hundred different ways."

This was true on every team, but Ferrari seemed to put his drivers at particular risk by fostering competitive pressures, a kind of sibling rivalry. He did so by lining up more drivers than cars, then leaving the drivers to fight for a place in the pecking order. To him, an insecure driver was a fast driver.

Newspaper headlines announcing the death of handsome young drivers — and the collateral damage in grandstands — only added to the brand's mystique. The drivers themselves never talked about danger, except obliquely and with darkest humor. For example, the rugged Targa Florio in Sicily contained a curve so perilous that Peter Collins called it the "back to England in a box turn." When friends said, "See you next week" to Stirling Moss, his standard response was, "Well, I hope so."

Moss preferred the sport perilous because it set the drivers apart in a nobility of daring. More than skill, it was danger that made them elite. "Without danger there wouldn't be any point to it, really," Moss said. "It would just be a game that anyone could play. It would be like climbing a mountain with a net ready to catch you if you fell. What's the point to that?" Though it should be noted that Moss faced the dark uncertainties with a protective parcel of superstitions: He carried a Saint Christopher medal and a horseshoe on board, and he tried to avoid racing on the thirteenth day of the month.

Moss and the other British drivers carried themselves with the studied indifference of RAF pilots half a generation older. They lived by the adage, "swallow your emotions or they will swallow you." In newspaper and magazine interviews they voiced the same platitudes about peril concentrating one's mind on the here and now. "The very uncertainty sharpens the appetite," said Colin Chapman, a driver who later founded Lotus, the British race car manufacturer. "The danger makes the value of life all the more appreciable."

Phil Hill was having dinner with a group of drivers one night when he noticed a restaurant window shaking menacingly in a strong wind. "The racers were the first ones to flee the window before it shattered," he said. "They are always the first ones to flee an accident on the track. They don't want to die. They just want the possibility of death. It is their way of reaffirming their life. Without racing they don't feel they are really alive. Of course this is not rational."

They went through mental gymnastics to convince themselves that they were impervious. Otherwise they would be unable to compete. When a driver died his friends explained his accident as the result of faulty judgment or freakish mishap. The victim *got his,* as the drivers said, by missing a gearshift or hitting a patch of oil at an awkward moment. The survivors were blithely confident it would never happen to them. Death would visit the next man.

Hill, the sober-minded technocrat, knew that was not necessarily true. Too many possibilities lay beyond their control. He was acutely aware that racing was a form of Russian roulette, and it showed in his perpetually grim-faced demeanor. Hill had mostly outgrown his ulcers, but he still slept poorly before races, if at all. A thousand dark possibilities crowded his mind as he tossed and turned in hotels all over the world. He paced the pits, smoking and wiping and re-wiping his goggles and biting his lower lip as he worked out mechanical problems in the back of his mind. Tetchy and high-strung, he glared at anyone who disturbed the unsmiling rhythm of his pre-race jitters. "I've been described as anxious in four or five languages," he said.

Denise McCluggage described Hill as a "Hamlet with goggles and gloves." She once told him that he was better suited to working as the second oboist for the Cincinnati Symphony.

"Exactly," Hill answered. "But I can't play the oboe."

Drivers were not supposed to reveal their anguish. It spoiled their image as the 1950s equivalent of Spitfire pilots. Hill broke the taboo by expressing his anxiety without restraint. "A racer should have, as they say in German, his nerves close to his skin," von Trips said. "Phil has that quality, but he can't seem to control his nerves as well as he should. He seems so tense, so concentrated."

Hill openly voiced his safety concerns to the press, which sometimes antagonized his Ferrari handlers. "Pheel, you 'ave spoke too much," race manager Romolo Tavoni would tell him while menacingly gripping a button on Hill's polo shirt. To the British drivers, in particular, Hill's fretting seemed unmanly and out of keeping with the stoic code. Mike Hawthorn ridiculed Hill's hand-wringing, calling him "Auntie." But when it came time to drive home from dinner or drinks, Hawthorn wanted Hill behind the wheel.

In Hill's view, the chivalric tradition of bravery and bloody sacrifice that von Trips espoused was obsolete. It was, in Hill's opinion, better suited to von Trips' ancestors than to Ferrari drivers of the 1950s. Hill believed himself to be a more accurate reflection of what he called "the age of anxiety." In the Cold War era of spy satellites and H-bombs, speed had acquired an intimation of dread. In keeping with the paranoid mood of the day, Hill was both obsessed with and unsettled by the quest for speed.

"I had been to many races and many funerals," Hill said, "and a battle was mounting within me. There was an inner drive to race, to excel; but there was also a tremendous drive to stay alive and in one piece. . . . Some drivers never seem to entertain that conflict. I think Wolfgang von Trips was one of them. He was tremendously turned on by everything about racing, the driving, the adoration. His inner image of himself seemed to be as a racing hero."

When the beat reporters gathered over wine, they often talked about Hill as if his psyche were a riddle to be solved. How could a man so doom-conscious get in the car and drive unflinchingly through heat and rain? Behind the wheel Hill's apprehension mysteriously vanished and he turned into a racing robot coldly calculating time, distance, and engine performance. He had learned by now to use his nervous adrenaline to quicken his reflexes and heighten his sense of movement and maneuvering — a faculty known today as situational awareness. "I have no lack of confidence," Hill said, "when I have the wheel in my hands."

As long as Hill was in the car he was in control and blissfully free of the awkward social interactions of everyday life. "All doubts, all anxieties, all memories of past painful struggles fade away before the magic of this occasional purity," he wrote in *Sports Illustrated,* referring to morning practice laps on an empty track, "and I am at one with the car." It was as if there were two Phil Hills — one a neurotic hand-wringer, the other a hard-minded hero — each strangely disconnected from the other.

If Hill was happiest behind the wheel, von Trips was the opposite. He looked forward to the moment when the struggle ended and he could step from the car with a wan smile of relief. Like a mountaineer descending from the peaks, he was glad to have faced down the danger. "Happiness lies in mastery," he said. "It's not the thrill of speed that makes us happy, but the fact that we go through 120 or 180 kilometers an hour and return home."

Both men found it hard to face the danger,

but they found it harder to quit. Racing was all-consuming, and therefore addictive. "Once the game has become life," Ken Purdy wrote in 1962, "and life has become a vestibule, unimagined courage is required to renounce the game — because renunciation is suicide."

Peril had its compensations. Drivers generally had their run of the well-tanned camp followers who sat pretty in the pits in capri pants and floppy hats. Before he met Louise King, Peter Collins' personal car was a Ford Zephyr with a bumper sticker on its rear fender that read, "I like girls!" That might qualify as one of history's great understatements. Collins was a dashing figure, and before settling down with King he used his charm to full advantage. For example, while Stirling Moss gave a speech from the winner's podium at the 1955 Targa Florio in Sicily, Collins disappeared under the stands with Miss Targa Florio.

Like Collins, Stirling Moss was as famous for womanizing as racing. "I got more column inches by taking out crumpet than winning races," he later said. Moss met his first wife after spotting her in the crowd at Le Mans. He waved and signaled for her to meet him in the pits. He got engaged to his second wife, Katie Molson, a Canadian beer heiress, shortly after Collins married Louise King. At an engagement party at the Savoy Hotel in London, Moss told guests, "Of course, I realize this is a foolish time to get engaged because Peter Collins has just got married and has released such a flood of crumpet onto the market, and now I can't do anything about it."

When Mike Hawthorn's car broke down at the Monte Carlo Grand Prix he spotted a blonde watching from a hotel window. He asked her for a glass of water. When she went to fetch it he climbed in the window.

With women, as with most things, Hill was the cranky voice of dissent. He all but vowed celibacy, saying those who live close to the limit should not live close to women. "A wife would worry too much about my driving," he told the *Times* of London. "I'll drive and worry alone."

He had grown up in a marital war zone, and he did not want relationship problems clouding his mind. Besides, he found it easier to drive if he knew that he could die with a clear conscience. "Look at them," he once told a friend, nodding toward a handful of wives holding stopwatches and binoculars in the pits. "Don't they know that their husbands are going to die?"

Hill sometimes found it hard to keep his

distance, given the pack of determined women that followed the drivers from city to city. A woman with designs on him once shrewdly arranged to attend a pre-race party in Monte Carlo with neither money nor a means of returning to her hotel. She knew that Hill had brought a car, and she coyly asked if he could help her. "Sure," he said, and he reached into his pocket. "Here's 50 francs for a taxi."

He spent so much time with Denise Mc-Cluggage, the gamine American correspondent, that acquaintances assumed they were involved. But Hill denied it. His abstinence was so conspicuous that it was suspected he might be gay, though that was not the case. Hill was often seen with a pretty French schoolteacher named Michele Albert, though she, like McCluggage, never officially became a girlfriend, at least not publicly. "When I'm away from the track, I forget about racing," von Trips said. "But Phil, he just hangs around Modena. He has no home over here. He just hangs around hotels all the time. It must make him sick."

Von Trips was never one to languish in a hotel. He had not entirely outgrown his sickly childhood, but workouts and weight-lifting gave him a robust, barrel-chested presence. No racer of the time looked more handsome in a polo shirt and goggles, his cheeks colored by sun and smudged with exhaust. Hearts fluttered. Women gravitated to him, and he returned their flirtations in gentlemanly fashion. "If he saw a girl he liked he really zeroed in on her," Louise King said. "He was good-looking, glamorous, and of course, he was a count."

One evening Louise King was having drinks on the aft deck of a yacht docked in Monte Carlo with von Trips and a couple of girls. With barely a parting word von Trips slipped off with a redhead named Zoe. "He always went off to some quiet place with them to make out," King said. "He always kept them away from us."

Von Trips had a wealth of affairs, none of them serious. As if to capture everything about his new life — as if to savor it with a survivor's relish — he traveled with a 16mm movie camera. Viewed years later, his home-made movies are a montage of preposterously beautiful women in bathing suits and ski outfits, all of them laughing and turning fond eyes on the cameraman.

He scampered to evade groupies as the Beatles would a few years later. Girls drove uninvited into Burg Hemmersbach's forecourt and asked for him. The boldest knocked on his hotel room door, and they were surprised when he did not invite them in. On at least one occasion a woman claimed an attachment that probably did not exist. Salome Ringling, the granddaughter of circus producer Henry Ringling, worked as a translator with Maserati in the mid-1950s. She was slyly nicknamed "gearbox," ostensibly for her willingness to hold tools for the mechanics as they worked. Years later, after she had moved home to Wisconsin, she claimed to have been engaged to von Trips, but there is no record of it.

No driver bedded more women than Hill's and von Trips' teammate Alfonso de Portago, a Spanish nobleman with black eyes and a thick head of curls that cascaded over his ears and collar. He kept a spacious apartment on Avenue Foch, one of the finest addresses in Paris, with a Ferrari parked out front. The apartment was practically empty except for stacks of Latin music albums and silver bowls won in bobsledding, polo, and steeplechase. He stayed out all night in bars and nightclubs, chain-smoking and, oddly enough, drinking only milk. Reporters gravitated to him because he could be relied on to speak poetically in a near whisper about the meaning of racing and risk. "Adventure is like religion," he said, "and in religion you have to have faith."

In reaction against his silken upbringing, Portago wore dirty shoes, a black leather jacket, and an unbuttoned black Lacoste polo shirt. He had an inexplicable reluctance to bathe and shaved every four or five days. Hill called him "a Spanish James Dean without some of the brooding."

Portago was rarely seen without his sidekick, Edmund Nelson, a quiet light-heavyweight boxer and former merchant marine who had worked as an elevator operator at the Plaza Hotel in New York when Portago lived there with his mother. Nelson taught Portago sparring and introduced him to the novels of Jack Kerouac, which might account for his willfully disheveled appearance and roughneck posture.

Not that it dampened his appeal. "That man was so busy with women," Louise King said, "I don't know how he had any time for racing."

Portago's wife, an American showgirl named Carroll McDaniel, eventually tired of his public affairs, most notably with model Dorian Leigh, and decamped to an apartment at 1030 Fifth Avenue with their two children. Portago then took up with B-list actress Linda Christian, the ex-wife of actor Tyrone Power. She appeared in the last of Johnny Weissmuller's Tarzan movies and a 1954 television adaptation of the Ian Fleming novel *Casino Royale,* which makes her the original Bond girl. She told friends she would marry Portago as soon as he got divorced, but as a Catholic he would never divorce.

The drivers called him "Fon," but his full name was Alfonso Antonio Vicente Eduardo Angel Blas Francisco de Borja Cabeza de Vaca y Leighton, Grandee of Spain, 17th Marquis de Portago. His ancestors fought off the Moorish invaders and sailed to the New World in search of El Dorado, the legendary city of gold. One of them, Álvar Núñez Cabeza de Vaca, was shipwrecked near Tampa Bay, Florida, in 1528 and led a small group of survivors on an eight-year march through wilderness and swamp to a Spanish outpost in Mexico. His father was a loyalist hero in the Spanish Civil War. He died on the polo field.

The twenty-eight-year-old marquis tried to outdo them all by pursuing a series of high-risk sports, which he intended to use as a steppingstone to a political career. At seventeen, Portago won a $500 bet by flying a borrowed plane under a causeway bridge near Palm Beach, Florida. He rode steeplechase and played polo, but gave them up when he gained weight from dining in Paris restaurants. He took only two or three practice runs in Switzerland before buying a $1,000 bobsled, recruiting his cousins from Madrid, and entering the 1956 Winter Olympics at Cortina d'Ampezzo, Italy. Veteran bobsledders dismissed him as a dilettante, but he came within 0.17 seconds of winning a bronze medal.

His first taste of car racing was in the 1953 Carrera Panamericana, where he acted as Luigi Chinetti's navigator. "It spins so slowly," he said after their car slid off the road and crashed. "You have plenty of time to think." Three years later Portago joined the Grand Prix circuit, where his driving was all acceleration. The front of his car was dented from nudging rivals out of the way at 130 mph. He was too brash and impetuous to observe the subtle etiquette that allowed experienced drivers to maneuver without causing accidents. The press called him "fast and fearless Fon" and "the madcap Marquis."

He seemed unequipped for the rigors of the sport. Before one of his first races he and his co-driver took apart the gear mechanisms housed in the transmission. When they reassembled it they unaccountably found fifty-four nuts and screws left over. Portago's best friend on the circuit was Harry Schell, one of the most cautious drivers. Schell predicted that Portago would not live to be thirty. Portago answered that he expected to win the World Championship by thirty and move on to politics by thirty-five. "The trouble with life is that it's too short," he said. "But I'm certainly not going to spend the rest of my life driving race cars."

His impatience showed. Portago was known as a driver who tried to overtake in curves where overtaking was impossible, and he pushed cars beyond their capabilities, like a rider who punishes a reluctant horse. He consequently burned out or broke one car after another. But he had suffered only one serious accident: In 1955 he skidded on a patch of oil at Silverstone, England. He was thrown from the car at 90 mph and broke his leg.

Fangio and some of the older drivers tried to coach him. They showed him what line to take into a curve and how to throw the car into a drift turn. But they came away convinced that he was not listening — not really listening, anyway. He was too impatient to learn the nuanced inner game. He was in too much of a hurry to heed the limit.

Like other fashionable figures who found their way onto the sports car circuit, Portago conducted himself with an air of entitlement. He once asked through a mutual acquaintance why Enzo Ferrari had not invited him to join his team. Ferrari responded by mailing two photos of Portago's car in a ditch.

"I am considered quite an expert on the subject of going off the road," Portago acknowledged in an article for *Sports Illustrated* published in May 1957. He died while that issue was still on the newsstands.

For all his thrill-seeking, Portago never wanted to race in the Mille Miglia. He dreaded it for the same reasons as other drivers — the debilitating length, the erratic amateurs in souped-up Renaults and Fiats, the spectators spilling onto the road, the uncertainly about what lay around each hill, hummock, and swerve. "Unless you're Italian you can't hope to know the roads," Portago said, "and as Fangio says, if you have a conscience you can't drive fast anyway. There are too many places where a car can go off the road and kill a dozen people."

But Portago had no choice. By 1957 Enzo Ferrari had finally hired him, and Ferrari needed Portago to fill out a sports car team left shorthanded by Castellotti's death two months earlier. Ferrari had won all but two Mille Miglia since the war. Enzo Ferrari was determined to win another. Nothing was sweeter than winning before his country-men.

In her memoir, Linda Christian described a premonition she had while vacationing with Portago in Spain before the Mille Miglia. His car was number 531, which adds up to nine — a numeral that she believed foretold tragedy. "If you go into this race," she told him, "you'll be brought back here and put in the grave with your father." Portago had his own presentiments. "My early death," he wrote to Dorian Leigh, "may well come next Sunday."

In the week leading up to the race, while the mechanics prepped the cars, Ferrari gathered Portago, von Trips, and the rest in a hotel in Manerbio, a town just south of the starting point in Brescia. For Ferrari, it was a chance to play on their insecurities and pit them against one another. Over a series of meals he goaded Portago, saying he expected Portago's 355S to finish behind his teammate Olivier Gendebien, even though Gendebien would drive a less pow-erful 250 GT. Portago formed an implacable resolve to beat Gendebien, no matter what. He would prove Ferrari wrong.

Portago and von Trips spent most of the last day together talking about how racing heightened their sense of life and fulfilled an inborn need for physical tests. Their philosophy, hashed out over cigarettes and coffee, held that fighting ennobled the spirit and helped strengthen a new generation of leaders to tackle the dangers of the nuclear era. Racing, they agreed, was "beautiful and necessary."

"We philosophized until we were over the moon," von Trips said. "In discussing these things I found confirmation of what I always felt but was never able to clearly express."

No doubt their chivalric ancestors would have endorsed their brand of bravery, but it was unfashionable in the Europe of the 1950s where wariness and conciliation were the order of the day. Progressive Europeans tended to reject physical courage as backward, even barbaric. It was considered a vestige of a discredited old order that had led to two world wars. In the Cold War culture of long-range ballistics and biological warheads, daring was a liability. Risk was in disrepute.

That night a group that included Portago, von Trips, Collins, Louise King, and a handful of others pushed two restaurant tables together for a group dinner in Brescia. It was noted that they totaled thirteen, an unlucky number.

"Life has to be lived to the full," Portago said that night. "It is better to be wholly alive for thirty years than half-dead for sixty."

Shortly before midnight the first cars took off in one-minute intervals from the Viale Venezia. At 5:30 a.m. Portago and Edmund Nelson heard their names announced over the public address system. They rolled down the floodlit starting ramp, past a flag-draped grandstand, and into the night. Spectators stood behind hay bales and wooden barricades on both sides of the street, leaning in to touch the car as it passed. They skittered down cobblestone streets and jounced over tram rails while peering through a thin ground fog for red taillights ahead.

By the time they reached Verona the sky was brightening, and the mists hanging over the fields began to burn off. In the half-light they could see broken-down cars smoldering by the roadside. They blazed east at 150 mph through the flat countryside of Vicenza and Padova, then south over the bridges of Rimini to Pesaro. Now they could see white sand beaches and the sparkle of the Adriatic to the left as they wove through Ancona and Pescara. Portago was in fourth place and moving up fast. He was running less than two minutes behind the leader as he turned inland and thrashed his car back and forth through the switchbacks leading up and over the Apennine Mountains.

Linda Christian was waiting in Rome when Portago pulled in at late morning for refueling and to have his card stamped by race officials certifying his position. Dirt and sweat streaked his face beneath his goggles. She passed him a note: *Te quiero mucho.* I love you very much. She obliged the paparazzi by leaning in for a kiss. "I had to lean to touch him," she later wrote, "and I had a strange sensation with that kiss; it was cold. And it caused me to look for the first time at Edmund Nelson seated beside him. He seemed to be like a mummy, gray, ashen, as if mesmerized. He had the eyes of someone who had suffered an enormous shock."

"I'll see you tomorrow night in Milan," Portago said. They planned to meet von Trips for dinner. They would drink to the next win, in Monte Carlo, he promised. Champagne for Christian, milk for Portago.

He then roared off and Christian headed for the airport to catch her flight to Milan. She asked the driver to stop at the Church of Santa Francesca Romana, where she and

232

Tyrone Power had married eight years earlier. Beneath the altar was a crypt containing the body of Santa Francesca, the patron saint of drivers. She lit a candle. "As I prayed, a sharp pain seared through me, almost more than I could bear," she wrote. "Then it subsided into a dull, throbbing ache that was to stay with me for days."

A crowd was waiting at the foot of the passenger stair when Christian stepped from the plane in Milan. Flashbulbs crackled. A reporter from a Milan newspaper climbed the steps to speak with her. "Miss Christian," he said. "Have you heard yet?"

He led her into a small private room inside the airport and told her. They got in his car and drove through a hard rain to the crash site. A policeman described how they had found half of Portago's body on the left side of the road, the other half pinned under the car on the right. The crushed hulk of the car still sat in the ditch surrounded by shreds of clothing and shoes.

Hours earlier, at the final checkpoint in Bologna, mechanics had warned Portago that a broken shock absorber was causing the front left tire to rub against the bodywork. He waved them off. He was in fourth place with Gendebien muscling up from behind. If he paused for a tire change

Gendebien would pass him, as Ferrari had predicted.

After driving for thirteen and a half hours Portago set off on the final run to Brescia, a stretch through the Po Valley sometimes called the Death Road. This, wrote the French journalist Olivier Merlin, was "where the fastest cars in the Mille Miglia, scenting their stables after 900 miles journeying, rose to speeds of over 160 mph."

With thirty miles to go, Portago flew down a flat, narrow road toward the stone village of Guidizzolo. The villagers had stood all afternoon near a farmhouse on the outskirts of town listening for the sound of approaching cars. They cheered as he came into view. Children watched from their fathers' shoulders or from between their legs. "Ferrari, Ferrari," they shouted.

On the edge of town Portago swerved, probably because the abrading tire blew. The rear of his car fishtailed to the left, toppling a stone kilometer marker and snapping a telegraph pole. The impact drove the hood backward, slicing Portago in two. The car then spun fifteen feet into the air and severed the overhead wires. It caromed into a crowd on the right side of the road, coming to a rest in a drainage ditch half filled with water. Nine spectators died, including five children.

Von Trips was in the lead, miles ahead and unaware of his friend's crash. He had spurted to the lead with an average speed of 119 mph over the first two hours. After 250 miles he gradually fell back as his blood sugar crashed. He was so feeble that he could barely push in the clutch and work the brake pedal, which in those days required some manhandling. He retrieved a sandwich stashed in the cockpit and recovered.

It was a familiar pattern. "At first I drive well, but then suddenly I can't do it anymore and I fall back," he said. "I'm then simply worn down, and must very quickly have something to eat. Somehow the energy goes through me too quickly. When racing I always have a decent sandwich with me, because food is my biggest problem."

The final stretch through the Po Valley was a duel between von Trips and his teammate Piero Taruffi, a prematurely white-haired Italian known as the Silver Fox. At age fifty-one, Taruffi had entered his country's most prestigious race twelve times without winning. He had come out of semiretirement for one last try. He almost dropped out at the midway point when his transmission failed, making it difficult to switch out of fifth gear. "I had intended to give up because the car didn't seem very safe to me, in its crippled condition," Taruffi said. "But I had promised my wife that I would give up racing if I won a Mille Miglia. So I took a chance."

Taruffi and von Trips came into Brescia side by side. The spectators congregated on both sides of the road screamed when the two Ferraris barreled into town. With the finish line in view, Taruffi pointed to his rear axle, signaling to von Trips that he had a transmission problem. Then, Hermann Harster wrote, "he put his hand on the steering wheel for a moment, as if in prayer." In response von Trips pulled back to let Taruffi win. It was an act of sportsmanship and respect for a grizzled teammate. Finishing second behind Taruffi, von Trips told reporters, was the same as winning.

For Taruffi, it was a win of the sweetest satisfaction. He stood on the podium in black coveralls and silver helmet smiling and waving half a dollar bill. Before the race Bernard Cahier had ripped the bill in two, saying they would reunite the halves in Brescia to buy a celebratory glass of champagne.

Ferrari took first, second, and third, but its sweep was overshadowed by recriminations. Two days after the race, the bishop of Mantua stood in Guidizzolo's small parish church imparting absolution at a funeral for the nine bystanders killed in the Portago accident. A row of hearses stretched down the street, some waiting to carry the miniature coffins of the children struck down by the spinning car. For once Ferrari had shown up. He sat in the front row flanked by women in black and enveloped in incense. As always, his countenance was impenetrable behind his dark sunglasses.

Ferrari probably would have stayed in Modena if not for the public outcry. Italian politicians called him a murderer and several national newspapers printed editorials urging the government to abolish the Mille Miglia. The government complied, banishing Italy's premier race thirty-one years after it started. (It resumed in 1977 as a vintage car event.) Manslaughter charges were filed against Ferrari. In court hearings Ferrari acted indignant and hurt. He raced to ennoble Italy, he said, and this was how the government repaid him. The charges were eventually dropped, but Ferrari's sulk lasted for years.

As the outcry subsided the Ferrari drivers returned to the demands of the upcoming season. The rhythms of Modena resumed.

"When Castellotti and de Portago died it was because they were trying to be great drivers and going beyond their limits," Louise King said. "Life went on."

With Portago's death, Hill and von Trips moved up a rung on the Ferrari ladder. It was a dubious promotion considering what befell their predecessors. It was only a matter of time before they led the lineup — if they lived long enough.

The question of survival applied to von Trips more than Hill. He was the more erratic of the two, alternating head-turning performances with the kind of maddening mistakes that had plagued him from his earliest days. If he were to succeed on the Ferrari team he would have to break the pattern of accidents and mount a winning streak that would dispel his reputation as Count von Crash.

If there was a perfect place for von Trips to solidify his credibility as a frontline driver it was the Nürburgring, where he would race in the familiar Eifel Mountains surrounded by cheering Germans. Two weeks after his second-place finish in the Mille Miglia he was there, warming up for a 1,000-kilometer race in a Ferrari 250 GT. Like most sports cars configured for racing, its accelerator sat on the floor between the clutch and the brake. He drove a few laps, then, at the request of a team manager, switched to a showroom model, which had the clutch on the right. It was an arrangement he was familiar with, since he owned a showroom Ferrari for private use. He wound through the steep forested hills, tapping and pumping the brakes as he made his way through seventy-two turns per lap on the longest racecourse in Europe. At the Breitscheid curve, an abrupt drop obscured by a bridge, he became momentarily confused by the pedal configuration and hit the gas instead of the brake. He missed a turn and shot through a hedge. His car rolled down a hill and crumpled against a wall.

Von Trips was unconscious when ambulance workers pulled him from the car. Doctors at the local hospital treated him for a broken nose, bruised breastbone, and two broken vertebrae in his lower back. He was moved to a Cologne hospital and fitted with a body cast that extended from his chin to his backside. For three weeks he lay immobilized, reliving the mistake in his mind and worrying that Ferrari would lose faith in him. He could feel himself falling from grace.

Mike Hawthorn (left) and Peter Collins, the mon ami *mates, after Collins won the British Grand Prix in 1958. It was his redemptive race after falling out of favor with Enzo Ferrari. (© 2011 LAT Photographic)*

8
TEN-TENTHS

Every morning for more than a month von Trips woke in his hospital room to face another day spent flat on his back, his torso encased in plaster. He passed the hours opening mail and receiving well wishers with feigned cheer. All of June and into July they marched down the bright hallways of the Cologne hospital — school friends, girlfriends, family. They deposited flowers and food packages on his bedside radio and handed him newspapers in three languages that he flipped open to the motor racing pages. Among other things he read that Hill had come in second at a 12-hour race in Reims, France, and would soon be competing in Sweden, Venezuela, and the Bahamas. The season was continuing without him.

In addition to shooting back pain, von Trips bore the agony of uncertainty. He had no way of knowing if he would race again. And if he did, could he muster the nerve for the scrum and tussle of competition? The margin between winning and losing was so thin, particularly at the elevated speeds of Grand Prix, that the slightest flinch would eliminate him from competition.

Drivers measured their proximity to the limit in tenths. A manager might order his team to practice at no more than eight-tenths of the limit, meaning fast but not reckless. If they accelerated to nine-tenths they were pushing the edge of control. At ten-tenths they were on the limit, where even the most stoic drivers trembled and perspired. Too often von Trips had transgressed to eleven-tenths and flipped or spun off the road. He would now have to prove that he could reliably drive at ten-tenths, and that he could overcome his crash habit.

In late July 1957 doctors released von Trips from his cast. A few days later he walked out of the hospital to begin his comeback, his second within a year. It would be a slower recovery than expected. When he returned a month later for a check-up, an X-ray showed that the fractures in his vertebrae had not fully healed. He went back into a body cast for three more weeks.

On August 4, friends helped relieve his

boredom by pushing him in a wheelchair to watch the German Grand Prix at the Nürburgring. They propped him up on a low wall overlooking the backstretch, not far from where he had gone off the road two months earlier. His teammates Hawthorn and Collins had given him a set of yellow, blue, and white flags so that he could signal the location of Fangio, their most lethal opponent. "I had my job to do," von Trips wrote in his diary. "So I signaled them. 'There he is!' "

From the sidelines von Trips observed a master class. Fangio had filled his red Maserati's fuel tank only half full so that he could take the turns faster than the heavy Ferraris, which were fueled to brimming so that they could go the distance without stopping. It was a gamble: Fangio's lightened car leapt out front, but it was unclear if his lead could withstand an early fuel stop. Fangio coasted into the pits with a 30-second lead. His crew struggled to replace his tires, costing him more than a minute. By the time he returned to the road he was 45 seconds behind Collins and Hawthorn. Everyone assumed Fangio could not make up the deficit, but he broke and rebroke the course record nine times as he closed the gap. He crossed the finish line 150 yards ahead of Hawthorn, clinching his fifth world championship. Afterwards Fangio said that he never wanted to drive like that again.

If there was something humiliating about waving flags from the sideline, von Trips didn't show it. Days later his cast came off and he began physical therapy and a regimen of massage and electric impulses designed to relieve pain. He was driving again too, placing second in a hillclimb through the highest stretches of the Italian and Swiss Alps. He was eager to prove that he had not lost his edge, and he asked Ferrari if there might be a car for him at the Italian Grand Prix at Monza in early September.

Romolo Tavoni, the team manager, confirmed by letter that a car had already been reserved for him. "As long as you have an interest, you drive," Tavoni wrote. "This car is only for you. Just watch out if you get tired." Von Trips did not tire. On the contrary, he drove doggedly, chasing the leaders, Fangio and Moss, to a third-place finish. He was the first Ferrari across the line. More importantly, he appeared unaffected by his crash four months earlier. It is easy to imagine Ferrari smiling to himself as he listened to the radio coverage in his dimly lit office. Like the prodigal son, von Trips was back.

Meanwhile, the steadfast Hill had to agitate for his due. At the start of the 1958 season he received the summons for his annual meal with Enzo Ferrari. Il Commendatore never attended the races, and he showed up sporadically for practices at the Modena *autodromo* in a linen cap, baggy trousers, and suspenders. The drivers mostly knew him as an enigmatic figure who issued edicts through Tavoni, the perpetually harried team manager and Ferrari mouthpiece. Reed-thin with thick-framed glasses and a pronounced widow's peak, Tavoni looked more like an accountant than a race official. He had the unenviable job of mediating between a bellicose boss and a pack of distrustful drivers.

The drivers never knew for sure where they stood in the team hierarchy. An invitation to dine with Ferrari was a rare chance to gauge one's standing, like a faltering student invited to eat at the headmaster's table. "You would go, wait the standard half an hour or so, and then be shown in for a light bantering exchange," Hill said. " '*Come stai?* How are you? How's your love life?' That sort of thing. And Ferrari's language could be X-ratedly blunt."

Then they walked out of the factory gate

and across the street for dinner at Il Cavallino, where Ferrari parked his bulk in a straight-backed wooden chair. It was his custom to keep his heavy-rimmed sunglasses on even in the gloom of the dining room. They were part of his ensemble of intimidation.

Hill had a point of contention to discuss over his antipasto. He and von Trips had both joined the Ferrari team a year earlier. Von Trips had gone directly to Formula 1, the most prestigious racing class, while Hill toiled away in sports cars. Day after day he had stood in the pits, helmet in hand, hoping Tavoni would ask him to take practice laps in Formula 1. He never did. Wasn't it time he got a shot? Had he not proven himself?

"I began to feel that perhaps I was not ever going to be a really first-rate driver, that something in my makeup might prevent me from reaching the ultimate stage in motor racing," he said. "There are several drivers who do well in sports cars but can't seem to do well with a Grand Prix machine. I was beginning to be haunted by the fear that maybe I'd be one of them. I had to find out."

Ferrari was noncommittal. *Aspettiamo, vediamo.* Let's wait and see.

"Yeah," Hill later told a friend. "You wait and we'll see." Like his father, Ferrari was impossible to please.

In Ferrari's mind, Formula 1 was a form of divine madness. It called for nerveless sprinters — *garibaldini* — who flung themselves to the fight without calculation. That was not Hill's style. Ferrari considered him better suited to long-haul sports car campaigns, like the 12-hours at Sebring or the 24 Hours of Le Mans, where his mechanical acumen and instinct for survival ensured consistent finishes.

It was hard to quibble with Ferrari's reasoning. While one driver after another skidded or somersaulted off tracks, Hill barely dented a fender. His achievement was not winning at the greatest speed, but winning at the slowest. He was what the racing community called a "sympathetic" driver. He could detect the strain of an overpushed engine with his ear and absorb its mood through the vibration of the wheel. He never bullied a car beyond its capability, choosing instead to nurse it. "He had a terrific feel for the soul of a car," McCluggage said, "and he was very good to them." As a result he finished about 80 percent of races he entered. Most drivers finished only half.

"I would rather drive with Phil than any

other driver," said Collins, who drove a sports car in tandem with Hill for part of the 1958 season. "When you get the car from him it is as if it had been sitting in front of the pits all the time."

Then, as now, Grand Prix races usually took place on Sundays. On the three mornings before a race, Hill steered his car out on the empty track for ten or so laps at a time, edging up to the limit with progressively faster runs. Afterwards he pulled into the pits to discuss tire pressure, balance, suspension settings, and camber. His dark, intense eyes bore down on the mechanics. Don't you hear that? he demanded, cocking his ear to some faint click or rumble. Third gear might be too low, or maybe fourth gear was a tad too high. His manner was that of a man utterly determined to get the chassis tuning, springing, and wheel angles right — exactly right. Garage etiquette barred Hill from touching the car himself. That was the exclusive role of the mechanics. But he could lean over their shoulders, listening as they tightened or tweaked. More, he told them. A little more. There. Perfect.

The mechanics were unaccustomed to working with so skilled a diagnostician. They welcomed his feedback, up to a point. Like Italian tailors or furniture makers, the mechanics were proud craftsmen. They took it as a personal insult when Hill, the agitated perfectionist, diagnosed a problem and prescribed its remedy all in one impatient breath. Tune-up sessions were frequently adjourned for cappuccino, croissants, or wine. Seated on stacks of spare tires, the mechanics smoked cigarettes and cut thick slices of sausage and cheese. Hill glared at them. He was indignant when they put down their tools before solving the problem at hand.

Hill was not constituted for coyness or dissembling. He had an ingenuous American way of speaking his mind. But over time he learned the Italian manner of diplomacy, dropping clues so the mechanics believed they had fixed the problem on their own.

The mechanics spoke only Italian, which complicated matters. By 1958 Hill was fairly fluent, but he hid his proficiency so that he could listen in when the mechanics discussed team politics. "Whether my open eavesdropping really made any difference or not, it at least gave me a sense of being one-up, a confidence builder that I needed," he said.

Hill gradually came to understand that much of the communication at Ferrari was conducted in a baffling code language.

When he arrived, he was continually urged to go slow — *piano, piano* — so as not to damage the car. But when he eased off, Tavoni and the engineers looked displeased. He eventually decided to ignore them and follow his instincts. "I understood now that although they said *'piano, piano'* they meant let it all hang out."

As the 1958 season got under way, Hill would use all his mechanical mastery to prove that he was qualified for Grand Prix — and to prove Ferrari wrong. He recorded the fastest practice time for the 1,000-kilometer sports car race in Buenos Aires in mid-January, beating Fangio, the perennial winner, who had the advantage of driving on his home course. He and Peter Collins won the race, with Hill twice breaking the course record.

Hill not only won, but he helped von Trips and Gendebien secure second place. "During the closing stage," Hill said, "having lapped the other cars, I held off Moss who was trying to pass Gendebien into second, thus assuring our team of a few more points. That was a very successful afternoon for us."

Ferrari agreed to let Hill practice in Formula 1 for the Buenos Aires Grand Prix, which took place a week later. On consecutive mornings Hill lowered his body into a half-reclining position inside the low fuselage of the single-seat Ferrari Dino 246. It was "a cute little thing with a terrific pull," he told the British magazine *Autosport,* "and I just loved to drive it."

"Cute little things can get you into trouble," he added.

It was an unnerving adjustment to a flyweight car with lightning-quick responses, as it had been for von Trips a year earlier. "The turns rushed up at a far greater rate than I was accustomed to, and it required a new kind of perspective to deal with this," he said. "I was spinning around, sliding off the road and so forth."

By the end of the week Hill had cut his Formula 1 lap times by more than three seconds, tying him with von Trips. Seizing on these practice runs as proof of his proficiency, Hill convinced Tavoni to let him take over von Trips' car for the second of the two heats.

Unfortunately for Hill, von Trips never got that far. He attacked Fangio in the early going and edged by him. Von Trips was so surprised to pass the world champion that he glanced back to see if Fangio was in trouble. That split-second distraction caused him to fishtail off the track and crash through a barrier. "That was the end of my Formula 1 introduction," Hill said.

Things didn't go any better for them in Cuba, where political unrest again disrupted the Gran Premio. Shortly before dinnertime on the eve of the race, three Castro rebels with scruffy beards stepped up to Fangio, the heavy favorite, as he chatted with a group of men in the lobby of the Lincoln Hotel in downtown Havana. They called his name. When he looked over they identified themselves as members of the July 26 Movement. One man pressed a .45 Colt revolver to Fangio's back and hustled him into a Pontiac idling around the corner. The rebels assured Fangio that he was safe. The abduction was meant only to embarrass the Batista regime. No ransom was demanded. They deposited him in a house with a woman and crying child.

That night von Trips led a group of drivers on a tour of Havana's seamy side, visiting clubs where drag queens performed and couples had sex onstage. "He knew where every sex club was," said Bruce Kessler, a young American driver, "including the gay bars."

The next day President Batista sat rigidly in the grandstand with his family while police searched frantically for Fangio. Hill, von Trips, and the rest waited for ninety minutes at the start area after an announcer excitedly reported that Fangio had been released and was on his way. When Fangio failed to appear the drivers were ordered to their cars. Fifteen minutes into the race a privately owned yellow-and-black Ferrari driven by Armando Garcia Cifuentes, an inexperienced twenty-seven-year-old Cuban, skidded on a patch of oil as he was coming out of a turn. He sailed into a grandstand outside the U.S. embassy, killing seven spectators. "It seemed only an instant," Hill said, "and bodies were being mowed down." A cloud of dust went up and curious spectators rushed in to ogle the skid marks streaked across the sidewalk and pools of clotted blood drying on the grass.

The bloodshed was too much even for Ernest Hemingway, who was then living in Cuba. "A matador bears only his own risk," he told a reporter. "But these ne'er-do-wells are always tearing into one another."

That evening the rebels turned Fangio over to the Argentine ambassador. Once freed, he made a point of saying that his captors had treated him well. They fed him steak and potatoes and invited him to watch the race on television. Nonetheless, it was an unnerving reminder that racing and politics were entangled in a changing world. "I think we were all glad to get out of there," Hill said.

In late April 1958 von Trips taught a three-day racing class in Germany. He was by now a leading figure in German sports, and he felt a responsibility to help restore the country's racing culture with a series of clinics. His students included Juan Carlos, the future king of Spain, and Bernd Rosemeyer Jr., the son of von Trips' childhood hero. They paid 240 deutsche marks to learn basic sports car handling — how to accelerate through a turn, how to match revs while upshifting, how to pass cars on the inside of an oval track. The course's motto was, "Fast driving is not only a pleasure, but an art, and only the few can master it."

Von Trips must have wondered if he could master it himself. He qualified eleventh at the Monaco Grand Prix on May 18, 1958, but his engine gave out in the last few minutes. He performed well in long-distance races in Sicily (despite hitting a dog) and the Nürburgring. But he was unsure if he could overcome his inconsistency, and he worried that Ferrari would give up on him. On June 6 he wrote Il Commendatore to ask if he should expect to drive Ferraris in the remaining Grands Prix of the 1958 season. If not, he would like permission to speak with Porsche and Maserati. "I've had a lot of bad luck with Grand Prix cars," he acknowledged.

Ferrari was a master at letting his people stew in their own uncertainties, and he took his time writing back to say that, yes, he would provide von Trips with cars — but it was a wan endorsement.

While von Trips' confidence dwindled, Hill was hitting his stride with wins in Buenos Aires and Sebring, the latter with brakes so worn that they would hardly have stopped a bicycle. Ferrari was known for innovation, but he was conservative by nature and slow to abandon the fragile and ineffective drum brakes for the newer disc technology developed in England. On the straights Hill continuously pumped the brakes with his left foot, hoping to keep the brake shoes near the wheel drums without boiling the brake fluid or tearing the brake lining.

A day after the Sebring race, Hill left for New York in his 1939 Packard Twelve, one of a handful of cars that he had restored for his own use. Finding himself stuck behind a plodding truck, he dropped back, considered his timing, and shot around the truck, missing an oncoming car by half a second.

He had no way of knowing that an off-duty policeman drove the approaching car. The cop made a U-turn, pulled Hill over, and handed him a $15 ticket. In typical fashion, Hill thought a logical explanation would absolve him. "This car develops astronomical torque right off of its idling," he explained to the cop.

"If you want to speed," the cop answered, "why don't you go down to Sebring with the rest of those nuts."

Each win on the sports car circuit made it harder for Enzo Ferrari to deny Hill a shot at the Grand Prix. If he won at Le Mans on June 20, Ferrari would surely relent, or so Hill thought. He was well positioned for a top finish at Le Mans, but it was a hard race to predict. Too many things could go wrong as the race ground on through the heat of a June afternoon and the gloom of night, particularly with the dubious Ferrari drum brakes facing a 2,500-mile test at speeds approaching 200 mph.

The drums may have been suspect, but the car was formidable. Hill and Olivier Gendebien shared a 250 Testa Rossa, one of the most beautiful sports cars ever made. It was named Testa Rossa, or redhead, for the red valve covers on the 3-liter V12 engine, but it was most noticeable for its curvaceous pontoon-shaped fenders and generous cockpit with leather upholstery.

Even before the race Hill and Gendebien found a brake problem. A scrap of metal had found its way into the drum, the cylindrical housing for the brake mechanism. "We could feel the problem," Hill said, "and knew when the brake was damaging itself." The scrap might disable the brake long before it had a chance to wear down on its own.

At 4 p.m. Gendebien ran the short footrace across the track to the car, the traditional mode for a Le Mans start, and set off on the rectangular course unsure how long the brakes would last. Stirling Moss charged to the front in his green Aston Martin, trailed by Hawthorn and von Trips in their Ferraris. Gendebien hung back in fifth place, nursing his brakes. "Little by little we manipulated the errant brake so that it wasn't destroying itself," Hill said. "In the meantime, most of the front runners broke or crashed."

Moss's Aston Martin consumed itself trying to set an impossible pace and gave out after two hours. With a top contender gone, von Trips stepped up to challenge for the lead with Gendebien trailing. Hill replaced Gendebien after two and a half hours and took off after the front pack.

Shortly before sunset a blanket of clouds darkened the summer sky and a squall wind whipped the fairgrounds. Flags snapped. Tents shuddered. A sheeting rain flooded the track and cars skidded their way through the dusk, kicking up mud and spray.

The rain would pour down hard for the next sixteen hours. Nothing is more hair-raising than sliding and slipping on a wet road in the dark, but the rain helped Hill in one respect: The slower pace put less strain on his doubtful brakes. Stepping gingerly on the pedals, he caught up to von Trips by the third hour, after 103 laps, and passed him to take the lead.

With twenty-one hours to go, Hill steeled himself for a hellish night spent squinting into the rain from his open cockpit and glancing over his shoulder at von Trips' headlights. The rearview mirrors were useless in the deluge. Headlights and taillights blurred to a fuzzy glow or blinked out altogether. "The volume of rain was amazing," he said, "but I discovered that if I sat on the tool roll to prop myself up — no, we didn't use the seatbelts — and then tilted my head back and looked just over the tip of the windshield and under the bottom of my visor, the view wasn't too bad."

At times, Hill was forced to navigate by sound alone. He sped down the long Mulsanne Straight at 150 mph listening for the grind of downshifting gears. Like a foghorn in the night, it was a signal that he was approaching the 300-degree turn. Through the shrouds of rain he could occasionally see a friend's car wrecked by the roadside. He drove on without knowing their fate.

At 10:40 p.m., after more than six hours of racing, von Trips made a right-hand turn at the end of a long straightaway. He saw a flash of light and car parts scattered by the roadside. A French driver named Jean Hébert had rolled his Alfa Romeo and was lying unconscious on the road. Von Trips pulled over. In a letter to Hébert written later that summer he described what happened next:

I saw you half-lying on the road, and then moved you, with some effort, a few meters over on the grass. You seemed to be unconscious and groaning — at least you were not responding to questions I was asking. You lay on your back and did not seem to have any external injuries except to your face, at least as far as I could see it by the glow of your burning car. I moved the largest parts of the car from the racetrack. I couldn't see any other drivers (I thought there might be another car involved) and when I saw people with lanterns — and help for you — I drove off again.

A dozen other cars crashed that night, including a Jaguar D-Type driven by the Frenchman Jean-Marie Brousselet. He lost control entering the first turn after the pits and died when his car hit the banking. Bruce Kessler, an American in a privately owned Ferrari Testa Rossa, swerved to avoid the wreckage. He jumped from his car moments before it hit a retaining wall at more than 100 mph and exploded. Kessler landed at the top of a low roadside hill with a collapsed lung, a pair of ugly hematomas, and a severed nerve at the base of his back. With the ambulances already in use, spectators carried him away on an old door and drove him to a hospital in the back of a pickup truck. "That was worse than the accident because the road was so rough," Kessler said. "That was a painful ride."

The hospital attendants struggled to get him to the upstairs operating room because the door wouldn't fit in the elevator. As they shifted him to a stretcher a priest showed up and began administering last rites. "I

told him, 'No, no, no. I'm not dying,' "
Kessler said.

When the nuns unzipped his raincoat in the upstairs operating room they found pieces of roast chicken that Kessler had tucked away to eat during the long night at the wheel. They mistook the chicken for intestines or mangled body parts. Kessler tried to explain what it was, but he did not speak French. "Finally I picked up a piece and ate it to show them it was chicken, and one of them just went down like a rock."

One by one Hill's rivals crashed or dropped out. While von Trips napped in the drivers' bunkhouse, his co-driver, Wolfgang Seidel, drove off the road and had to quit.

Just before midnight, Hill woke up from a nap in the bunkhouse to learn that a Jaguar was gaining on Gendebien, his co-driver. Jaguar had won Le Mans five of the previous eight years, and it was intent on extending its dominance. By the time Hill trudged through the mud to the pits Gendebien's lead was down to 26 seconds. When the cars came around again Hill could see through the gloom that the green Jaguar had taken over the lead.

On the next lap Gendebien pulled in and turned the car over to Hill, who gave all-out chase through the blackness. The tinny loudspeakers crackled to life as an announcer alerted dripping clusters of die-hard spectators to the pursuit. Peering through the rain, they watched Hill close the gap. Within seven laps Hill was harrying the Jaguar, and finally passed it to reclaim the lead. By 2:30 a.m. Hill was ahead by an insurmountable lap and a half.

Dawn revealed a string of ashy hulks abandoned on the muddy verge, like sea creatures left by a receding tide. Spectators emerged from tents and tiptoed across fields of mud. At noon, after 251 laps, Hill was poised to lap the second-place Jaguar, driven by Duncan Hamilton, for the second time when a small French Panhard abruptly slowed in front of them. Hamilton swerved, turned over, and bounced sideways across the road. Hamilton's Jaguar flew "so high in the air," Hill said, "that I could see its underside and thought at one point it might hit me."

Hill drove on unscathed. By afternoon, the rain stopped and the sun burst through, drying the road and bathing the French countryside in a glowing light. "We had some laps in hand," Hill said, "the tension from the driving in the wet was gone and we knew we could win."

He crossed the finish line at 4 p.m., his

hand raised in triumph, with an average speed of 106 mph and a 100-mile lead on his closest pursuer. Movie footage of that day shows him smiling broadly as Gendebien, checkered flag in hand, clambered onto the hood for a victory lap. It was a gutsy display of driving in what might qualify as the toughest racing conditions of all time. Only twenty of the fifty-five starters finished. Hill later called it "my favorite race and the most rewarding to me."

For all his anguish, Hill came away with a reputation as a nail-tough endurance driver. Within six months he had won at Buenos Aires, Sebring, and Le Mans, almost single-handedly securing the sports car championship for Ferrari. He had every expectation that his tour de force at Le Mans would secure him a start in the French Grand Prix two weeks later, on July 6, but no offer came from Modena.

The next afternoon Hill drank tea in the dining room of the Hotel de Paris in Le Mans with McCluggage and other friends. They told him he was loyal to the point of foolishness, and that he should not allow Ferrari to take advantage of him. They urged him to force the issue. Bonnier offered Hill the use of his two-year-old Maserati 250F. "We all said, 'Phil, you should do that,' " McCluggage said. " 'I'll show you' wasn't his style, but we tried to give him backbone."

In the end, Hill agreed to borrow the Maserati. It was outdated, with six fewer cylinders than the Ferraris, but it would allow him to make his Grand Prix debut. "At least I'd call some attention to myself," he concluded. "I was tired of waiting in the wings for an onstage call."

Peter Collins endured his own frustrations in the wake of Le Mans. He and Hawthorn disliked the race more than most. They hated its circus atmosphere and Gallic chaos. Before the 1958 Le Mans they joked that they could not abide the race for its entire twenty-four hours. They would be home in England, they said, in time for Sunday lunch. Ferrari's spies reported these words back to Modena, where they burned in Il Commendatore's ears.

Collins was one of the few drivers whom Ferrari took to his heart. He had a sunny, openhearted disposition and he embraced the local Modenese ways. Most British drivers stationed in Italy subsisted on steak and French fries and learned just enough Italian to order a Campari and soda. Collins, on the other hand, spoke fluent Italian and relished the local menu of Lambrusco, tortellini, and steamed meats. He seemed to fit effortlessly into Ferrari's world.

When Ferrari's son Dino lay dying of muscular dystrophy in 1956, Collins paid daily visits. According to Tavoni, Collins treated Dino as a brother:

Dino would say, "Peter, are you going to the movies tonight?"

"No, I will stay here with you. Why?"

"Because if you go to the movies, tomorrow morning you can tell me all about it. I cannot get out of bed. I am like a small bird in a big cage."

So Peter would go to the cinema and the next day he would describe to Dino the movie he had seen. Naturally this kindness created a very good impression with Enzo Ferrari and the Signora, although Peter did not do it for this reason.

After Dino died, Collins became a surrogate son to Enzo Ferrari. Ferrari loaned him Dino's apartment above Il Cavallino and looked in on his way to work. Laura Ferrari swung by in her chauffeured car to do laundry and tidy up.

Their relationship cooled after Collins

married. By April 1958 Collins and Louise were spending most of their time on their new forty-three-foot motor yacht, which they docked at the exact spot on the Monte Carlo harborfront where Alberto Ascari had driven into the water three years earlier. They christened her Mipooka, an Irish name for goblin. They hosted Hill and von Trips often, serving Pimm's Cups and throwing coins to the musicians strolling the harborfront.

"[Collins] had become unhappy living under the Ferrari yoke at Modena," Hill said. "No matter who you were, when you lived there you had to toe the Ferrari line and like so many other people Peter became uncomfortable at always having to please Ferrari — for everything to have to be his way."

The bond between Collins and Ferrari further unraveled after Hill's victory at Le Mans in 1958. Collins shared a Testa Rossa with Hawthorn, who mangled the clutch in the surge to get ahead at the start and brutalized it chasing Moss in the early going. "Mike always screwed up the clutch," Hill said. "I think he had more to do with clutch development at Ferrari than anyone else."

By 7:30 p.m. the deteriorating clutch

required a repair stop of twenty minutes, a delay that left them six laps behind Hill. By midnight they were hopelessly mired in the rear pack. At 2 a.m. the clutch gave out entirely. He left the car by the roadside and walked back to the pits in the downpour. A few hours later Hawthorn, Collins, and Louise drove to Paris, took the boat train to London, and continued on to Hawthorn's family home in Farnham, Surrey. They arrived in time to hear the coverage of Hill's victory on the radio.

When word of the Collins-Hawthorn withdrawal reached Modena, Ferrari fulminated. To lose was bad enough, but to abandon the car and leave the race grounds was in his view unforgivable. To make matters worse, the Ferrari mechanics retrieved the Testa Rossa and found the clutch working, possibly because it had cooled overnight. If Ferrari's special regard for Collins dampened when he married Louise, it now ended in recrimination. Collins had sullied the Ferrari name. He was persona non grata.

It has been said that the long campaign to uphold the empire ingrained in British schoolboys a heightened respect for national teamwork. As a result their approach to racing and other sports was fundamentally different from the gladiatorial spirit instilled in

Italians. Collins and Hawthorn had an unbreakable allegiance, but only to each other. It was their slightly subversive way of expressing British patriotism within an Italian organization. In the pubs and pits they called each other "mon ami mate," a term borrowed from a popular British comic strip. On the track they maneuvered in cahoots, taking turns running in the lead while the other blocked anyone from passing. They were a team within the team.

In the weeks after Le Mans, their teammate Luigi Musso complained to Ferrari that Collins and Hawthorn conspired against him. Standing at the bar with a tweed jacket and pipe, Hawthorn told Musso that he and Collins would ensure that the next champion was British, not Italian. What the British might consider schoolboy teasing, Musso took as harassment.

Musso was a swarthy Roman, the son of an Italian diplomat, with light eyes and the charismatic disposition of a gentleman sportsman. With Ascari and Castellotti dead, he bore the burden of national expectation. Ferrari called him "Italy's last world-class driver in a long line of stylists."

Musso struggled to live up to that role. On the night before races he closed his eyes and let his memory wander through the rooms of his childhood home, conjuring the walls, furnishings, and paintings. He never knew why, except that it calmed him.

He also struggled financially. He had left his wife and two children for a twenty-four-year-old dark-haired beauty, and in the process fell badly into debt. His arrears mounted after he signed a deal to import a thousand Pontiacs to Italy. It had not occurred to him that Pontiacs were too big for narrow Italian streets, or that their brakes would fade halfway down an Alpine descent. "It was a disaster," Tavoni said. "The day before the [French Grand Prix] he received a telegram from his partner in Rome saying, 'You must win so you can pay off your debt.' "

Ferrari promised Musso that Collins and Hawthorn would not gang up on him at the French Grand Prix. When the Ferrari drivers arrived at the Lion d'Or Hotel across from the great cathedral in Reims, they were dumbstruck to learn that Ferrari had dropped Collins to Formula 2, a lower-ranking class run with smaller 1.5-liter engines. It was a shocking demotion, considering that Collins had won the French Grand Prix two years earlier, and an obvious punishment for the Le Mans fiasco.

With Ferrari holed up in Modena, Collins

took his objection to Tavoni. In a heated argument in his hotel suite, Collins accepted blame for ruining the clutch at Le Mans. He begged Tavoni to restore him to the Formula 1 lineup if he performed well in the Formula 2 race held earlier in the day.

Tavoni tried to talk Collins out of it. "I told him that it was going to be a very hot day and this was not a good idea," Tavoni said. Eventually, after consulting Ferrari by phone, he agreed to let Collins drive in the Grand Prix if he felt up to a second race.

The tensions were put aside the night before the race as drivers went out to dinner together. When they returned to the Lion d'Or, the group, led by Hawthorn, Hill and Musso, spotted a little white Vespa 400, one of the lightest cars ever made, belonging to Harry Schell, a popular Franco-American journeyman driver. Flush with Bordeaux, they hoisted it from its parking place, carried it through the lobby and up a flight of stairs. "They looked like a gang of ants carrying a dead grasshopper up a sand bank," McCluggage wrote.

They had hoped to drive the Vespa down the corridor, honking the horn outside Schell's room. When they found that he was out celebrating his girlfriend's birthday, they deposited the car in a second-floor parlor where it stood beside gilt-framed mirrors and antique card tables with a For Sale sign on its roof. They then called the concierge to complain that Mr. Schell's car was bothering guests trying to play cards. Would they please ask him to remove it?

"A short time later Harry called the concierge and told him he knew exactly who the parties involved in the caper were," recalled Cahier, who was one of the perpetrators, "and if his car was not in front of the hotel in the morning each of theirs would be terminally sabotaged." Fangio considered driving it down the stairs, but in the end they carried it back, Cahier wrote, "with what seemed like a lot more effort."

The next morning Collins placed second in the Formula 2 race, prompting Tavoni to make good on his promise and restore him to Formula 1. He lined up in the second row of the starting grid. Hill's practice times earned him a place in the fifth row, a respectable spot given that he was in Bonnier's outmoded Maserati 250 F. His defection drew threats from the Ferrari camp, which had not believed he would go through with his disloyalty. "If you get in that Maserati," Tavoni had said before the race, "you'll never get in a Ferrari again."

"So be it," Hill said.

Hawthorn muscled his way into first as the pack rounded the initial turn and set off across the rolling French farmland. Musso drove with feverish aggression, desperate to close the gap. He trailed Hawthorn by just two seconds as they flashed by the pits on the tenth lap. Half a lap later Musso tried to pull even as they snaked through a little twist known as the Muizon curve. He went through that tricky stretch flat out, without braking — clearly over the limit. He lost control, appeared to recover, and overcorrected. Through his rearview mirror Hawthorn watched Musso's Ferrari jump over a white curb and somersault three times. The car was thirty feet in the air, red against blue sky, with Musso soaring above it. He hung in midair for a moment, like a toy tossed high, then landed in a wheat field, twisted and broken. When Hawthorn whizzed by the pits on the next lap, Musso was no longer trailing him.

At every race the congregation of women — wives, mistresses, girlfriends — holding clipboards and stopwatches in the pits prepared themselves for the moment when a car failed to appear. There was no way to know what might have happened on the far side of a track that wound for miles through empty forests and fields. The track announcers were no help; they dismissed accidents as "shunts" or ignored them altogether. So when Musso did not come around, the women waited, stricken, listening for sirens or the whirring of a medical helicopter.

"No one said a word and I was scared to ask," Musso's young girlfriend, Fiamma Breschi, later wrote in a memoir. "I started to pray, 'please God . . . please God . . . please God.' " An ambulance scrambled. Minutes later a medical helicopter landed, flattening the wheat with its propeller blast.

The drivers were masters of tunnel vision. Hawthorn pushed Musso from his mind as he drove on to win — he led all fifty laps — with an average speed of 126 mph, followed by Moss. Near the end Hawthorn was an entire lap ahead of Fangio and was about to pass him, but stepped on the brakes out of respect. "There was no way I was going to lap Fangio," he told Cahier after the race. "He's the greatest and I certainly didn't want to hurt his feelings."

Afterwards Fangio announced his retirement, ending one of racing's greatest careers. It is not known how much Musso's devastating accident influenced his decision, though he did say he was lonely. Roughly thirty of his fellow drivers had died over the course of his career. He had started in

Grand Prix exactly ten years earlier on the same course. "Here I started," he said. "Here I finish."

As Fangio's Formula 1 career ended, Hill's had just begun. He came in seventh — the top finish by a privately owned car and an impressive showing in machinery ill-equipped to keep up with the strapping Ferraris. He was vindicated, and he uncharacteristically rubbed it in. "I can remember being so gauche and inconsiderate as to rush over to the pits afterwards," he said, "looking for some sort of approval from Tavoni, knowing full well that they were worried sick about Musso."

Musso was hanging on with severe head injuries when Breschi arrived at the Maison Blanche hospital in Reims. His condition was grave, doctors told her, but there was hope. "I took his hand and squeezed it," she wrote, and felt a faint response. "He did not have one scratch. He was handsome. God how he was handsome."

She returned to the hotel room that she had shared with Musso and waited for news with some of the other wives and girlfriends. A few hours later one of the Ferrari managers knocked on her door. Musso had died.

"I ran for the window, which was open because it was July and very hot," she later said. "I tried to throw myself out. I was already halfway out when Beba (Fangio's girlfriend) and Lulu Trintignant (Maurice Trintignant's wife) grabbed me and pulled me back. They didn't leave me alone that night or the next day."

Shortly after Musso died, Breschi saw Collins and Hawthorn kicking an empty can around a piazza. "For a brief moment the hate for those two was stronger than the pain I was feeling. I would have wanted them dead," she wrote. "Why were they alive and Luigi was not? Damned Englishmen. Why were they laughing?"

Four days later, as Musso's body was flown back to Rome for burial, the Vatican asserted that the Ferrari win, like so many others, was built on the backs of the dead. *L'Osservatore Romano,* the semi-official Vatican newspaper, published a sharply worded editorial denouncing the "usurious, crazy, inhuman price" paid simply to glorify the carmakers. Racing, it said, had become "a ruthless idol that demands increasingly heavy sacrifices of blood" and compared Ferrari to Saturn, a devourer of his own children. It was a cruel comparison given that Dino Ferrari had died barely two years earlier.

Catholic law had prevented Musso from

divorcing and marrying Breschi. As a result, she inherited nothing. She was now destitute and directionless. To make matters worse, Musso's wife showed up in Rome before the funeral to retrieve the jewelry and other gifts Musso had given her. "There was an ugly scene where she literally tried to tear the jewelry given to Fiamma by Luigi from her neck and wrists," Cahier later recalled.

A month after Musso's funeral, Breschi received a letter from Ferrari written in the violet ink he used for all correspondence. "He said I would always have friends at Maranello and that I could go back whenever I wanted," she said. "So when I recovered, I went to see him."

In the summer of 1959 she took a train to Modena and checked into the Albergo Reale. Tavoni picked her up and drove her to a restaurant where Ferrari sat waiting at a table. His driver Peppino was seated nearby in case Il Commendatore needed anything. "For me, the meeting with Ferrari was a sort of work interview," she said.

She wept as she described how lost she felt without Musso. Her grief was made worse by her grandmother Elisabetta's recent suicide. Ferrari also wept as he shared the anguish of Dino's death. He told her that he relived the tragedy every time a driver died. He described what he called "his terrible joys," a term he would use six years later as the title of a memoir.

"He was a constructor of cars and a destroyer of souls; and yet, if you entered into his orbit you would have given anything to never leave," she wrote. "That is how I entered into his life and he into mine."

Ferrari set Breschi up with her own boutique, first in Bologna, then Florence. He visited her apartment every Thursday afternoon. Ferrari's liaison with Breschi became an open secret, along with the household he kept with Lina Lardi. "One day I arrived at the factory to meet with Ferrari and I was told by his personal secretary, Franco Gozzi, that he had good news and bad news," Cahier later wrote. "The bad news was that Il Commendatore was going to be late for our meeting as he had gone to Bologna. The good news was that when he returned he would be in a very good mood, which indeed he was."

Because Ferrari never went to the races and rarely attended practice, he needed spies as much as mistresses. It was not long before Ferrari sent Breschi to the racetrack to mingle, and possibly more, with drivers and mechanics. Ferrari, she said, "was not satisfied with the information that he would receive through official circuits. He wanted news firsthand, not only expert opinions. I lent myself to this work, I know the atmosphere well and I knew how to distinguish a champion from a good driver."

The summer of 1958 was a season of vindication. Hill had ignored Ferrari's threats and proved himself in a borrowed Maserati. In doing so, he had shown that Formula 1 lay well within his abilities. "They built up such a mystique about Formula 1, as if one must serve a novitiate for it," he said. "Nonsense. My skills were as ready for Formula 1 in 1955 as they ever were. All one had to do to dispel the mythic aura around Formula 1 was to drive Formula 1." With Musso gone, Ferrari forgot his threats and invited Hill back to fill the vacancy.

Von Trips also had reason for encouragement. He had lined up last on the starting grid for the French Grand Prix, then in typical fashion stalled his engine at the start. By the time he got under way the entire field was out of sight. From the distant back of the pack he made a lightning run to beat out Fangio for third place. His through-the-pack surge was better than a win — it was an impassioned comeback that stole the day. The German magazine *Auto Motor und Sport* put von Trips on its cover, calling him "The Fastest Count in the World." *Der Spiegel* wrote that he had "made his mark and fame right there, becoming a celebrated star."

Peter Collins had also worked his way back into Ferrari's good graces. After his morning Formula 2 race at Reims, he finished fifth in Formula 1. On July 19 he took the British Grand Prix, steadily widening his lead while Hawthorn protected him by badgering Moss. His standing would be fully restored with a decent showing at the German Grand Prix.

Before going to the Nürburgring for the race on August 3, he and Louise spent a happy interlude on their yacht in Monte Carlo, swimming and drinking Pimm's Cups in the cockpit. They had made a £500 down payment on a Georgian house owned by a ninety-year-old bishop in Kidderminster, a sign that Collins was thinking of retirement. "Peter was a fun-loving and happy human being," Louise said. "We never discussed the possibility of something interrupting our perfect lives."

Race weekends were highly social, with raucous dinners and parties thrown by local dignitaries. They were particularly lively at the Nürburgring, where drivers stayed together at the Sporthotel built beneath the grandstand right beside the starting line. On the morning of the race Hawthorn barged into the Collinses' room for breakfast, as he usually did. Louise was up, but Collins was still asleep and snoring loudly. In his memoir, *Champion Year,* Hawthorn recalled looking down at Peter that morning and feeling happy. "He is one that won't die, I thought," Hawthorn wrote. Hawthorn roused Collins and the three ate a late breakfast in the room. Hill showed up and helped Collins complete an elaborate wooden puzzle that he had been working on for days.

Hawthorn and Moss were deadlocked in the championship standings, and a huge crowd had turned out to see them duel for the lead. As usual, Moss bolted ahead in the early going, then dropped out with a faulty magneto. That left Collins and Hawthorn swapping first place as a cozy tandem until their countryman Tony Brooks mounted a charge. His British-made Vanwall lacked the Ferrari muscle — it was 15 mph slower on the straights — but the British brakes and suspension gave him an edge in maneuvering the twists and drops through the Eifel Mountains. By the eighth lap they had formed a three-car caravan — Brooks, Collins, Hawthorn — climbing and winding through the forest.

The red cars scrambled to keep up with Brooks as they ground into a tricky serpentine stretch known as the Pflanzgarten. All three crested a hill in third gear, then touched the brakes and shifted to second as the cars leapt momentarily into the air on the downslope. After a dip they accelerated up a short, steep rise leading to a right-hand turn. From his rear position, in third place, Hawthorn could see that Collins was entering the bend too fast and too wide. As Collins tried to swing his car back into line, the rear wheel hit a low embankment on the left side. Hawthorn braced for a collision; he expected Collins to bounce off the embankment and spin across the road and hit him. But he didn't. Instead Collins' car flipped in the air and landed upside down in a cloud of dust. As Hawthorn passed he glanced over to see that Collins had been thrown out.

Brooks expected Collins to challenge him on the straight after the Pflanzgarten. "I had no idea what had happened and I was expecting Peter to come alongside on the straight," he said. "When I got there I had a good look in the mirrors and was rather surprised not to see him. I realized that I had achieved my objective of getting away from the Ferraris, but I didn't know how."

Hawthorn chose not to stop when he came to the pits three miles later. He had no concrete information to share, and he didn't want to alarm Louise, who was waiting patiently in the pits. Four miles later his transmission failed and he pulled over. He stepped from the car and asked a race official to call the pits for news of Collins. Word came that he was roughed up, but all right.

When the race was over Hawthorn got a ride back to the pits, stopping at the Pflanzgarten to retrieve Collins' helmet and gloves. There was no sign of blood.

Louise was in the pits logging her husband's lap times on a clipboard when he failed to come around. "But that had happened many times in the past," she said. "Besides, word had gone around that he was walking back to the pits."

She wasn't too worried, at least not until Hawthorn returned. "Mike came back to the pits and I turned around and looked at him and he turned away from me," she said. "That was when I knew something had happened."

Tavoni came over and told her that the accident was more serious than originally thought. Collins had landed headfirst against a tree trunk. A helicopter was flying him to a hospital in Bonn where one of Germany's top brain surgeons was waiting to operate. Tavoni would take her in his car. It was an agonizing drive. They crawled through traffic exiting the racetrack. Tavoni spoke only a few words of English. She spoke no Italian. They sat in silence, trying not to imagine what they might face at the end of the drive.

When they reached the hospital, a doctor told Louise that her father was on the phone from New York. He had learned of the accident from a UN contact. He wanted to be the one to tell his daughter that Collins had died in the helicopter.

When the awful fact had sunk in she asked to see him. "I wanted to see Peter but everybody said no, you don't want to do that." She insisted. A receptionist took them down to a basement morgue. Louise could see a bluish-white foot sticking out from under a white sheet. "I said that's enough. I knew Peter was gone," she said. "I'm glad I turned around then." They had been married for eighteen months.

Hawthorn also asked to see the body when he arrived at the hospital. "The doctor pulled back the sheet," Tavoni said, "and there was Peter, like he was asleep. Mike took one look, turned and went out into the corridor and slid down to the floor. He just sat there, saying nothing."

Back at the Nürburgring, Brooks had won, but nobody celebrated. Ten or so drivers and friends gathered in a hotel room at the Sporthotel to await word on Collins' condition. There was subdued talk interrupted by bursts of anxious laughter. Denise McCluggage cut Bonnier's hair. It was, McCluggage later wrote, "an understood but unacknowledged waiting." They expected the worst, but it was still a shock when the news came. "I do remember sitting on my bed that night," she later wrote, "holding in my hand the one shoe I had just removed, and then finding myself exactly like that 45 minutes later, stiff and bone chilled."

The Pflanzgarten was not a particularly dangerous curve, and Collins was known as a safe driver. Had the continuing pressure to redeem himself caused him to exceed the limit in his pursuit of Brooks, or was it a simple mechanical failure?

German authorities concluded that driving error caused the crash, but Hill suspected the brakes gave out. Ferrari was so obsessed with building powerful engines that other components were often discounted. As every Ferrari driver knew, the outdated drum brakes had a tendency to wear out, or "fade," as the drivers termed it. As friction heated the saucer-shaped drums they expanded and edged away from a corresponding piece known as the brake shoe. The driver consequently had to stomp successively harder on the brake pedal to bring drum and shoe together.

It didn't take long for the brakes to lose their bite altogether. Von Trips had pulled in with fading brakes after just two laps. The mechanics threw up their hands. He managed to finish fourth by downshifting as he approached each turn, using the braking power of the engine itself to slow the car. He went ten laps without touching his brake pedal at all.

Hill's brakes also died, causing a near accident at the steep descent to the Adenau Bridge. "I had to throw the car sideways and slide it through," Hill said, "and from then on I was finished. I had no brakes."

Five days after Collins died, Horst Peets, one of Germany's most prominent sports commentators, published an article headlined "Peter Collins: For What?" in *Die Welt,* a leading newspaper. It was once accepted that advances in race technology directly contributed to safer, better-engineered cars for the public. By the late 1950s, Peets argued, the improvements no longer justified the deaths:

A number of motor sport experts — mostly men who are in offices, or men who represent a particular sphere of this industry — make it sound like horsepower and cylinder pressure go together with death on the racetrack the way a collar-button fastens to the collar. They take this kind of death as a function: someone must be ready to die in order for us to live a little bit better. . . . Collins was a fine young man, as are basically all his peers. We should convince them, however, that there are quiet things that make chivalry and manhood.

In the 1930s the great Italian driver Tazio Nuvolari, known as the Flying Mantuan, said that "death will catch us all." Since then, Peets wrote, "almost every big-time driver, young or old, has died in one gruesome way or another. Something drove each man up to that diabolical point where he finally overestimated himself."

Four days later Peets followed up with an appeal for safer, stronger cars: "This is not a sport but a show, where you wait to see who dies. . . . So vulnerable and exposed is the driver, so helpless in the moment where something goes wrong, so incredibly naked in the whirlpool of death."

He quoted from a letter Countess von Trips had sent him in response to his first article: "I hope that your article helps me to get my son to quit this cruel sport."

It would take more than a pair of newspaper columns to dissuade von Trips. Two weeks later he rebutted Peets in a letter to *Bild,* a popular German tabloid, arguing that even in the modern world physical courage was an important virtue and a corrective for a culture grown soft on suburbs, television, frozen food, and other postwar comforts. He espoused a Nietzschean view of racing as an expression of man's drive to excel, even if it cost a driver's life. The editors splashed his letter across eight columns below the headline "Therefore I Must Race On!":

That we race cannot be explained by the necessity of sports for industry, but by the indefinite urge in men to compete and succeed in doing perilous things. Things that really serve no purpose, but still require the entire dedication and force of his personality. . . . Danger and fear have become anonymous and invisible — radioactive clouds floating around us. That doesn't change the fact that there are people who thirst for action, to overcome risk and danger by force of will, who are born to fight. These are the characteristics of the man who will help build our contemporary worldview.

A few days after this public exchange, Louise Collins returned to Modena to sort out her affairs. She stopped to see Ferrari, as widows often did. Speaking through an interpreter, he told her that Collins had been like a son to him. He could not continue the racing program without him, he said. The Italian Grand Prix on September 7, 1958, would be the last race for Ferrari. After that, *finito.* He never attended the races, as she knew, but he would join her for this one last race if she would accompany him.

Ferrari and Louise together visited Hill, who was being treated for a kidney ailment in a Milan hospital. "Ferrari wept at my bedside," Hill recalled years later. "He told me he was going to watch the race and that Louise would be by his side. It all sounded very melodramatic and I used to believe —

and tell people — that he faked it all. Now I don't think he did. I think it was a sort of drama he created in his mind and believed it."

Whatever Ferrari believed, he failed to show up at Monza, leaving Louise to attend the race alone. Years later she would see his absence as a benign form of manipulation, Ferrari's way of thrusting her back among old friends one last time before she resumed her acting career. Seated in the grandstand for the first time since Collins died, Louise watched as Mike Hawthorn, her husband's "mon ami mate," lined up on the front row of the starting grid, the lone Ferrari among three Vanwalls. As always, he was wearing a bow tie and green jacket. But he was not the same person. Collins' death had erased Hawthorn's schoolboy smirk. In the weeks before the race he had sat with friends weeping and broken.

At noon on race day he had languished in bed at the Palace Hotel in Milan, trying to pull himself together for the midafternoon start. He and Collins had made a pact that if one died the other would keep racing. In honor of their agreement he squeezed himself into the car. He may also have been encouraged to return by his position in the Grand Prix standings. If he could hold off

Moss he would win the championship.

Von Trips and Hill lined up in the second row with orders to protect Hawthorn. With Collins gone and Hawthorn shaken, it was becoming clear that they would inherit the Ferrari mantle, but for now they played supporting roles.

Hill exploded out of the start to an early lead — the first time an American had led a Grand Prix race. His maneuver was a deliberate provocation to Moss, who had a tendency to run his cars down with aggressive starts. The rabbit act worked: Moss flashed ahead to ride Hill's tailpipe and withdrew seventeen laps later with a busted gearbox. His departure left the way open for Hawthorn to finish second, giving him an edge over Moss in the season tally. Meanwhile von Trips had tried to power his way to the fore in a car muscled up with a robust new engine but he didn't last a lap. As the lead pack rumbled down the opening stretch at 125 mph, von Trips drifted to the left looking for a way to pass the green Vanwall driven by Tony Brooks before they braked and swung right into a bend known as the Lesmo Curve. "The Vanwalls are built really high," von Trips wrote in his diary. "So beside me was a really high green wall. We were barely centimeters apart."

Von Trips slid safely ahead of Brooks, only to collide with Harry Schell, who was passing Brooks on the other side. "Schell passed the Vanwall, lost control in the curve on the left side and I immediately started going up his backside," von Trips wrote. While Brooks followed the Lesmo curve to the right, Schell and von Trips skittered off the left side of the track, their cars locked together. As they slid into the underbrush Schell looked over, aghast that von Trips had rammed him. "Von Trips must have been totally crazy," he later said.

Schell was unhurt, but von Trips flew from his car and landed in a rose bush. "I felt something like a funny bone in my left calf. I couldn't see the car but it couldn't be far. Because I wouldn't be able to save myself if there was a tank explosion, I yelled. Then a paramedic pulled me out of the rose bush."

The "funny bone" turned out to be a severely torn and stretched knee cartilage. His car didn't fare much better: Its chassis had snapped in two. Von Trips spent two months in the hospital, first in Milan and then Cologne. For the second time in as many years he faced a long and complicated convalescence, relieved by teasing from friends. "What are you thinking?" a former schoolmate wrote from Berlin. "A car is not a tank or a snowplow. It is intended strictly for roads and not for test drives through ditches and trees!"

While lying in the hospital he wrote a long soul-searching letter to an old girlfriend in Munich revealing loneliness and self-doubt. He confessed that he had begun to question whether his campaign for a championship was worth the isolation and emotional sacrifice. Almost none of the drivers had a family life, and he understood why. Racing made it almost impossible to cultivate real relationships. She wrote back to say that he must accept that he was human, and not a superman:

You have the ability to love already in you — it's only, I believe, that over time you have simply forgotten how to analyze those feelings properly. And so you have misled people. I'll bet there are women who complain of insensitivity and cold-ness in you, women who have wanted or hoped for things you could not give them, because your whole self, your whole life, your yearning and suffering under your motto and creed can tolerate no rival. The racers — you are in some place obsessed, and that is not good, because you sacrifice too much, you are too much fixed on one thing.

She went on to congratulate him for growing beyond what she called his "lovable recklessness":

In you there is already a little of the maturity, the detached observation that only very old people have. It is probably because you have looked death in the eye so often that you are already finished with your life! . . . Wolfgang — I am very pleased with you. You have become much more mature, and even if the lovable recklessness is gone — so are you dearer to me. I have never believed the frivolity of which many accuse you.

Von Trips was recovering at Burg Hemmersbach when word arrived that Ferrari had dropped him. After a total of eight accidents, Ferrari's patience had run out. "I'm not amused by drivers who smash up my cars," Ferrari told a reporter. "I expect them to win."

If he were to race again, von Trips would have to recuperate yet again and find a team willing to take a chance on him. Prostrated in his castle bedroom, he was unsure if he had the stomach for another comeback. From his window he could see the seasonal workers turning the loam in well-tended fields. In the hothouse his carnations pushed up through rich Rhineland soil. At 5 a.m. each morning a truck ferried the flowers to a wholesale market twenty-five miles north of Cologne. His pet project, a newly planted cherry orchard, yielded fruit sold to local bakeries. After thousands of hard miles of racing he could succumb contentedly enough to the unhurried rhythms of planting. It was hard for him to know if he had at last accepted the farmlands as his rightful place, or if he had given up on racing the way a drowning man accepts his fate.

Hill didn't win in Formula 1 that year either, but he played a key role in Hawthorn's push to succeed Fangio as world champion. According to the complicated calculus of Grand Prix, Hawthorn could claim the championship by finishing first or second in the Moroccan Grand Prix. Otherwise Moss would win. The British press called it the "showdown in the sun."

Hawthorn eluded the press by arriving in Casablanca on a separate flight from his girlfriend, a twenty-one-year-old model named Jean Howarth. His first stop was to inspect the Ferraris covered in tarps at a rented garage. The car assigned to him had the number 2 painted on it, the same number Collins and Musso had when they died. Hawthorn would not race with it, he said. Gendebien agreed to switch with him.

Once again, Hill's job was to induce Moss to damage or wear down his car by setting a fast pace. Moss bolted fast from the starting line, as always, and took off down a sun-baked road that ran by turbaned Arabs and white minarets on the sandy outskirts of Casablanca. Hill pecked at Moss from behind while Hawthorn hung back to preserve his engine. On the fortieth lap Hill eased back so that Hawthorn could finish second and beat Moss by a single point in the season tally. Moss led the race from beginning to end and recorded the fastest lap, but Hawthorn became the first British world champion.

When Hawthorn rolled into the pits after his cool-down lap, Tavoni rushed to congratulate him. *Bravissimo, bravissimo!* Before stepping from the car, Hawthorn told Tavoni that he was retiring. He was done. He made a perfunctory showing at the post-race ceremonies, then whisked Howarth to the hotel. At the age of twenty-nine, Hawthorn had resolved that he would be the one Ferrari driver to escape alive. He would marry Howarth and move back to Farnham to run the family garage.

In leaving, Hawthorn turned the team's hopes over to Hill, with the caveat that Hill had to stay alive long enough to fulfill them. "Let me make a prediction," Hawthorn told the press in a farewell statement. "The combination of Phil Hill and Ferrari will be heard from over the coming seasons. I think Phil has an excellent chance of becoming world champion — if his luck doesn't run out."

The first months of retirement went much as Hawthorn planned. He and Howarth were engaged and were to marry the following year. At Christmas he gave her a boxer dog named Ferrari. On January 22, 1959, he set off for London to attend to some business and meet Louise Collins, who had just completed a run in a traveling production of *Romanoff and Juliet,* a Cold War version of the Shakespeare play written by Peter Ustinov. A few days later Hawthorn would go to Paris to meet with lawyers about making provisions for an illegitimate son he had fathered in France. It was a complication that he had to resolve before finalizing his marriage to Howarth.

He left Farnham in his highly tuned Jaguar Mark 1 on a wet winter morning with squalling winds, heading northeast through the rolling Surrey countryside. As he drove along a ridge known as the Hog's Back he caught up with a Gullwing Mercedes driven by Rob Walker, heir to the Johnnie Walker whiskey fortune and owner of a stable of Grand Prix cars. Hawthorn pulled alongside and waved. For all his talk of retirement and marriage, he could not resist a tussle — especially with a Mercedes.

The two cars plunged neck-and-neck down a long hill slick with rain. They went flat out, each driver working his way up the gears to a speed of about 100 mph. Easing into a right-hand turn at the bottom, Hawthorn slid and smacked the curb. The impact spun his Jaguar 180 degrees. Now he was going backwards at 100 mph. The drivers were still traveling side by side, but facing opposite directions. Their eyes met for an instant before Hawthorn nipped the median. The collision flung him onto the shoulder, where the Jaguar wrapped itself around a tree. Walker reached him in time to see his eyes glaze over and go still. Hawthorn had escaped death in a Ferrari only to find it on a Guildford bypass three months into retirement. It didn't take long for news of Hawthorn's death to reach Burg Hemmersbach, where von Trips waited in exile. Within nineteen months, four of his former teammates had died: Portago, Musso, Collins, and now Hawthorn.

"We drivers of the Scuderia family were always a small family," he wrote to Ferrari, "and if we quarreled sometimes, so also do we have steadfast ties and an awareness that to drive for Ferrari is something that keeps us together. Even when someone like me is no longer a team member, the memory is still very much alive. It was a time when I was in your cars and in the company of many dear friends, no longer living, racing on tracks around the world."

His wistful tone suggests that he did not expect to race again, at least not for Ferrari. Drivers who came close to dying, like those who married, were no use to Ferrari. They rarely mustered the nerve to face the limit.

For the moment, von Trips found a measure of peace walking on crutches under the chestnut trees and tending to his flowers. Once again his parents pressured him to stay home. His mother in particular voiced her hope that the accident — his second serious crash at Monza — would sway him to retire from racing and take up his long-deferred agricultural duties. Supervising the farmlands was a full-time job, and his parents were getting too old to manage.

Besides, he was an only child and the last son of the Trips dynasty. Hawthorn's death was a reminder that the ancient bloodline would expire with von Trips if he died. The other branches of the family had long since withered away. Von Trips was fond of saying, half jokingly, that his ancestors were all robber-knights who came to violent deaths.

There was no shortage of women hoping to settle down with him, many from the network of aristocracy spread across Europe like an extended family. He had a long casual affair with Princess Maria Gabriella of Savoy, the tall blonde daughter of Italy's last king. He met her through Juan Carlos, the future king of Spain and a pupil in the driving clinics von Trips occasionally conducted. He and the princess saw a lot of each other in Paris, where she was studying painting with Oskar Kokoschka, an Austrian expressionist known for swirling psychedelic portraits and landscapes. She was a genteel bohemian and the kind of free spirit that would be called a hippie few years later. She avidly pursued von Trips — avidly enough to give him a nude watercolor self-portrait. In the end, he decided that she was too far above his station.

Besides, von Trips was uncomfortable with the prospect of a marriage founded on the perpetuation of his noble pedigree. His mother came from a bourgeois family, and he had grown up with an awareness of slights and subtle condescension from those who considered him a half-blood count (though the aristocracy was only too happy to claim him when the press christened him "the fastest count on earth"). Racing had always appealed to him as an escape from the issues of birthright and entitlements. It was a meritocracy where Fangio, the son of a potato farmer, rose to the top and any number of titled pretenders failed. "The racetrack had its own aristocracy," said Taki Theodoracopulos, the journalist who was then an amateur tennis player and a frequent companion on evening excursions. "You couldn't tell the difference between the highborn and the lowborn."

Von Trips spent his recuperative months in his study, a private hideaway tucked beneath the mansard roof, writing letters and listening to George Gershwin and Stan Getz. He sat on the floor and recorded ruminations into an audio diary and for fun dubbed the roar of engines onto the soundtrack.

He also listened to an LP recording of an interview with his friend Alfonso de Portago. Like a voice from the grave, the soft-spoken Portago made the case for racing as the invigorating pursuit of a modern nobility. It was a philosophy borrowed equally from Jack Kerouac and their knightly ancestors. "The racer is happier, luckier than other men," Portago said, "because he lives through a stronger sense of the nearness of death. The racer is in a world that only a few understand."

It looked as if von Trips might be forever becalmed in his castle when his early supporter, Huschke von Hanstein, wrote with an invitation to join Porsche for the 1959 season, just as he had when von Trips was bereft two years earlier. "If your daredevil spirit knows no end," von Hanstein wrote, "I'll again extend my offer to you to satisfy it."

The letter landed like a hand grenade at Burg Hemmersbach, where von Trips was just beginning to resign himself to a life spent fussing over the potato and turnip harvests.

With von Hanstein's backing, he went to the Monaco Grand Prix on May 10, where he did little to redeem himself. Within the first five minutes he lost control in a bend where the road climbs steeply to a hillside casino. As von Trips spun out the British driver Cliff Allison rammed him with his

Ferrari. The silver Porsche 718 crumpled against a wall. Von Trips exited the race before the first lap ended, just as he had at Monza in 1958. "The young ladies can rest assured," a radio broadcaster said, in a nod to von Trips' female following. "Nothing's happened to him."

Von Trips nursed a badly gashed cheek on the roadside as Hill whisked by on his way to a fourth-place finish. Von Trips' abysmal showing could easily have been the concluding episode of his career. "We've seen a lot of great moments from the Count," *Der Spiegel* wrote, "but we've repeatedly learned that in the decisive moment he does not have the necessary perspective. It's not the first time that failure's come by hasty, even reckless action."

While von Trips tried to resuscitate himself with Porsche, the ranks of Ferrari drivers continued to thin. Jean Behra, a short, stout Frenchman hired by Ferrari for the 1959 season, became paranoid and surly as he strained to meet Ferrari's expectations. At thirty-eight, he had survived a dozen crashes. His body was laced with scars. A French magazine published a full-page photograph of him with a dense display of arrows identifying his broken bones. A collision three years earlier had torn off his right ear. Behra endured it all with a Gallic shrug. "Only those who do not move do not die," he said. "But are they not already dead?"

Nobody doubted Behra's toughness, but he was temperamentally unsuited for Ferrari. He fried his clutch at the 1959 French Grand Prix, then overstrained the car until smoke billowed from the engine. At a party held in a restaurant after the race, he accused Tavoni of assigning him cars that were mechanically unsound. Tavoni responded by saying that Behra himself had trashed the engines with sloppy driving. Behra slapped Tavoni, and would have pummeled him if his wife had not pulled him off. When Ferrari heard about the scrap he immediately fired Behra. Behra then tried to buy a Ferrari to race independently, but Ferrari refused to even see him.

Desperate to prove that he could still compete, Behra entered his own Porsche Spyder RSK in a sports car race run on a 2.5-mile stretch of West Berlin road known as AVUS. Two long parallel straights ended in a thirty-foot banked hairpin surfaced in a rough layer of brick. The race carried no real importance; it was staged only to rouse local interest in the German Grand Prix held the next day. Behra was in third place when his car skidded on the wet hairpin turn at 110 mph. He entered the turn on the proper line, but the tail of his car slid higher and higher on the banking until it flew off the edge backwards and crumpled against an old anti-aircraft bunker. Behra was thrown clear. For a moment spectators could see him writhing in midair, his arms outstretched as if swimming to safety. He struck a flagpole and rolled down a slope, coming to a stop near a street where drivers were practicing for the next day's race. He died of a skull fracture.

Even by Ferrari standards, it was a cruel ending. "We abandoned this man to his despair," the Ferrari engineer Carlo Chiti said. "We had obliged him to take refuge in his own desperation."

At a wake held in Berlin, von Trips laid his hand on Behra's forehead inside the open casket. It was a tender parting gesture captured by a gaggle of press photographers. Behra was buried a few days later with his checkered helmet placed on his coffin.

Behra's final race marked the beginning of von Trips' latest comeback. Moments after Behra died, Hanstein held out a chalkboard with an "X" by Behra's name. He intended the signal as a warning: Von Trips had better slow down on the wet course. But von Trips held his speed and won. It was an insignificant race but it helped restore his confidence.

"I remain best of friends with the House of Ferrari, but after my accident in Monza '58 and the many fatal crashes on the Ferrari team I was not in the mood to be on the Formula 1 circuit this year," he wrote to an acquaintance. "It simply takes a little time before the wounds delivered by blows of fate — for which the death of an entire racing team certainly qualifies — heal on their own. Still, I believe I've found the old form and strength again."

Enzo Ferrari agreed. Following the races from his Modena stronghold, he could tell that von Trips' instincts had returned, along with signs of a new maturity: He had finally learned how to keep his impetuousness and overreach in check. It had taken a crisis of confidence for Von Trips to understand what Hill had known all along: Going faster sometimes required slowing down.

The horrific death toll of the previous two years had depleted the Ferrari lineup. As a result, Ferrari may have needed von Trips more than von Trips needed Ferrari. In the fall of 1959, Il Commendatore invited von Trips to Modena. Over the customary lunch of tortellini and Lambrusco at Il Cavallino he offered to reinstate von Trips. All was forgiven.

On December 12, von Trips was back in the fold, competing in the U.S. Grand Prix at Sebring. His return almost ended before it began. He crushed the nose of his Ferrari by running into Tony Brooks, but righted himself for a sixth-place finish. The mishap notwithstanding, it was clear that he was a shrewder and more circumspect driver.

The redemptive race, the one that demonstrated his new maturity, took place the following March when he overcame a pack of Coopers, Porsches, and Lotuses to win the Syracuse Grand Prix in Sicily, making him the first German to win a Grand Prix since 1939. "Wolfgang was once an erratic driver," wrote Louis Stanley, an automotive historian. "Blessed with great bravery, the Count drove fast, sometimes too much so, with the inevitable result. . . . In 1960, he stood in front of us, mature, with a great sense of responsibility."

More important than the win itself was the way he won. He didn't try to do too much, instead relying on control and tactics to outlast the competition. When he crossed the finish line a laughing Ferrari mechanic lifted him from his seat. The black, red, and gold German flag was hoisted and the German national anthem, "Das Lied der Deutschen," was played.

"Finally, a victory," he wrote in a telegram to his mother. "Am happy. Wolfgang."

The 156 Sharknose was Ferrari's answer to the nimble British cars of the late 1950s. Built in secret, with the flared nostrils of a predator, the Sharknose returned Ferrari to dominance. (Klemantaski Collection)

9
BIRTH OF THE SHARKNOSE

"Speed is the keynote of our age," Alfonso de Portago wrote just before his fatal crash. They were prophetic words. On January 2, 1959, a 250-ton Soviet rocket lifted off from the desert steppes of Kazakhstan and roared into space. It broke Earth's gravitational pull, the first man-made object to do so, and passed the moon at 5,500 mph on its way to solar orbit. Three weeks later the jet age officially began with the first scheduled transcontinental flight of a Boeing 707 from Los Angeles to New York. In February, Texas Instruments requested a patent for the integrated circuit, an initial step in the computer revolution.

On the cusp of the 1960s, the modern world beckoned with supersonics, sex, and disquiet. But time stood still in sleepy Modena. *Paisanos* drove bullock carts down empty cobbled alleys. Balsamic vinegar aged in chestnut casks, as it had since Roman times. Nine miles up the Via Abetone, in Maranello, teams of grizzled Ferrari artisans in brown coveralls made pistons, cylinder heads, and crankshafts by hand.

Nobody clung to the old ways more than their boss. The man who built a global brand synonymous with speed was oddly averse to the pace and practices of modern life. Enzo Ferrari refused to travel in airplanes. He avoided elevators, and he would see movies only if he could sit by the door. He clung to small-town habits — the barbershop gossip during his morning shave, lunches of boiled meat with his cronies, the daily visit to his son's tomb.

For the first time the Ferraris themselves looked old-fashioned. In the 1960 Belgian Grand Prix, Hill chased Jack Brabham, the 1959 world champion, for lap after lap as they snaked through the Ardennes Forest at 150 mph. Brabham flicked periodic glances over his shoulder to see Hill crowding his tail. In the end, the pace was too much for Hill's Ferrari. On lap 29 the engine ignited. Hill jumped out, patted down his singed coveralls, and doused the engine fire with a tiny extinguisher. The flames fed the impression that the Ferraris were straining to keep up. And they were.

It was a startling reversal. For years

Ferrari had dominated with a succession of bullying, bellowing engines. The British marques had seemed alarmingly fragile by comparison. British racing was practically a cottage industry with homegrown production shops scattered across the Southeast and Midlands. British Racing Motors, known as BRM, was set up behind the founder's Lincolnshire home. Lotus operated from an old stable behind a London hotel. Chassis were stacked outside under a tarpaulin.

By 1959 the tables had turned. The British answered the Italian hysteria for speed with a cool and calculated efficiency. The engineers at Cooper and BRM had produced a new species of Grand Prix cars with the engine positioned in the rear. By 1960 Lotus followed. With the weight centered just behind the driver, the cars were more balanced and agile as they slipped around corners. They also had an aerodynamic advantage: Without an engine up front to see over, the driver could sit lower, greatly reducing the car's wind resistance.

The Ferraris still rocked the grandstands with their banshee blare. They still looked like felines poised for the pounce. But they now seemed comparatively heavy and ungainly, like woozy heavyweights. With weight positioned way up front, they waddled around turns and labored to keep up with the lighter, nimbler British cars, even on tracks that favored a wealth of horsepower.

Ferrari brushed off foreign innovations. He dismissed Cooper and the other British outfits as *garagistas.* No, he told friends over grappa, the red cars would always house beastly, gut-pounding engines up front. "It's always been the ox that pulls the cart," he said.

The ox might have pulled the Ferrari cart forever had the Ferrari engineer Andrea Fraschetti not spun and flipped while testing a prototype at the Modena *autodromo* in August 1957. He died the next day. In his place Ferrari hired a rotund Alfa Romeo engineer with thick-framed glasses named Carlo Chiti. He moved into an apartment next to Ferrari's above the old Modena workshop at 11 Viale Trento e Trieste. Together they looked like an Italian version of Tweedledum and Tweedledee. The craftsmen joked that Ferrari and Chiti wore glasses because their protruding stomachs required them to stand at a distance.

The provincial Ferrari circle received Chiti with suspicion. He came from Florence, just sixty-four miles from Modena, but it might just as well have been Moscow.

Mechanics muttered an old Modenese proverb under their breath: "Better to die in bed than to have a Tuscan at the door." Nor did they welcome Chiti's progressive ideas about suspension geometry, weight distribution, and aerodynamics. Ferrari had its set way of doing things, and it did not welcome change.

Chiti brought an artist's disposition to the drafting table, working extravagant hours and erupting into volcanic fits when his new methods met resistance. Not surprisingly, he favored moving the engines aft, and he bought a Cooper chassis to demonstrate how it might be done. Ferrari was unimpressed. "He was unwilling for us to try, even at the level of a mere project," Chiti said, "because he believed this would be a betrayal of the technical philosophy of his firm."

Ferrari might have curbed Chiti's experiment once and for all if not for an unexpected change in the Grand Prix specifications. On October 29, 1959, the Royal Automobile Club threw a formal party at its 258-room clubhouse in the St. James's neighborhood of London to honor Vanwall, a British manufacturer that had won six Grands Prix that season. After years of chasing red cars, the British had dominated.

This was their victory party.

At evening's end, after the awards had been handed out, Augustin Pérouse, president of racing's governing body, stepped to the microphone. The room went silent as his announcement sank in. New regulations for Formula 1 would limit engine capacity to 1.5 liters, a reduction of 40 percent. To discourage the construction of fragile cars, a weight minimum of 450 kilograms would be imposed.

The British racing establishment had drunk rounds of toasts that night, and the hall was syrupy with patriotism. It came as a shock to learn that now, with British racing green finally dominant, the ground rules would be upended. The British jeered.

In one sense their indignation was puzzling. The new rules, to go into effect in 1961, were roughly equivalent to those governing Formula 2, where the British had thrived. It might well benefit the British to extend the rules to Formula 1. But the reaction was based more on nationalism than logic: Delegates from Monaco, Holland, France, Germany, and Belgium had voted for the change. Italy alone had joined Britain in opposition. The British felt that their European neighbors had ganged up on them in their moment of triumph. They objected, as well, to the prospect of Pérouse, a Frenchman, imposing a gutless reduction of power and spectacle.

Over the next year the *garagistas* drafted a series of complaints to the sport's governing body, the Fédération Internationale de l'Automobile in Paris. The federation's "structure is slow and cumbersome even as your sport is fast and alive," said Moss, who must have felt doubly frustrated. A London judge had just revoked his license for a speeding violation. The arresting constable asked him, "Who do you think you are, Stirling Moss?"

The British were in no position to rush new machines into production, even if they wanted to. Their budgets and workshops were too small. As the months passed the British delegation offered counterproposals and compromises and huffy condemnations — all the while assuming that they would prevail.

But the federation held firm. By September 1960 it was clear that they would not rescind the new 1.5-liter rules. Cooper and Lotus gave up and began work on new engines and cars, knowing that they could not produce them in time for the 1961 season.

While the British were arguing, Ferrari

315

was quietly plotting a surprise. As soon as Pérouse announced the new regulations, Ferrari had sequestered Chiti in a secret Modena workshop, away from the Maranello factory, to develop a rear-engine car that complied with the new rules, giving him a six-month head start over the British. "Ferrari had agreed to try," Chiti said, "even though he wasn't really in agreement."

In February 1961 the automotive press came to Maranello to see Chiti's secret weapon. The Ferrari 156 was a stripped-down screamer with tapered torpedo lines and wide-splayed wire wheels. It descended from earlier Formula 1 models, but with a more modern aspect: Its physiognomy expressed a sinister form of Space Age speed. The 156 possessed the beauty of a design reduced to its essence. Beneath the polished red skin a 400-horsepower V6 engine nestled behind the driver. Chiti sank the engine deep, near the middle of the chassis, so the car would have a lower center of gravity and handle more deftly than its precursors. The result was a harmonic convergence of power and weight. The reporters standing in the factory's cobbled forecourt nodded. *Bellissima, bellissima.* This was a car to carry Ferrari back to the podiums.

Chiti shaped the 156 with the aid of a wind tunnel, a new technique for Ferrari. It consequently had a swept-back jet age profile with drivers reclining like Mercury astronauts behind a low wrap of windscreen. It was a new look for a new era of technological advance. The 156 looked dazzlingly fast, and it was. In test runs von Trips touched 180 mph. It would take its nickname from the twin intake nostrils fitted on either side of its sinister snout: the Sharknose.

Chiti had engineered not just a car, but a reversal of fortune. The Sharknose all but assured that Ferrari's dominion would be restored for the 1961 season. He had won the race for horsepower and handling before the first starting flag dropped.

The only remaining question was which Ferrari driver would ride the Sharknose to the championship. The coming season shaped up as a two-man race: Hill versus von Trips.

In March 1959, *Sports Illustrated* put Hill on its cover with the tagline "Sports Car Driver of the Year." He was photographed leaning against the hood of a 250 Testa Rossa with his legs crossed and a smile on his tanned face. After years of anguish he

317

looked happy and confident. "I'm always afraid when I race," he told the magazine, but he persisted "because I do it well." That was Hill's career in distillate — a debilitating apprehension overcome by the draw of automotive distinction. He was ready for a summer-long push to prove that an American, an outsider and misfit once relegated to sports cars, could earn the highest laurel of a European sport.

Hill had become a star in spite of himself. At one of the many cocktail parties preceding the races a pretty girl sidled up to Graham Hill, a British driver with a David Niven pencil mustache. "Oh, I'm sorry," she said, blushing when she realized her mistake. "I thought you were the famous Mr. Hill."

Fame gave Hill something else to stress about. In his book *Cars at Speed,* Robert Daley described a pack of shouting, excited German boys clamoring for Hill's autograph as he left a restaurant near the Nürburgring:

"I'm nobody," Hill said.
"You're Phil Hill," the boys chorused.
"No I'm not," asserted Hill firmly. He slid into his car and drove off.

While Hill holed up in his hotel room

listening to music on his Concertone, von Trips made a warm and likable impression as a television correspondent at the Brussels car show and appeared in advertisements for motor oil, car parts, and eyeglasses. Like President John F. Kennedy, who took office a month before Ferrari unveiled the Sharknose, von Trips had an instinct for the casual élan of the early 1960s. He was almost Edwardian in his gentlemanly bearing, but his magnetism burned bright in television interviews and magazine photos. He could talk to reporters in four languages; in all four his enthusiasm for racing was infectious.

Most team owners would have named Hill the lead driver for 1961 and ordered von Trips to stand back, or vice versa. But Ferrari refused to designate either one. He had a long history of extracting the utmost by pitting his people against one another, whether it was in the machine shop or on the racetrack. So the two men faced a gauntlet, an ordeal of one-on-one struggle that would last through the season. "The tension was excruciating and could not be relieved by a frank expression of competitiveness, not acceptably anyhow, between friends and teammates," Hill said.

Hill and von Trips weren't smoothed-face

novices anymore. They were in their mid-thirties with crow's-feet and creases earned by years of strain and hard driving. They had reached the peak of their powers. This was their moment.

Both men expected to drive hard up against the limit until a breakdown or accident decided the contest for them. They knew that death might be the arbiter.

*The start of the Monaco Grand Prix, May 14, 1961.
For Phil Hill and Wolfgang von Trips, it was the beginning of an agonizing summer. They knew that a fatal
accident might well decide the championship. (Getty
Images)*

10
1961

One cold night in the first week of January 1961, Wolfgang von Trips stood at a doorway, suitcase in hand, and rang the bell. He lingered in the chill air, listening for signs of stirring within.

Three years earlier he had hired a former tax advisor named Elfriede Flossdorf to type his diary entries and manage the details of his endorsement deals and appearances. He teasingly called her "the racing secretary" because she dashed to keep up with the growing workload. Flossdorf was so busy, in fact, that von Trips installed her and her husband Willi in a small house on the entrance road to Burg Hemmersbach so that she would be close at hand. He had come to their door in the middle of the night to pick up his key. "Guess where I've been," von Trips asked when they had roused themselves.

They looked puzzled. "Well," she said, "in

South Africa . . ."

"I was walking with the Almighty," von Trips interrupted.

"Where?"

"I celebrated the new year in absolute heaven," he said. "Astounding, isn't it?"

He was making a facetious reference to the Aga Khan's home in South Africa where he had spent the holiday with Gabriella, Princess of Savoy. In the coming months he faced a murderous campaign for the championship, but he began the year in the arms of a blue-eyed princess.

The next morning von Trips unwrapped a set of plates sent by Huschke von Hanstein of Porsche, a steadfast friend throughout his rise and fall and eventual redemption. Hanstein had given the plates as a Christmas gift and to show that he accepted von Trips' decision to leave Porsche and return to Ferrari at the end of the 1959 season.

"I've just unpacked your Christmas present and note to my great regret that the large plates have broken into three clean pieces," von Trips wrote to Hanstein. "My next difficulty is to interpret what this oracle could mean. Shards can mean luck, or it could be a wink at my decision to go with the Reds."

As von Trips noted, broken plates are

considered propitious. He may have carried the luck with him to Sicily for the Targa Florio, a rugged mountain race preceding the Grand Prix season. Hill chased von Trips through the harsh countryside on rutted roads caked with dung and caught up to him on a rocky plateau 2,000 feet above the coast. He tried to pass but the road — no more than a paved track for donkey carts — was too narrow. Von Trips might have edged over to let Hill pass, but he was unaware that Hill had pulled so close; the engine howl drowned out the sound of Hill's car. Hill announced himself with a series of bumps and shoves delivered from behind at 120 mph. One rough nudge sent both whirling off the road and into the weeds. After a heated exchange, they pulled back onto the road, with von Trips leading again. Now driving in a fit of anger, Hill muscled past von Trips and skidded his way down a long switchbacked descent to the sea, flashing by ancient stone churches and old men riding mules. At the bottom of a steep stretch he hit a blind bend and lost control, sliding through concrete guardposts and crumpling his Ferrari in a ditch. He crawled out of the wreck in time to see von Trips rumble by on his way to a win. It was a taste of the dogfight to come.

Sicily was a prelude to Monaco, the first of nine Grands Prix that would decide the championship. Von Trips glowed with confidence at the pre-race galas and the house party thrown by Bernard Cahier at his home in Villefranche-sur-Mer, six miles down the Riviera coast. He was a bit shy, as always, with a hint of sadness in his eyes, but his charm and good humor seemed to inoculate him against misfortune. He was too nice to die.

Von Trips had the winner's demeanor, but a betting line would probably have favored Hill due to his consistent record. "This is Hill's year," Moss said. "He has the ability . . . and the car." Though you wouldn't have known it to see Hill on practice days. As usual, he was a knot of nerves, pacing the pits with a cigarette and wiping his goggles. At every turn he exchanged sharp words — punctuated by animated Italian gestures — with the Ferrari mechanics buzzing about the cars in buff-colored coveralls. When he was not practicing, Hill burned off nervous energy and built stamina with long swims off the Monaco beachfront. The warm, wet Mediterranean was his antidote to days spent staring at blacktop.

Hill, the incessant worrier, did not accept the common view that a Ferrari championship was inevitable. "There was always an uncomfortable feeling in the team," he later wrote, "and while the car was very competitive, I never was convinced that the championship was going to be easy or even possible to win."

Among other things, Hill feared that Stirling Moss might steal the race, or the season, with one of his sensational dark-horse performances. Moss was flinty-eyed and muscled, with almost superhuman discipline. He once said that he abstained from sex for a week before each race so as not to soften his resolve. His eyesight was so acute that he could read newspapers from across a room and scan the crowd for pretty girls while entering a curve at 85 mph.

Moss had won fourteen Grand Prix races — more than any other active driver — but he had yet to win a championship. His shrewd, cold-blooded precision made him a perennial threat, despite his refusal to join a manufacturer's team. Aside from a stint with Mercedes, Moss relied on privately owned cars a year or so out of date. He enjoyed the underdog role, just as he relished driving cars painted British racing green, but he knew that he might never win a championship that way. In one race after another the obsolete cars broke down under his punishment.

"I like to feel the odds are against me," he said. "That is one of the reasons why I do not drive for a factory. I want to beat the factories in a car that has no right to do so. If I had any sense I would have been driving for Ferrari all these years. Year after year Ferrari has the best car. But I want to fight against odds, and in a British car."

Moss took particular delight in beating Ferrari. Ten years earlier, when Moss was a twenty-two-year-old sensation, Ferrari had courted him. After some negotiation Moss had agreed to race a sleek new four-cylinder Ferrari with a tapered nose in a race at Bari, a port city on the heel of the Italian boot. Moss and his father, a prosperous dentist, made the long trip from London, only to be rebuffed at the Ferrari garage. "The mechanic said, 'Who are you and what are you doing?' " Moss recalled. "I said I was going to drive that car. He said, 'I'm afraid you're not.' "

Moss telephoned Ferrari, who unapologetically explained that he had changed his mind and given the car to the veteran Piero Taruffi. Ferrari was most likely punishing Moss for taking a tough stance in their negotiations. Moss took it as a barefaced insult — to England as much as to himself — and vowed revenge on the racetrack. Indeed, the affront gave him extra incentive over the following decade. "It gave me great pleasure to beat Ferrari," he said.

If Moss could beat Ferrari anywhere, it was Monaco. In the narrow streets winding above the blue Mediterranean, the driver counted at least as much as the car. The course contained only one straight where the Ferraris could unleash their decisive horsepower. Racing a Ferrari against Moss in Monaco, Hill said, was "similar to seeing which is quickest round a living room, a race horse or a dog." Monaco was not considered dangerous. The cars reached only 120 mph or so as they twisted their way up and down the hilly principality. It had been nine years since a driver had died there. The circuit might not be fast, but it was demanding. One hundred laps of short bursts and tight hairpins punished the clutch — and the driver. They changed gears about once every five seconds.

Monaco was the only Grand Prix run in city streets, and the smallest slip could send a car into a storefront or streetlamp. Pedestrians stood unprotected on the curb, almost within reach of passing cars. Six years earlier Alberto Ascari had driven his

Lancia into the harbor, and a driver once missed a sharp left turn and rammed his hood into the ticket office of the train station. "To go flat-out through a bend that is surrounded by level lawn is one thing," Moss said, "but to go flat-out through a bend that has a stone wall on one side and a precipice on the other — that's an achievement."

Race day felt like a fresh start for a sport afflicted by so many recent deaths. As the Sunday church bells tolled, tanned spectators gathered on balconies and in open-air cafés. The city was bright with lilies and bougainvillea. White yachts bobbed at their moorings with pennants fluttering and girls sunbathing in bikinis. Many of the yachts had moved a safe distance from their quayside slips. Rescue divers waited on small boats in case a driver flew off the harbor-front promenade.

At 2:30 p.m. the mayor of Monte Carlo arrived at the grandstand in a chauffeured convertible, a sign that the race was about to begin. Mechanics rolled a pair of Shark-noses onto the third row of the starting grid for Hill and von Trips. They sat one row behind Richie Ginther, Hill's Santa Monica friend and a former mechanic.

At Hill's urging, Chiti had hired Ginther

to test drive the Sharknose prototypes. He would now race the latest version with a new engine configured with V-shaped cylinder banks spread at 120 degrees. Ginther's cylinder banks were 55 degrees wider than those found in the other two Sharknoses, allowing the engine to sit lower in the chassis. With a lower center of gravity, the 120-degree version should in theory handle better on Monaco's hairpins and switchbacks. Chiti wanted the new version assigned to Hill or von Trips, but Ferrari did not trust it. He insisted that it go to a second-tier driver. Hill and von Trips would drive the more thoroughly tested model. "It was a typical piece of Ferrari meddling — jealous of a possible project of which he hadn't approved," Chiti later said. "He was almost afraid of a good result, after having said, over and over, for months, that the future didn't lie with rear engines."

Ferrari's reservations proved unfounded. The 120-degree engine was blindingly fast over three days of practice, earning Ginther a place beside Moss on the front row.

As usual, Moss was badly handicapped by an obsolete car, though it never seemed to bother him. The year-old Lotus was 20 mph slower than the Ferraris. It had undergone a series of hasty repairs, the last of which took place on the starting line. Minutes before the start Moss noticed a crack in the chassis. He stood by calmly sipping water as a mechanic covered the fuel tanks in wet towels and welded the fracture closed.

With five minutes to go, the drivers pulled their helmets on and lowered themselves into their seats. They stretched their legs inside the hollow cars and checked the alignment of rearview mirrors. They twisted wax earplugs into place to muffle the engine noise and pulled on string-backed gloves dusted with talcum powder to absorb sweat. Up and down the starting grid drivers yawned in response to nervousness and swallowed to slake dry throats. Some spat for good luck. A helicopter buzzed overhead, ruffling palm fronds. Team managers leaned in for parting words. *Viel Glück. Bonne chance. Buona fortuna. Good luck.*

A minute to go. The drivers adjusted goggles, snapped helmet straps, and scanned gauges. The hornet shriek of exhaust reverberated off the tiers of hotels and grand homes ringing the semicircular harbor. Hill and von Trips put their cars in gear and held the clutch to the floor, eyes fixed on the starting flag.

When the flag dropped, sixteen cars leapt from a billow of blue exhaust and the gray smoke of burning rubber. Ginther squeaked into the lead as the cars sprinted the first 300 yards and abruptly slowed to 30 mph for the first turn, a 180-degree hairpin known as the Gasometer. Moss and a young Scotsman named Jim Clark shadowed Ginther with the pack strung out behind. They moved like a herd of red, silver, and blue thoroughbreds, darting left and right but never touching. The drivers switched gears every three or four seconds, leaning out to watch as they placed the front wheels on a precise line.

They climbed the switchbacks to Casino Square, passing between the green-domed Casino and the Hotel de Paris, two Belle Époque wedding cakes at the clifftop. A wrong turn here and a car would fall eighty feet. The pack fought and wove for advantage as they funneled downhill through zigzagging legs ending at a dark, curving tunnel that opened onto a long waterfront run back to the starting line.

Clark dropped back on lap 11 with a faulty fuel pump, leaving Moss to shadow Ginther. Moss pressed, hoping to force Ginther into a mistake. On lap 14 Moss made his move. He slithered by Ginther coming out of the Gasometer to steal the lead. Eleven laps later Ginther yielded to

Hill, who had worked his way up from seventh.

Von Trips never joined the lead pack. A faltering battery reduced his revs, causing him to miss a gear shift on the last lap and smack into a guardrail at Mirabeau, a hairpin leading down to the tunnel. He was unable to finish, but he would be awarded fourth place based on the number of laps completed behind the winner.

Now it was a three-car race: Moss chased by the Ferrari tandem of Hill and Ginther. Hill closed to within four and a half seconds of Moss, waiting for the spot where he might pass. But he never found it. Moss was hitting his stride, smoothly shifting gears ninety times a lap. "What I remember about that race," Hill later said, "was the frustration of busting my ass and not being able to catch Moss."

By now Moss was lapping the slower cars, weaving among them for protection from his pursuer. "It was rather like a fighter plane being chased by a superior enemy and being saved by dodging into the clouds," he said.

With brakes worn by the punishing twists and turns and his carburetor faltering, Hill motioned to the pits that Ginther should take over the chase. "Richie was going much faster than I was," Hill said. "I kept waving for him to go by."

Tavoni agreed. On the seventy-fifth lap — the three-quarter mark — he flashed Ginther a sign marked "Go." It was his signal to move up into second place and assault Moss's seven-second lead. The two men flung themselves all over the road, swooping down the hills and peeling along the harborfront, the Ferrari edging closer by tiny increments. Ginther jawed hard on a wad of gum, his face set with determination. Billows of exhaust hung in the narrow streets.

Moss kept the lead, but that was not necessarily an advantage. "It's much easier to chase a man than to be the one being chased," Moss said. "If a man is following you really closely — within a couple of yards — he's learning an awful lot about your techniques and where he might be able to pass you. If you have a particularly unusual line around a corner you immediately show it to him. So unless you can break away from the pack it's not a good thing to lead for 99 out of 100 laps and then have the bloke pull out and pass you on the last one."

It looked as if Ginther might do just that. With sixteen laps left he spat out his gum and stepped up the attack, closing to within four seconds. The Ferrari pit crew held out a sign marked "Bravo." In cafés and on verandas the spectators stood. All of Monaco watched to see if Ginther would pass Moss in the final minutes. "The last few laps I stopped watching," said Rob Walker, who owned the car Moss was driving. "I couldn't look anymore. I couldn't stand it."

Even in the midst of the race Moss held the steering wheel with his fingertips and lifted a hand to wave at the crowd, which gave him a deceptively nonchalant appearance. "At Monaco in 1961 I was on the limit," Moss later said. "One doesn't very often run a race flat-out ten-tenths. Nine-tenths, yes. But at Monte Carlo every corner, every lap as far as I can remember, I was trying to drive the fastest I possibly could, to within a hair's-breadth of the limit, for at least 92 of the 100 laps. Driving like that is tremendously tiring, just tremendously tiring, most people have no idea what it does to one."

Before the final lap Tavoni held out a pit sign that said "All." On the final lap Ginther mounted one last frantic blitz. He came within 2.8 seconds, but Moss held him off. He had snatched the win from the Shark-nose pack in an aging car. Ginther and Hill followed Moss in that order.

"Until I saw the checkered flag I wasn't sure what would happen," Moss said.

The British boats blasted their horns. Moss received congratulations from Prince Pierre in the royal box and held the trophy aloft while a band played "God Save the Queen." His mother tried to push her way in for a hug, but the police turned her away. She watched with tears as her son lit a cigarette and took a victory lap, waving to the crowd with that distinctive British parade gesture. Moss called the race "my greatest drive."

Hill was so exasperated as he talked with reporters that he looked as if he might break down. Ginther wiped his grime-streaked face with a rag and smiled ruefully. "Embracing him, it seemed to me that [Ginther's] overalls were completely empty," said Franco Gozzi, one of Ferrari's aides. "He was shattered, all in, he had really given everything."

Ferrari wouldn't have to wait long for revenge. Within days the teams packed up and moved to the Dutch Grand Prix at Zandvoort, a resort hard against the North Sea. The setting could not have been more different than Monaco. The Dutch track's broad, sweeping turns wound among massive sand dunes studded with scrub grass and scoured by cold sea winds. It was fast, with one side flattened to form a half-mile straight where the Ferraris could cut loose.

If they showed up. In the first practice session, held on a Saturday morning, the other teams whipped through biting wind and rain showers. There was no sign of Ferrari. The Lotus and Porsche crews conferred in hopeful tones — had the punishing maze of Monaco exposed a flaw in the Sharknose, sending Ferrari engineers back to the drawing board?

Minutes after the Monaco Grand Prix ended, Chiti had phoned Ferrari. Based on Ginther's performance he urged that 120-degree engines be installed in all three cars in time for the Dutch Grand Prix. After a short pause Ferrari said, "No, not even worth discussing." Chiti was livid. He went to Maranello and demanded an explanation. Ferrari convened a meeting to discuss the proposition. Not surprisingly, Ferrari's deputies unanimously sided with Ferrari. Chiti dug in: Either the new engines go in, he said, or he would quit. Ferrari backed down. "Do you as you like then," he said.

The Ferrari team missed the first morning of practice as the new engines were prepared and installed. At lunchtime a red Ferrari car transporter, a double-decker truck shaped like an oversized fire engine, pulled up to the paddock and unloaded three Sharknoses. No longer constrained by the tight Monaco turns, the Sharknoses put on a display of raw speed. They were easily fast enough to earn Hill, von Trips, and Ginther side-by-side positions on the front row — a blockade of red. Moss would line up directly behind them.

After practice Hill, as usual, dickered with the mechanics. Von Trips noticed a ten-year-old Dutch boy sitting on the roof overhanging the low pits. He stepped onto a bench and pulled himself up, tousling the boy's hair and sitting with him for a few minutes, trying to glean warmth from the wan sun glimmering through the cold fog. It was the kind of spontaneous gesture that came easily to him.

On the morning of the race Prince Bernhard and Princess Irene arrived by helicopter and shook hands with the drivers. It did not go unnoticed that the princess wore a headscarf with the Ferrari logo. During the final tune-ups Hill found that his car had developed a tendency to oversteer, which caused him to turn more sharply than intended. It was the sort of glitch that unhinged Hill, particularly when it arose during last-minute preparations. To make matters worse, his clutch conked out on the final warm-up lap. The mechanics swarmed, rushing to repair it five minutes before the start. Hill tried to "calm his palpitating heart with his right hand," *Motor Racing* reported, "while he unwrapped a stick of gum with his left."

Moss, who was not known for jokes, chose this moment to goad Hill. "Push that thing away," he said. "It will only jam up the rest of us."

"Oh, look Phil," he added. "They're taking the whole bloody back end out of your car." Hill had tried to ignore Moss, but now he turned in a panic. In the end the mechanics fixed the clutch and Hill got into his car on the front row. Moss chuckled just behind Hill, knowing that he had unsettled him.

After the start the cars vanished among the sand dunes. When they reappeared at the end of the first lap von Trips was leading. He had surged ahead while Hill tried to manhandle his errant steering through the rolling gray landscape. He was, by his own description, "all arms and elbows."

"I was going around oversteering all over the place," Hill added. "You can just oversteer your way around that course so long before you've done in your tires — and run out of adrenaline."

With von Trips five seconds ahead, Hill sparred for second with Jim Clark, the Scot who had briefly challenged him in Monaco. Chiti and Tavoni were working their stop-watches when Clark ripped by an inch from the pits, forcing them to jump back. Clark's message was as unmistakable as it was intimidating. Even though Clark's Lotus handled the turns adroitly, it couldn't compete with a Ferrari whistling down the long straights. For the first time in the season, the Sharknose showed what it could do. With twenty laps left Hill pulled away. Chiti exhaled in relief. Il Commendatore could no longer question the 120-degree engine's capability. It looked unbeatable.

Now Hill was finding his rhythm, and he began eating into von Trips' lead. Just as Hill drew up behind von Trips, the phone rang in the pits. It was Ferrari calling from his office. On his orders Tavoni held out a message board dictating the order of finish: "Trips-Hill." With the first Ferrari win of the season within reach, Tavoni would not risk any tangles. "They just didn't want us ripping each other up once the thing was stabilized," Hill said. Von Trips led all seventy-five laps, scoring his first Grand Prix win — the first by any German in two years — with a dominating performance. Cheers erupted in beer gardens and raths-kellers all across Germany.

Prince Bernhard and his daughter, Princess Irene, were supposed to present the winner's trophy, but the crowd surged onto the field and formed an impenetrable throng around von Trips, who pulled Hill under the victory wreath with him. Von Trips had agreed to a post-race interview with Hermann Harster, the German journalist who was covering the race for a Hamburg tabloid, but von Trips had no way of getting to their meeting place. He borrowed a bicycle from a teenager and rode with the teen sitting on the handlebars. "It was a big day for him," Harster wrote. "How many kids are ridden around on their bicycle by a Grand Prix winner?"

Moss and von Trips had each won a race. The pressure was now on Hill to keep pace at the Belgian Grand Prix, held at Spa on June 18. "Trips wanted it very much, and so did I," Hill said. "And despite the fact that we were members of the same team we each knew that we'd have to fight with everything we had to win the title. The tension continued to build from race to race."

If Hill were to win he would have to

prevail on the fast and unforgiving track at Spa, where drivers rocketed through the Ardennes Forest at an average speed of 130 mph and slid around turns on asphalt softened to a slippery sheen by an early summer heat wave. As if to prove up front that he was in the fight for good, Hill scorched the practice laps and recorded the first lap under four minutes in track history. The fastest practice times earned him the right to start in the pole position, the inside spot on the front row that guaranteed an edge as the pack entered the first turn. Von Trips would line up beside him. Completing an all-Ferrari front row was Gendebien, who, as a Belgian, was driving a Sharknose painted yellow, the Belgian racing color.

The lead switched back and forth between Hill and von Trips as they swung through curves at 150 mph. Hill eventually pulled away, three times recording track records. A heavy rain closed in and the pack slowed by about ten seconds a lap, impeding von Trips from challenging Hill, though he surely would have pressed had he known that Hill was vulnerable. A tiny pebble had lodged in Hill's eye on the twentieth lap. He drove the last third of the race half blind.

Once again Tavoni held out a sign freezing the positions, this time with Hill beating

343

von Trips by barely a half-second. Hill looked embarrassed as the laurel wreath was laid on his shoulders. Victory displays always made him uncomfortable and he slipped away as fast he could. More than anything he was relieved to have done it — relieved to be back in the mix — but he called it "more of a joke than a race" because of Tavoni's orchestration.

The win in Belgium propelled Hill to the top of the standings. He now had nineteen points, one more than von Trips. He had shown his mettle by scrapping from behind in the tally, and it looked as if he would add to his lead two weeks later at the French Grand Prix in Reims, a race on public roads looping through the patterned geometric fields of Champagne country. His car ran particularly fast in warm-ups, giving him "a guilty surge of pleasure."

Hill's car was so fast that it became a point of contention in the elaborate game-within-a-game that preceded each race. Von Trips groused to Tavoni that Hill had an unfair advantage. Hill knew that von Trips was right. "God, my car was clearly superior to Trips'," he said. "I mean, my car was a full half-second, three quarters of a second faster."

Von Trips demanded that Hill take a few laps in his car to demonstrate its slowness. If Hill also logged sluggish lap times it would prove that the problem lay with the car, not the driver. "I didn't really want to," Hill said. "After all, it might not be running right and they might fix it so that it would be faster than mine."

Ferrari normally prohibited drivers from handling a teammate's car for fear of sabotage. In this case Tavoni relented under pressure from von Trips. "Sure," he told Hill, "take it around." Hill only agreed because there was an oil spill at Thillois, a hairpin turn just before the pits. If he drove slower than von Trips, he figured, he could blame it on the oil. In fact, he drove three blazing laps, beating von Trips' lap time by half a second, a generous margin by Grand Prix standards. "I really let it all hang out," he said. "I flew. When I came into the pits, Trips was the picture of gloom. I said, 'I'm sorry I wasn't able to turn in a good one with all that damn oil all over, but it doesn't feel half bad, to tell you the truth.'" Hill compounded the insult by winning the hundred bottles of champagne awarded to the driver with the fastest practice lap.

As if that weren't humiliating enough, von Trips looked back on the next practice lap to see Moss riding an out-of-date Lotus in his slipstream so that the more powerful Ferrari would suck him along in its wake. Moss and other British drivers had perfected the technique during those many difficult years when their cars could not keep up with the Italians. When Tavoni waved in warning from the pits, von Trips sped up, hoping to shake Moss, but he succeeded only in pulling him along faster. Moss's practice times were consequently much faster than they would otherwise be — the speediest among non-Italian cars by two seconds — assuring that he would start near the front. On his way back into the pits he flipped the Ferrari crew the two-fingered up-your-arse gesture.

On the morning of the race the July sun scorched the blond wheat fields like a blowtorch. The thermometer touched 102 degrees in the shade and 120 degrees on the circuit. Women clutched glasses of cold champagne beneath broad-brimmed hats. The drivers lingered in the pits, dousing their coveralls with water. Ferrari mechanics wiped the cockpits down and removed body panels to allow cooling air to flow around the drivers' legs and bodies. Hill put a rubber bag of ice water on his floorboards with a jury-rigged hose snaking up his shoulders. When he stepped on the bag a cold spritz trickled down his back.

The heat softened the black tarmac, loosening bean-sized pieces of gravel. It was like "driving on a spill of ball bearings," Hill said. Two years earlier, on the same road, a bit of gravel had bloodied Hill's nose. "I was drinking blood for about five laps and couldn't feel a thing," he said.

As expected, the Ferraris jumped out front with Hill leading comfortably, followed by von Trips. After eight laps Hill eased back. Five laps later von Trips pulled up and Hill let him pass. It was still early and Hill could afford to sit back and spare his engine exertion and overheating.

On the other hand, Hill may have been ordered to give way to von Trips. Denis Jenkinson, a long-bearded correspondent for the British magazine *Motor Sport,* wrote that Tavoni had told Hill in a pre-race meeting that he would have to step aside for von Trips, despite Hill's faster practice times. Hill had accepted the order, according to Jenkinson, but with an eruption of anger. Hill's frustration is understandable. For five years he had accomplished everything asked of him, only to see Ferrari repeatedly favor von Trips. Hill's rage would only have pleased Ferrari. An angry driver, he knew, was a fast driver.

As it turned out, von Trips would not win, with or without Hill's help. He pulled into the pits on the eighteenth lap with his engine smoking and steam spewing from his right-hand exhaust. A piece of gravel had punctured his radiator.

Spectators saw a broad smile of vindication under the tinted visor of Hill's helmet as he reclaimed the lead. The race was now his to lose. With a 16-second lead he could afford to slow down and play it safe. He could coast home without incident. Ginther, in second, was too loyal to challenge him. Moss was laps behind. Hill was now all but assured of extending his lead in the Grand Prix tally and extinguishing some of the crushing pressure.

The race appeared locked up for Hill until he came out of a long downhill straight — among the longest and fastest on the entire Grand Prix circuit — at 160 mph and swung into the notorious Thillois hairpin expecting to drift his car around. Maybe he was too relaxed. Or maybe the heat had wilted his reflexes. Either way, he committed a rare miscue and skidded clockwise 180 degrees directly under the gaze of a grandstand. He might have quickly recovered if Moss, still struggling with his brakes, had not plowed into the Ferrari's nose, spinning Hill another half turn. Hill then stood mid-track, cars whizzing by on either side, push-starting his car. He shoved it into motion with one hand and threw it into gear with the other. In the process the car ran over his foot. By the time the engine shook to life he had dropped to ninth place, which is where he finished.

Hill still led von Trips by a point, but he had fumbled his chance for an insurmountable lead. "My golden opportunity to make a decisive leap in the point standings was lost in one stupid move," he said, "but perhaps a certain Calvinist notion of retribution had been satisfied."

The charcoal skies hung low with a cold spit of rain when Phil Hill set out alone to walk the three-mile track at Aintree, site of the British Grand Prix and home of the Grand National, the country's most famous steeplechase. He had come a week early to inspect every detail — the pebbled texture of the road, the windy stretch near Bechers Bend, the sightlines into Cottage Corner. He had come to absorb the feel of the place, to visualize it. If he learned anything from the frustrating Reims episode of the previous week, it was that anything can happen.

Wolfgang von Trips, the presumptive world champion, after winning the British Grand Prix on July 15, 1961. For a divided Germany, he was a hero on the verge. (Cahier Archive)

He wanted to eliminate uncertainties.

Hill walked along a dead-flat black asphalt road separated from the steeplechase course by high hedges and white fencing. It was a grim expanse, as featureless as a pool table, overlooked by a double-decked Victorian grandstand with a deep overhang to shelter spectators from persistent drizzle. Along with bland food, the cold Lancashire rain was Aintree's most distinctive aspect. Rain sprinkled on the practice runs and poured in sheets fifteen minutes before the start, sweeping the track with puddles. Dark roiling squall clouds mingled with factory smoke from Liverpool five miles to the south. Mechanics rushed to exchange smooth-tread tires for wet-weather versions with deep grooves for traction. Hill and von Trips stood in drenched coveralls adjusting their helmet visors.

Spectators huddling under umbrellas hoped the rain would help Moss pull off another upset. He had grown up in the damp British weather, and his wet-road skills had earned him the nickname "Rain Master." But when the Union Jack dropped it was Hill, not Moss, who jumped out in front. He led for the first six laps with von Trips driving into a forty-foot plume of spray thrown up by his rival's Ferrari. Hill drove with great authority, safely negotiating flooded sections at Country Corner and Valentine's Way.

Before the race, while the track was still relatively dry, Hill had adjusted his car's brake balance so the front wheels had more braking force. He regretted it now as his front tires began losing traction on the flooded tarmac. On the seventh lap he gained speed on the long backstretch, then braked in a tricky spot known as Melling Crossing, where a road crossed the track. He skated at 100 mph toward a massive solid oak gatepost, spinning first one way, then the other. His championship prospects seemed to vanish as he slid hopelessly closer to the post. He had unwillingly entered the state drivers feared most: He was a passenger without control, waiting for the slide to play itself out.

At the last second, as the gate loomed beside him, his front tires found grip through the puddle. He engaged a low gear and dodged the post by an inch. It was a near miss, but the fright played on his nerves. "A few years earlier it would have been forgotten — like a letter dropped in a mailbox — the instant the wheel caught hold," he said, "but by 1961 it stayed with me."

Consciously or not, Hill drove more cautiously after his close call, allowing von Trips to nip by. Then Moss came up from behind to badger Hill. On the tenth lap Moss blew by him, drawing cheers from the grandstand. Badly shaken, Hill dropped to third.

Now it was von Trips' turn to see Moss looming in his rearview mirror, waiting to pounce like a wolf on the smallest mistake. Moss was an endlessly resourceful fighter with British veins of ice. In the past, his unnerving presence, combined with the foul conditions, might have provoked von Trips into an impetuous blunder. But by now von Trips knew how to keep his composure, and he drove a nearly flawless race through unrelenting rain. "Sometimes I lost my Ferrari at 150 kilometers an hour and we skipped through the puddles like a stone thrown flat on the water," von Trips said.

Still, Moss kept turning up the heat. Lap after lap he hounded von Trips. By the twentieth lap Moss had closed to less than a second — an arm's reach away. He made his move at Tatts Corner, a 90-degree turn at the far end of the backstretch, but von Trips closed the door on him.

Moss would have tried again, and might have succeeded, but he suffered his own skid at Melling Crossing, spinning an entire 360 degrees on the wet road. Five laps later he dropped out with a broken brake rod.

Half an hour later von Trips saw a tire appear through the wall of rain ahead of him. A second tire emerged along with the red body of a Ferrari. The rookie driver Giancarlo Baghetti had pulled close to another car to shield himself from the water spraying onto his windshield and goggles. When the other car unexpectedly braked, Baghetti went into a spin. "Suddenly I saw the eyes of the Italian coming out of the rain curtain toward me," von Trips said. "It was ghostly, eerie. He came closer and closer. Finally I flicked past him. On the next lap I saw Baghetti on the edge of the track. Without a car." Baghetti had spun five times and rammed into a wood fence.

By now the clouds had parted and the road dried. The sunlight shone on von Trips as he crossed the line in first, seven seconds ahead of Hill. More than any other, this race made von Trips look like a champion in waiting.

Minutes later the two men flanked Laura Ferrari on the podium. She smiled and linked her arms in theirs, a show of Ferrari unity. Von Trips wore a laurel wreath. He held his cup aloft and sipped champagne from it as the crowd whistled and clapped. Hill, who had led the standings until this moment, stood by in a suede windbreaker looking as if he had aged ten years.

Halfway through the Grand Prix season Hill and von Trips began wearing down. Neither could gain the upper hand, and the deadlock put added pressure on both men to crowd the limit. Von Trips called their contest "the highest test, the high wire." Their rivalry played large on the front pages of newspapers. Everywhere they went people asked about it. Teammates stole sideways glances to see how they were holding up.

"As I had feared, Trips and I became involved in an increasingly bitter competition for championship points," Hill later wrote. "Because the championship was at stake, I was not able to be reasonable and sensible about every race. After all these years I should have been, automatically, but there was this continual counting of points. By midseason my concentration was suffering."

Hill joined von Trips for a midseason break at Burg Hemmersbach, where the count lightened the mood with funny stories about his upbringing in the castle and the Americans stationed there. It is not known what else they discussed, but Hill clearly made a good impression on the countess. He was the sort of earnest and articulate young man parents approved of. Most of her son's friends cared only about speed and girls, but Hill's inquisitive mind took in everything European culture offered —

wine, architecture, and history. The castle was like a museum, and she was his personal docent. In particular he shared her interest in music. It's easy to imagine him admiring the piano where she had played Chopin to von Trips as a boy. Hill and the countess agreed to attend the Salzburg music festival together later that month.

Back on the circuit, Hill and von Trips found it harder and harder to maintain a friendship under the strain of competition. In hotels and restaurants they were cordial, but they kept a protective distance. They greeted each other with tense smiles. "All year long it was him or me for the championship," Hill said. "It's not a normal situation race drivers are in: you try to beat the other guys all day, and then at night you're supposed to forget all that."

Their friendship was further strained by von Trips' driving. Too often he seemed oblivious to the subtle points of protocol that safeguarded drivers, and his tolerance for risk had a infectious quality that Hill struggled against. "I was very aware of staying within my limits, but Trips was unpredictable in this regard, and in a way I feared him," Hill said. "Racing against him, I soon learned that I was capable of being sucked into areas where I didn't want to be, even as I was having enough trouble knowing and sticking to my own limits."

A week before the German Grand Prix at the Nürburgring, von Trips found diversion in speed of a different magnitude. The 36th Fighter Wing of the U.S. Air Force invited him to ride in a supersonic F-100. Just before the Ferrari transporter delivered the cars for practice, he drove an hour to the Bitburg air base where he was "passed around the officers' club like a champion cup," said Harster, who accompanied him. A small, wiry major named Charlie Davis fitted him into the cockpit with a flight suit, oxygen, and radio. After the sickening G-force of takeoff, Major Davis gave von Trips an aerial view of the Nürburgring. "There was the track," von Trips said. "There was the start and the finish. Charlie put the bird at an angle so I could see everything exactly. Then we were on the straightaway directly in front of the grandstand, on it at more than 900 kilometers an hour."

"There was a green splash of color in the pits," he added. "Probably the sleeping Lotus belonging to Stirling Moss." (The Lotus would actually have been blue, the Scottish racing color.) "Thank goodness, no red," he said. "I didn't need a bad conscience. The Ferraris weren't there yet. My car wouldn't miss me."

Then the F-100 shot almost vertically through the clouds and into a dark blue sky. Major Davis rolled the jet and flicked on the afterburners. "About 30 seconds later there was a light tremor through the machine," von Trips said. "The needles with heights and speed began to dance like drunks." They broke the sound barrier over Burg Hemmersbach. Von Trips called it "a visit with the Gods."

He looked down from 40,000 feet at a serene and verdant countryside, but on the ground was a country in crisis. In August 1961 Germans fled East Berlin at a rate of fifteen hundred a day until Communist officials sealed the border with a barricade of barbed wire and jagged glass. Tanks patrolled the streets and police hauled thousands to detention camps. East and West faced off across the Berlin Wall, their fingers on the trigger.

Almost overnight von Trips' ambition to be the knight of a new Germany became closer to an imperative: He now carried the weight of national expectation. Divided and demoralized, Germany needed a uniting figure.

His countrymen had every reason to

believe von Trips was on the verge of a Grand Prix title. His win at Aintree gave him nine points, leapfrogging him ahead of Hill in the championship standings. He arrived at the German Grand Prix with a two-point lead. He also had the comfort of racing on familiar ground. The Nürburgring was sixty miles from Burg Hemmersbach and practically within walking distance of the family hunting lodge. He was at home with the scent of pine needles and the short, steep mountains patrolled by wild boar and red deer. It was here that Bernd Rosemeyer had first roused his interest in racing.

Not that anyone would call the Nürburgring welcoming. On the contrary, the drivers nicknamed it the Green Hell. It was a fourteen-mile roller coaster created exclusively for racing, with narrow, winding turns without guardrails and abrupt plunges that pitched cars airborne. The road ran up and down hills that a civilian road would skirt. An atmosphere of foreboding hung over the course with Schloss Nürburg, a medieval ruin, overlooking Butcher's Field, Pick Axe Head, Enemy's Garden, and other hazards. When an Australian driver was told (incorrectly) that Hitler himself had designed some of the features, he said, "I guessed as much."

Von Trips arrived for practice a few days before the race and checked into the Sporthotel tucked under the grandstand. The hotel was reserved for teams on race weeks, and it took on a clubby aspect, with drivers wandering among rooms for meals and drinks. They could stroll to the pits in minutes. The drawback for von Trips was that thousands of admirers hovered, even on practice days. They encircled him at every turn, thrusting programs for signatures and cornering him with questions. Girls lingered in the stairwell hoping to meet him.

The demands chafed on his goodwill. "I noticed that I had slowly but surely fallen into a state of nerves," he said. "I would like to leave the Nürburgring hotel and stay somewhere else, somewhere quiet, but I'm always there because it is practical. . . . This time it was simply too dangerous for me. I had to find some peace at any price."

Von Trips had a reputation for conducting himself as a gentleman, but "sometimes it's just too much," he told a friend. "When I give a nice lad an autograph, I immediately have a whole tribe of people around me. So I'll go back to using my old method — I look at the floor, three feet ahead of me, and walk through the area, try not to make eye contact with anyone. It's the best way to get through." He thrust his hands in his pockets and nodded to avoid shaking hands.

With practice under way, word spread through the paddock that Enzo Ferrari had issued an edict from Modena that Hill should hold back, permitting von Trips to win the race and collect nine more points. According to an anonymous source interviewed by Robert Daley, the decision was based purely on business:

> Von Trips is to win here and the world championship, too, in recognition of his splendid victory in the rain at the British Grand Prix in July and because this will sell many Ferrari touring cars in Germany. Ferrari's American market already is booming. He figures that a victory by Hill would not add anything in America.

At Reims Hill had reluctantly complied with the order to step aside for von Trips, though fixing the finish had struck him as a shameful European arrangement determined by pedigree more than merit. But this time, with Hill trailing in points with three races to go, the suggestion that he take a dive stirred him to defiance. On the eve of the race he told Daley that he had not received any such instructions. Nor would he obey them.

"Ferrari can make all the decisions he wants to," he said. "But the decisions wouldn't mean anything unless I go along with them. I don't intend to go along with them."

As if to prove his resistance, Hill went out and drove a near-perfect practice lap in eight minutes and fifty-five seconds, with an average speed of 95.2 mph. One report described him looking "starry-eyed and trembling" when he returned to the pits. It was the fastest lap ever clocked at the 14.2-mile Nürburgring and the first to break the nine-minute barrier, which many considered inviolable. Hill called it a "freak" performance that he would not likely repeat.

"Out of the car he seems colder, more determined than ever before," Daley reported. "There is an icy edge to his apparently friendly banter with von Trips."

Meanwhile von Trips struggled through a series of mechanical setbacks. "Madre Mia," he said as he pulled in after a practice run. Tavoni came over with the conciliatory air of a physician. "First, the transmission is bad," von Trips told him. "Second, the chassis sits miserably on the course. And what about the time?"

The lap time was indeed laggard. At nine minutes and twenty-nine seconds, he was thirty-four seconds slower than Hill. Tavoni assured him that the mechanics would work through the night to get things right.

Von Trips' mood lightened on the short walk back to the Sporthotel. "If the engine cooperates," he said, "I will also come in under nine minutes." He paused to book a private hour of practice at 7 a.m. the next morning, for which he paid 100 deutsche marks.

The reworked engine proved surprisingly swift, allowing von Trips to break the nine-minute mark the next day, as he predicted. Later that morning a light rain fell, preventing Hill and von Trips from duplicating their earlier times. Hill clocked nine minutes and seven seconds; von Trips was two seconds faster. It was a good sign for von Trips. "Now I know that under the same conditions on the Ring I am probably just a tick faster than Phil," he said.

A pack of photographers encircled him, each calling for a different pose. *Sit behind the wheel. Look under the hood. Share a laugh with your teammates.* "If they only knew how tired I am," he whispered to a friend.

That night von Trips snuck away to an old hotel in a nearby village. He ate in a private dining room and borrowed a bed from a mechanic who had booked a double room above a stable. "I slept three feet above the manure pile," he said. "No one wanted anything from me. It was just wonderful."

Shortly after noon on race day von Trips ate lunch in his room at the Sporthotel, then napped briefly. His shirt was unbuttoned. Around his neck dangled a gold chain with the Ferrari insignia of the prancing stallion. Hill was staying a few rooms down the hall, and he dropped by. Von Trips could see that Hill was in the same state of nervousness. "Now we'll start together once more," said von Trips.

"To a good race," he added.

"We'll have a good race," Hill said.

Von Trips bathed with cold water and ate a final snack to fortify his blood sugar. At 1:57 p.m. he walked through the tunnel leading to the track. He was greeted by Fangio, who would drop the starting flag. The former champion embraced the man who hoped to succeed him.

Three hundred and fifty thousand Germans stood on the wooded hillsides to watch their national hero flash by in a red Ferrari. By most counts it was the largest crowd gathered at the Nürburgring since von Trips' hero, Bernd Rosemeyer, had driven there in the 1930s. The crowd didn't seem to care that von Trips was driving an Italian car. He wore a silver helmet in honor of Germany.

"There were so many people around, so much excitement in the air," he said. "I would've preferred to crawl into a hole, to get away. But I had to be there in the thick of it. There was no other way."

On the damp starting grid Tavoni questioned whether to begin the race on dry or wet tires. Hill fretted along with him, pacing around the start area in his crewneck sweater.

With two minutes to go von Trips settled into his car and inserted his rubber earplugs. "The calm comes over me like redemption," he told Harster. "My helmet's strapped tight. The backup goggles are around my neck; the others are lowered over my eyes. The air valves are open. I slip on my gloves and turn the ignition. It sounds like Niagara Falls heard from far away."

Rumors had circulated all season that Britain's answer to the Sharknose would soon arrive on the Grand Prix circuit, diminishing the Ferrari advantage and possibly marking the start of a British comeback. At Nürburgring it finally happened, at least in part. A new V8 engine made by the British manufacturer Coventry Climax was fitted into a Cooper chassis for Jack Brabham, the defending world champion. "Doesn't it make a lovely noise?" asked John Cooper, the team owner. The new engine had 185 horsepower — enough to propel Brabham to the front row of the grid, alongside Hill and Moss. Von Trips started a row behind.

Von Trips had hoped to dart through the gap between Brabham and Hill, but Hill blocked his way. Instead, Brabham shot out to a quick lead as the front pack rounded the first curve and went up a straight behind the pits, around a left-hander, and through a serpentine series of downhill turns called the Hatzenbach. Then Brabham skidded on a damp, shaded patch and plunked his Cooper through a thick hedge and into a ditch, disappearing in a cloud of leaves. Passing drivers were "smiling happily to themselves as they saw Brabham climb out of the V8 Cooper-Climax," *Motor Sport* reported.

With Brabham gone, Moss inherited the lead and Hill tucked in after him. Von Trips shook loose from the trailing pack and moved into third. It could have been a snapshot taken three months earlier in Monaco: the dark blue Lotus chased by a pair of red Ferraris.

Like Monaco, the Nürburgring was known as a driver's track — a circuit where handling counted as much as horsepower. It was the kind of track where Moss could use his artistry to build an incremental lead, and he did. By the end of the third lap he had a 10-second edge on Hill.

Now von Trips was agitating from behind. On the sixth lap he closed on Hill with a time of 9:08, the fastest ever recorded at the Nürburgring during a race. On the next lap he bettered his own record by four seconds. "Suddenly everything was wonderfully simple," von Trips said. "Inside of me was a sudden lift, a buoyancy. I was playing with what the course was giving me, not forcing anything. I was in a good spot."

Von Trips was driving faster and faster, but Moss and Hill kept pace in front of him. On the eighth lap Moss bested von Trips' record with a time of 9:02. Then von Trips overtook Hill and reduced the record to 9:01. A sea of fans waved German flags and white handkerchiefs from the hillsides.

Von Trips' record didn't last long. Hill stirred himself from third place to break the record once more, recording the first lap under nine minutes during a race. Hill and von Trips had by now scrapped their way up to within seven seconds of Moss. They could see him weaving in and out of the curves ahead, but could they pass him? "Seeing Moss is one thing," *Motor Sport* wrote in its recap, "and catching him is something quite different."

Then, in a heart-stopping moment, Hill seemed to disappear at Bergwerk, a tight right turn at the end of a long, fast section. Von Trips lost him in his rearview mirror and assumed that Hill had spun out, or worse. It would take at least thirty seconds to recover from a spin. Hill would never catch him, von Trips thought. Moments later Hill reappeared, as if by magic. He had been there all along, lost in the vibrating mirror.

On lap 13, with two laps left, a soft drizzle began to fall on the dark cedars. Moss, who had insisted on rain tires, pulled away. He seemed robotic in his refusal to give in to exhaustion or make mistakes. He gradually padded his lead, leaving Hill and von Trips to fight their own private battle for second place and the six crucial points that came with it.

The two men raced side by side through meadows and dark tunnels formed by overhanging trees. On the penultimate lap Hill surged past von Trips. It was a critical maneuver. If Hill held on to second, he and von Trips would both have thirty-three points going into the Italian Grand Prix at Monza, where von Trips had a history of serious crashes. "When Hill went past me, I was very startled, appalled," von Trips said. "I tried to stay with it. It took a second for me to reconnect. . . . Moss is forgotten. For me, it is now only about how to pass Hill."

Von Trips slid in behind Hill with the intention of slipstreaming in his wake before shooting forward for a final surge on the last lap. He was puzzled when Hill slowed slightly ahead of him; it looked suspiciously like an invitation to pass. It took von Trips a few moments to see the trap. Hill wanted to be the one to mount a carefully timed lunge from behind. So von Trips slowed with Hill. They exchanged sly smiles. "We drove for a little while side by side, playing a game: After you, sir," von Trips said.

They rode shoulder to shoulder uphill at 160 mph and into the final stretch when the Rhineland sky turned a dozen shades of gray. A wall of thunderstorms swept in, like special effects for the closing act. Both cars skated sideways on pools of water. "We were both all over the road," Hill said, "and damn lucky we didn't take each other out." Von Trips straightened himself out first and edged Hill by 1.1 seconds for second place under the eyes of his countrymen.

Von Trips sprang from his car in front of the pits. All around him people stood and clapped in the driving rain. Von Trips was handed a bouquet of red and white carnations, which he impulsively passed to Moss in the winner's circle. Moss in turn pulled von Trips under the winner's wreath with him. "It was a barrage of cameras," von Trips said. "I was full of happiness and thanks and fatigue and hunger. I put on my best Sunday smile."

"I felt close to Moss in this very special moment," he added, "but not as close as I had felt a few minutes before with Phil Hill."

Moss had pulled off his second major upset of the season against the Ferrari juggernaut, but it was von Trips who won the day. The driver who often seemed too impulsive for prime time had at last proved himself a model of steadiness and control. Hill, who had built his career on consistency, slipped four points behind in the season tally. His analysis: "I screwed it up."

Their duet would continue on the high-banked turns of Monza, the Death Circuit.

Their summer of apprehension was almost over.

Phil Hill after clinching the world championship at the Italian Grand Prix. (Getty Images)

11
PISTA MAGICA

Von Trips spent the month before the Italian Grand Prix at Burg Hemmersbach planting tulip bulbs for spring. The oak and chestnut trees shrouding the castle had acquired a red tinge as the nights cooled and summer faded.

The obligations of celebrity intruded on his respite. A German television show interviewed him and he hosted a crew from *Life* magazine, which photographed him strolling the castle forecourt in a dark blazer and tie. Brazen fans occasionally showed up uninvited, only to be turned away by the vigilant Frau Flossdorf.

The count and countess could tell that their son was uncharacteristically tense. Unable to sit still, he drove his Ferrari convertible into Cologne in the evenings to buy *L'Équipe,* a French sports daily that printed more race coverage than German newspapers. The articles were sprinkled with mentions of driver safety. After so many recent deaths, it was clear that seat belts and other measures would soon be adopted. Von Trips weighed the issue. If he had worn a seat belt at the Nürburgring four years earlier he would likely not have broken two vertebrae. On the other hand, he might be safer without a seat belt in Formula 1 cars because they had no protective roof. Better to be thrown clear, he thought, than trapped inside.

Late one August afternoon he sat in his study surrounded by memorabilia — silver trophies, an Argentine saddle, a tabletop sculpture of the prancing stallion — and dictated notes on safety to Flossdorf. Cars moving at similar speeds rarely smash up, he said. Accidents more often occur when cars of differing velocities converge. "A mountain stream flows in a smooth bed to the valley, calm and quiet," he said, "and it's only a stone in the way or a bluff that takes the stream from out of its calm and starts it to foaming and rushing. It's the same with a road."

In late August, a fashion trade magazine named von Trips one of West Germany's best-dressed men. It was a nod to his magnetism more than his wardrobe, which favored polo shirts, slacks, and an Alpine hat. (Though he did seek the advice of his friend John Weitz, a German-American sportswear designer, who urged him to race in pale coveralls to complement the Ferrari red.) Von Trips hosted a party for the honorees at Burg Hemmersbach, where he mingled with actors, a conductor, a foreign minister, and former heavyweight champion Max Schmeling. After cocktails and grilled suckling pig, a guest stumbled outside and splashed about in the pond. Rejoining the party, his wet shoes slipped and he smacked his head hard on the floor. He was carried to von Trips' bedroom where he bled copiously on the count's sheets.

When his guests left, von Trips returned to the quiet of his moated sanctuary, tending his flowers and playing tennis on the private court shaded by overhanging trees just outside the moat. He was exhausted by a flood of letters and telegrams, and vexed by speculation that stardom was feeding his vanity.

"I feel like a thousand eyes are on me," he wrote to an acquaintance. "They watch me to see the point at which I become a prima donna, with the hope of seeing a prima donna. Not everyone who is suddenly forced into an extraordinary situation changes, but many do. They see things in a different light, they speak differently, and that's what ultimately makes me uncertain and leads me to conclude that I need to try and shut out the world."

The focus on von Trips intensified in the weeks before the Italian Grand Prix, where the *tifosi* expected him to secure the title. He led by four points, 33 to 29, and he was driving with authority. The season would not end until the October 8 finale in Watkins Glen, New York, but a third-place finish or better in Italy would clinch it for him. He would have to perform only passably to become the first German champion since the glory days of the 1930s when his heroes Rosemeyer and Caracciola made their names.

On August 29, von Trips left Burg Hemmersbach with his school friend Friedrich-Victor Rolff. They snacked from a sack of apples and sandwiches on the drive to Baden-Baden, where a newsreel crew trailed von Trips as he shook hands and signed autographs at a horse race. They swam, played bocce, and ate dinner in a two-hundred-year-old inn. The next morning von Trips belted out American spirituals as they drove. He and Rolff parted in Munich, with von Trips heading south to Monza where the Italian Grand Prix would take place at the Autodromo Nazionale, a combination of forest road and high-speed oval set in a royal park twelve miles north of Milan. It was known as the Pista Magica, the magic track. Coming late in the season, Monza decided fates. Championships were won and lost in its dark woods.

Von Trips led in points, but he had never won at Monza. Twice he had been carried away from ugly wrecks, both times crashing in the treacherous right-hand turns following the first straightaway. Hill, on the other hand, had won there a year earlier.

The day before the race, von Trips expressed concern about driving in close contact with Ricardo Rodriguez, a nineteen-year-old Mexican rookie recently hired by Ferrari. Von Trips saw in him a younger version of himself, a teen long on instinct but burdened by an undeveloped sense of judgment. Von Trips was eager to get the race over with. "If I drive fast, I'm so calm afterwards, free and clear," he told Harster, his biographer. "All the tension is gone."

After his final practice laps, von Trips joined Robert Daley and his wife for tea at a café behind the pits. They found him uncharacteristically reflective — and strangely prophetic — on the eve of his culminating race. "Every driver has a place deep inside him where he's afraid of death," he told them.

"This could all end tomorrow," he added. "You never know."

In a sense, von Trips had already cheated fate by the time he arrived at the track the next morning. Throughout his racing career he helped manage his family's farmland, and he was intent on modernizing its old-fashioned methods. With that in mind he traveled once or twice a year to agricultural events. Were it not for the Monza race, he might have joined a contingent of German farmers flying that weekend to an agricultural school in Chicago and to Wisconsin for a demonstration of new agricultural machinery. If so, he would have perished. Their charter flight from Düsseldorf crashed in a river after refueling in Shannon, Ireland, killing all but one passenger.

Before breaking away for final preparations von Trips slipped a few dextrose tablets in the pocket of his coveralls to boost his blood sugar. He smiled graciously, as he always did, and spoke with the racing press gathered around him in the pits. Had he become a better driver since crashing here in 1956, and again in 1958?

"No, only luckier," he said.

Why was he not married?

"I'm married to one of these," he said, gesturing to a Ferrari.

Was he looking forward to the race that afternoon?

"I love motor racing, where one has to fight to win," he said. "To do this you must drive close to the limit, which I am always prepared to do. There is a very thin line between winning and crashing; you have to walk it like a tightrope."

Hill, meanwhile, was as twitchy and overwrought as ever. His Sharknose had developed a glitch on the first day of practice. He could shift from first to second gear, but when he went for third it slid back to first. "Worse yet, nobody would believe me," he said. "I was throwing fits."

The mechanics eyed Hill with suspicion. They were not convinced the bug was real until one of them drove the car around the paddock. Afterwards, with Hill leaning over their shoulders, they uncovered a faulty gearbox. Hill missed practice while they replaced it. Even with the new gearbox the car was inexplicably sluggish. Hill was only fourth fastest in practice, placing him behind von Trips on the second row of the starting grid.

Hill was beside himself as the engineers probed the engine for answers. He paced around muttering to himself and waving away reporters. "Everything's gone wrong with my car," he said. "I can't talk. I can't even be civil."

After Hill complained that he couldn't compete in the car, Enzo Ferrari said, "Are you sure there isn't something wrong with your foot?"

Hill would have to dominate if he was to get back into contention with von Trips, and that would be impossible in a car he mistrusted. In desperation, he issued an ultimatum: He would not race at all unless the Ferrari engineers replaced the engine altogether. "Just change the damn engine," he said. Unable to come up with a better solution, they reluctantly agreed.

Hill returned to the Ferrari garage at 6 a.m. to find the mechanics bleary-eyed and slathered in grease. They sheepishly acknowledged finding a broken inner valve spring during their all-nighter. Hill had been right to insist on an overhaul. The racetrack was not yet open, so Hill furiously put the new engine through its paces on the streets near the quiet country inn where the Ferrari team was lodging. Over and over he accelerated from a dead stop, trying to break in the engine within a few hours — clutch thrown in, foot down, revs climbing to a falsetto shriek.

The sun rose on a mild and clear mid-September day. The drivers went through their pre-race routine wearing polo shirts and sunglasses. Hill asked a mechanic to splash a bucket of water on the back of his coveralls to keep him cool. Von Trips was as relaxed as ever, napping on a bench in the corner of the pits. He roused himself and ate a pear as the crew rolled his car into the pole position — the inside slot on the front row — marked with a white line on the gray asphalt. It was the only time that von Trips had earned the top spot. Before stepping into his car, he did something uncharacteristic: He slipped off his signet ring inscribed with the family coat of arms and handed it to a friend for safekeeping. "We may be teammates," he said of Hill as he adjusted his silver helmet, "but one has to fight. I love fighting."

Everything but the fight faded in the closing moments before the start. The notoriously officious Monza *polizia* chased off photographers and reporters milling around the start area. Mechanics darted about, shouting at one another in four languages. A heaving crowd of 50,000 packed the grandstands and bleachers. They pressed against wire fences at the edge of the 6.2-

mile course, drinking wine and singing. Some hammered spikes into trees and clambered up for a better view. It was their moment to see a Ferrari renaissance. The drivers emerged from the pits in Dunlop coveralls and lowered themselves one by one into their cars.

Five, four, three, two, one. The Italian flag swung down and the cars leapt. Hill's car still had "a stumble to it," he said, "but when the flag dropped I was gone."

Von Trips had a history of early faltering. It often took him a lap or so to shed his jitters and find his rhythm. True to form, he missed a few beats at the start and mired himself in a pack of six cars following Hill in tight formation, moving inches apart through the broad Curva Grande and the two sharp rights at the Curva di Lesmo. Von Trips was in fourth as the group charged down the long backstretch and around the big south curve to finish the first lap.

With Hill pulling away, von Trips surely felt an urgency to maneuver his way up through the tightly bunched field. It was still early, but if he got trapped in traffic he might forfeit his chance for a top finish, and with it his edge over Hill. With teeth bared he passed Jack Brabham and Jim Clark in two powerful blasts of acceleration.

382

On the second lap, von Trips sped out of the forest and through a bend in the back-stretch with Clark trailing behind and slightly to his left. The bend slowed them only slightly as they rolled into the fastest stretch, a straight where drivers could press the accelerator for nearly 30 full seconds. Moving at 150 mph, von Trips watched for his chance to pass Rodriguez directly in front of him.

Four hundred feet before the next turn von Trips swerved left to make his move. In his haste to catch Hill, he was unaware that Clark had stayed close. He may have assumed that Clark was slipstreaming directly behind him. In any case, von Trips "shifted sideways," Clark later said, "so that my front wheels collided with his back wheels. It was the fatal moment."

Von Trips committed a tiny miscalculation, a miscue of no more than an inch, but at 150 mph it was enough to sling him onto a grassy shoulder to the left. His wheels plowed the soft earth as the car rode up a five-foot slope where spectators stood two deep behind a chest-high chicken-wire fence. In an instant of explosive violence, the Ferrari slashed along the fence for about ten feet, shredding spectators like a big red razor, then bounced end-over-end back onto the track. The mauled car came to rest right side up with its wheels collapsed inward.

Five spectators standing along the fence died instantly, their skulls crushed by the threshing car. The survivors screamed in reaction to the death all around them. Bodies lay in scattered clumps. Ten more would die later. More than fifty were injured.

Meanwhile, Clark's car spun and struck the embankment several times before coming to a rest in the grassy stretch beside the road. The car was crushed, but Clark squirmed out unscathed.

The man who was supposed to be champion lay facedown on the track in bloodied coveralls, alone and motionless. His car had rolled on top of him, then, on the next bounce, flung him like a rag doll. His distinctive silver helmet had not saved him, nor had the flimsy roll bar.

Clark jumped from his Lotus and helped a race marshal drag von Trips' car to the shoulder. He glanced at von Trips, but could not bring himself to check on him. "I didn't really want to go over to where he lay," Clark said. With his helmet tucked under his arm, Clark went back to the pits, where he all but collapsed.

Von Trips had died of skull fractures by

the time an ambulance arrived. In a few savage seconds, no more than a few heartbeats, all his charm and promise, all the hope he offered to a troubled nation, came to a violent end.

A paramedic spread a sheet over the body. A bloodied forearm dangled from the shroud as von Trips was carried to the ambulance on a stretcher. It was the public's last glimpse of him. Laura Ferrari sobbed in the pits and asked to be taken to the hospital. There was nothing to be done, but she felt compelled to accompany the body.

All over Germany people had gathered in living rooms and bars with intent to celebrate. Now they froze over their coffee or pilsner as the radio sportscaster waited for a messenger from the Ferrari pit to explain why the count had not come around on the last lap. He broke the news in a wavering voice. With a choke of apology he said that he could not continue his coverage:

Ladies and gentlemen, dear listeners in Germany, I don't have to tell you how this event in all its elemental tragedy is affecting us and you'll understand that we have very little interest in current positions and lap times. Please forgive us if we do not wait for the end of the race. Please don't blame us if we sign off from the Grand Prix of Italy with the news about Wolfgang Graf Berghe von Trips, and in his memory and with thoughts of him, send you back to your home station in Germany.

In Horrem, Elfriede Flossdorf rushed from her home, but turned back before reaching the castle. She couldn't bear to tell the countess. A delegation of family friends, including Rolff and a local priest, broke the news instead. At first the countess refused to believe them. Wolfgang would recover, she said, just as he had overcome so many other accidents and illnesses.

At the hospital Laura Ferrari and Carlo Chiti lingered, as if in vigil, outside a long narrow room where bodies lay on a row of cots. Tony Helling, a newspaper correspondent, entered the room and found von Trips, his hands resting on a blanket. There was no sign of injury aside from drops of blood staining the pillow. "He lay there," she later said, "with eyes closed, with an incredibly relaxed expression — no smile, but even so I felt he could not have suffered, he could not have felt pain, and a deep calm came over me."

Meanwhile, the race flowed on with Hill

leading Moss by 18 seconds. Drivers wove through the smoke and debris, slowed by a marshal waving a flag of caution while the bloodied bodies were laid out on the roadside covered in tent canvas and newspapers. No announcement was made to the crowd.

Hill passed the scene forty-one more times that afternoon. On each lap he glimpsed the crumpled remains of the car, but he was uncertain whose it was until he saw von Trips' name removed from a scoreboard listing the order of drivers on the track.

After von Trips crashed, three other Ferraris dropped out. Watching on television in Modena, Enzo Ferrari said, *Abbiamo perduto.* We have lost. It was a curious reaction given that a Ferrari would win. Hill drove a nearly perfect race, a masterpiece of precision and pacing. Less than two hours after von Trips crashed, he raised his hand as he whipped by the checkered flag in first place, the only one of five Ferraris to finish. Moss, who started the race with a long shot at the title, dropped out with a collapsed wheel bearing.

The win gave Hill nine points, clinching the championship. He had overcome waves of obstacles — Ferrari's partisanship, a late-summer deficit in points, an eleventh-hour engine failure — to become the first American to win racing's greatest prize. Among other things, the win resolved the tug-of-war between anguish and ambition that had gripped him for more than a decade. It affirmed a pursuit that he had so often doubted.

Hill had arrived at the triumphant moment that had drawn him since childhood like a distant light. The realization that he had prevailed — the wondrous reality of it — came over him as "a warming relief, a soaring feeling. But it was to be a short flight."

Hill walked to the victory podium in a throng of pushing, swaying well-wishers. Sweat matted his hair and goggles dangled from his neck. He sipped from a bottle of mineral water. Chiti pushed through the crowd and hugged him. *Bravo, bravo.* Hill asked Chiti about von Trips. "He muttered something but I could tell from his face that it was not the truth," Hill said. "I suspected the worst, but it was not until after champagne and congratulations on the victory stand that I was told."

Sports Illustrated reported that Hill sobbed and dashed away as the flashbulbs popped. That was not the case. He was too inured for that. (According to one report, it was Wolfgang Seidel, a German driver, who wept.) Hill may have sagged. He may have paled beneath his sooty cheeks. But his face betrayed nothing but stony acceptance. "At the risk of seeming to be callous I can only say that my emotional defenses are pretty strong," he later wrote. "I can be stoical when I have to be."

Von Trips claimed all the morning headlines. The newspapers buried Hill, if they mentioned him at all. The insinuation was that von Trips was the rightful winner. Hill was merely an understudy, despite two first-place finishes, two seconds, and two thirds. The *New York Times* printed Daley's account of von Trips' death on its front page. Mention of the new champion waited until after the story jumped to page thirty-three. "He knows that his victory has been so submerged in the press under the death toll," Daley wrote, "that few people even realize he is champion."

On the day after von Trips died, undertakers dressed him in a light blue suit and laid him out for viewing. Hill passed silently before the body, pausing to place a bouquet of red roses beside the coffin. "I bow my head before him with a tearful heart," he said.

After the viewing, Hermann Harster locked himself in his hotel room to make notes for the book that he had collaborated on with von Trips, but would now finish alone. "Easily and quickly he died," he wrote. "His face showed it. It was very peaceful. No trace of a violent death." The next day the body was flown home to Burg Hemmersbach in a chartered plane.

Hill had no wife or family to celebrate with. Nor was he in the mood. He returned to his hotel in Modena and listened to Bartók and Shostakovich. He felt pride in his accomplishment but nothing like true gratification. "There was a certain amount of guilt on my part," he said, "that Trips was dead and I was alive and I had won the championship."

Meanwhile, Italian officials reacted with their usual paroxysms of reprimand and reproach. They impounded the mauled remains of von Trips' and Clark's cars in preparation for a lengthy inquiry. Clark made an official statement to police, then made a hasty departure on Brabham's private plane. Italian prosecutors would hound him for years. Newspaper editorials condemned Ferrari. *L'Osservatore Romano* published a pronouncement from the pope that "it would be criminal to allow absurd performances of death like this to repeat themselves."

In Modena, Ferrari put on another show of mourning, as if his lament shielded him from blame. A few days after returning from Monza, Hill met Ferrari in a café across from the factory. He looked "fatigued and hollow-eyed with the shadow of a beard," Hill said. Ferrari asked if Hill would return next season. Hill said yes.

"It was an emotional moment," Hill said. "Ferrari was capable of turning on great displays of emotion and one could not say that they were phony — any more than the third act of *Tosca* is phony. But there was something essentially theatrical about these displays — a great outpouring and then the curtain fell and it was over. La Scala might have lost a star when Ferrari went into tears."

Ferrari's mourning period did not include a trip to Horrem for von Trips' funeral. He stayed home, and he forbade Chiti and Tavoni from attending for fear that they might inadvertently give the press information that prosecutors could use in a criminal charge against him. In their place Ferrari sent his wife Laura, accompanied by Amerigo Manicardi, Ferrari's international sales manager.

Hill felt almost too guilty to go. Von Trips' photograph hung in classrooms all over

Von Trips' funeral cortège assembled in the forecourt of Burg Hemmersbach; Phil Hill (second row at right) with other pallbearers before the procession to the church. "It was a nightmare," he said, "acted out in daytime." (Associated Press)

Germany, as if the nation were mourning a martyred statesman. Hill dreaded the prospect of showing up as his replacement. "For all the Germans, Trips was going to be the new world champion," he said, "and I had to go as this terrible disappointment." In the end, the countess asked Hill to serve as a pallbearer, so he packed his bags. "I have never experienced anything as profoundly mournful as that day," Hill later wrote. "It was a nightmare acted out in daytime."

It was not a funeral so much as a Gothic death pageant. The day began with a mass in Burg Hemmersbach. Afterwards, a procession formed in the castle forecourt with the casket riding on a stand fitted like a ski rack on top of von Trips' dark green Ferrari roadster. Hill and seven other pallbearers walked coatless in the rain beside the car. Hill rested a hand on the driver-side door — von Trips' door — as the cortège crept along cobbled streets lined with rows of black umbrellas.

Local schools were closed for the day and ten thousand people turned out. Many laid garlands on the curbside. An old woman carrying a brass lantern led the procession. Behind her walked family and dignitaries from all over Germany. A band, dressed in black, played Chopin's funeral march.

A second lengthy mass was held at St. Clemens, a simple village church, where a three-hundred-year-old bell tolled, followed by a procession to the cemetery. To keep pace with the slow cortège, the mechanic driving von Trips' Ferrari had to ride the clutch, and it began to slip and wear down. The drivers marching beside the car exchanged worried looks. They knew the clutch might burn out before they reached the cemetery — a final indignity for poor von Trips.

It was raining harder now. The pallbearers shouldered the coffin and slipped and slid their way up a muddy hill where the final service was conducted and von Trips was entombed in the Gothic family tomb. Beneath the coat of arms was inscribed the Latin phrase *In Morte Vita.* In death there is life. Huschke von Hanstein said a final word: "About you, Wolfgang Graf Berghe von Trips, one can speak only good."

After the funeral, Hill returned to the home where he was lodging and took a long hot bath. Word came that the countess would like to see him that evening. They had struck up a friendship during his periodic visits to the castle. She teased him for not joining her at the Salzburg Music Festival earlier that month, as he had promised.

Since leaving Italy, Hill had suffered a painful stitch in his side. It was the kind of psychosomatic ailment that had afflicted him throughout his career. "I had felt it before," he later wrote. "It told me that I was tense, that I must relax."

Oddly, the cramp vanished as he talked with the countess. "I sensed, as we spoke, that she did not condemn racing," Hill wrote. "I knew she was terribly hurt by the loss of her only son, but he had chosen a dangerous career and now that he was gone she accepted the fact like a Spartan mother."

There were no flashbulbs when Hill landed at Idlewild Airport in New York en route to California. Between flights he called Denise McCluggage, who lived in Greenwich Village. He told her that he felt more like an afterthought than a champion. "He was slipping home essentially unnoticed," she wrote.

With the title wrapped up, Ferrari saw no reason to send his team to the final Grand Prix in Watkins Glen, New York. By skipping it, he denied Hill a chance to race before his countrymen as the new champion. "I was really sick about that," Hill said, "for that day should have been the crowning glory of my career, the biggest day of my life."

Instead, Hill went home to Santa Monica, where the World Championship barely registered. Americans knew about Grand Prix — they had glimpsed it in movies and magazines — but they just didn't much care. It was a distant European fixation that earned far less notice than the Indianapolis 500.

The Hill–von Trips rivalry, so feverishly followed in Europe, was eclipsed in America by that summer's home run derby between Mickey Mantle and Roger Maris. In a case of excruciatingly bad timing, Hill won the championship three weeks before Maris broke Babe Ruth's single-season record of sixty home runs. If Maris was an overgrown boy gamboling on grassy fields, Hill was like the shaken survivor of a distant war.

In December, Hill appeared on an episode of *To Tell the Truth,* a game show predicated on the obscurity of the guest's achievement. Asked in an interview if his life had changed, Hill said, "Not at all. If you mean do people recognize me and stop me on the street, they don't."

If Hill was an overlooked champion it was partially because he did not look the part. He was slight of build and grim-faced, with none of the swagger and easy bonhomie Americans expect from a winner. He seemed too articulate to be an athlete. Plus, there was a particular fragility about him in those months after the Italian Grand Prix, as if he were more affected than he let on. "Perhaps I am oversensitive," he wrote in

October, "but since returning to America this fall I have found that I am being treated with kid gloves."

At home in the Spanish-style house on the drowsy outskirts of Santa Monica he listened to minuets and concertos on his player piano. The fingers of long-dead masters trilled the keys. These were ghostly concerts performed only for himself. When the music stopped, the house fell silent.

The greatest year of Hill's life had found its bittersweet ending. Even in death von Trips had denied Hill the full satisfaction of winning. Over the short California winter Hill summoned himself. He would go back to Modena in the spring and try to do it all over again.

EPILOGUE

When Laura Ferrari saw Hill at von Trips' funeral she asked how he would be returning to Modena. She disliked her escort, Amerigo Manicardi, and she was clearly fishing for a ride home with Hill. In a moment of panic Hill said he was continuing on to a business engagement in Stockholm, though that was not the case. The next day Hill was driving his Peugeot 404 from the Milan train station to Modena with Richie Ginther when they spotted Laura in an adjacent car. Both men scrunched down so she wouldn't see them. Meanwhile, Laura had recognized Hill's gray Peugeot. Is that Phil Hill's car? she asked Manicardi.

"I don't know," Manicardi said. "There's nobody in it."

"Oh, that's all right then," she answered.

A few weeks later Ferrari's lieutenants gave him a letter demanding that his wife stay out of the factory. They considered her disruptive. The grievance had simmered for years, but it erupted into mutiny a month after von Trips' death.

Laura Ferrari had kept her distance while her son was alive. After Dino died, in 1956, she became a daily presence at the factory, where she ate sausage in the lunchroom with mechanics and lorded over financial matters. Throughout the 1961 season she attended races as her husband's proxy, a scarf tied over her hair in the manner of peasant women. She spied for him at parties and in the pits. Tavoni and Chiti looked over their shoulders for her, suspecting she second-guessed their tactics and bad-mouthed them to her husband.

Enzo Ferrari refused to intercede when his staff confronted him with their letter of complaint. (They also demanded raises, which could not have helped matters with their notoriously stingy boss.) "If this is how you feel," he told them, "there is the door. Here is your money. Out!"

Eight key managers and engineers walked out, led by Tavoni and Chiti, the two employees most responsible for the championship season. *Guerin Sportivo,* a weekly sports magazine, printed a cartoon of eight headless men leaving the Ferrari factory. Behind them stood Ferrari with eight heads bundled in his arms.

Within a year the eight exiles had formed a new race team, Automobili Turismo e Sport, or ATS, based on a farm west of Bologna with backing from Count Giovanni Volpi di Misurata, the twenty-four-year-old son of Mussolini's finance minister and founder of the Venice Film Festival.

Ferrari tried to compensate for the loss by inviting Stirling Moss to Modena for a solicitous talk. He sent a coupe to the Milan airport for Moss to drive and greeted him with a double-cheeked kiss. Over lunch at Il Cavallino, Ferrari made an extraordinary offer: If Moss signed on, Ferrari would build a Formula 1 car to his specifications within six months. "He said, 'I'll make it,' " Moss said. "Whatever you want I'll build it for you." Ferrari may have been the only car-maker capable of making good on such a promise. His craftsmen could fabricate a new car in months, a fraction of the time it would take the British *garagistas.*

Moss was intrigued, but wary. Ten years earlier Ferrari had offered him a car for a race in Bari, Italy, only to reassign it to another driver at the last minute. Moss had nursed the insult for a decade. Still, he could see the benefit of an alliance. They might not like each other, but they could help each other win. More than anything, Moss wanted a championship.

In the end, Moss agreed to race a Ferrari, but only if it was operated by Rob Walker's team and painted the dark blue of the Scottish Walker livery. That suited Ferrari perfectly. One of the best drivers in history, in the prime of his abilities, would race his car, but Ferrari would not have to pay him as a team member.

On April 23, 1962, a month before his Ferrari debut in Monaco, Moss entered a minor Formula 1 race known as the Glover Trophy at the Goodwood track in West Sussex. He was up dancing until 2 a.m. the night before, then rose, apparently unaffected, and prepared his pale green Lotus. On the eighth lap he pulled into the pits with his transmission stuck in fourth gear. By the time mechanics fixed it he had dropped to dead last. "What are you going to do?" a friend asked. "Have a bloody go," Moss answered.

In his urgency to make up time he flew down straights at 180 mph and swayed into corners at 75 mph. "He's pushing it," a mechanic said. On the thirty-fifth lap Moss neared a twisty right-then-left maneuver called St. Mary's Corner at 110 mph. His car unaccountably veered off the road, streaked across 150 yards of lawn, and smacked into an eight-foot embankment. A nurse held his hand for half an hour while mechanics sawed through the crumpled aluminum and removed his unconscious body. Blood smeared his face and dripped onto his white coveralls. The impact had crushed his cheekbone and shattered his left eye socket. That was the least of it. X-rays showed a severe bruise on the right side of his brain. He lay in a coma for a month with his left side partially paralyzed. In moments of delirium he spoke in French and Italian about women (*Connie, vous êtes une belle fille. Vous êtes très sympathique*) and racing (*É molto difficile per un corridore — molto difficile*). It was noted that his accent was far purer than when he was conscious.

On May 1, 1963 — a year and a week after the accident — Moss returned to Goodwood to test his reactions. He still slurred words and he still struggled to focus his left eye, but he was prepared to consider a comeback. He clocked decent lap times in a Lotus — about three seconds slower than normal — but something was not right. He may have found his motor skills lacking, or maybe he simply lost his nerve. Moss would not have been the first convalescing driver to lose his appetite for the limit. Whatever the case, he issued a blunt statement to the press that evening: "I have decided to retire; I will not race again."

Without Moss, Hill became the presumptive leader of the Ferrari team for the 1962 season. But there was little chance of him repeating as champion. Ferrari judged the year-old Sharknoses obsolete, and discarded them in favor of a new version. "We must inevitably replace it if we are to continue keeping just a little bit ahead," he wrote in his memoir. But Ferrari was not keeping ahead. Without Chiti, the new version of the Sharknose failed to measure up against resurgent engineering from the British teams.

Hill might have helped the new Ferrari management tune the new cars, but he found them unreceptive. When he suggested refinements, the mechanics made them reluctantly, or not at all. It was as if the clock had turned back five years: Once again nobody would listen to him.

When Ferrari introduced a lighter, slimmer Formula 1 car at the German Grand Prix on August 5, Hill refused to drive it. "It will be a better car some day," he said. "But it isn't yet. It has not been tested enough."

Tavoni's replacement, an imperious

twenty-six-year-old heir to a perfume fortune named Eugenio Dragoni, used Hill as a scapegoat for the team's downturn, beginning with the Targa Florio in May. Hill's throttle jammed during a practice run, sending him off a short cliff at 85 mph. Dragoni attributed the accident to Hill's "hysteria" over von Trips' death. When Hill had a persistent flu at the British Grand Prix in late July, Dragoni interpreted it as a lingering psychosomatic reaction.

Hill denied that von Trips' death had left an emotional scar. "I knew where I was psychologically," Hill said, "and I was no more nor less 'impressioned' by Trips' death than I had been by Collins' or Portago's or Musso's or Behra's or Hawthorn's."

After one race Hill overheard Dragoni reporting back to Ferrari by phone: "Your great champion didn't do a thing." Hill had never felt appreciated in his nine years with Ferrari, but by 1962 he found his position insufferable. He dined midsummer with Chiti, the defector, who was full of promising predictions for the new team. A spy reported their meeting to Ferrari, who likely punished Hill by assigning him inferior cars. It came as no surprise when Hill left Ferrari at the end of the 1962 season to join Chiti's team. That too was a disaster. Chiti's new

Grand Prix car was not ready for competition. Gearboxes, oil pumps, and fuel tanks failed, one after another. Hill's best finish in 1963 was eleventh in the Italian Grand Prix.

In 1964, with his reputation slipping, Hill accepted a pay cut to join the British Cooper team for one humiliating season. His seat didn't fit, forcing him to lurch awkwardly over the steering wheel and preventing him from driving from the shoulders as he preferred. The overheated cockpit gave him blisters. In Belgium his car caught fire during practice. A few days later the engine ignited on lap 14 of the race.

These mishaps were not his fault, but they shook his confidence. For the first time he began to commit serious driving errors. He was sparring with Brabham in the German Grand Prix when he fumbled a gearshift and trashed an engine. This time he accepted the blame.

Only three years removed from the championship, Hill's season became an embarrassment. On his first practice lap at the Austrian Grand Prix, held on a bumpy airfield in Zeltweg, he misjudged his speed going into a curve and skidded into a hay bale. The car hobbled back to the pits with a dislocated front wheel. John Cooper, the team owner, screamed at him, long and loud, within earshot of the other drivers, mechanics, and spectators. Hill crashed in the same curve during the race. The car erupted in flames just as he got out. Cooper fired him.

"There comes a time when every race driver becomes emotionally unsuited to this type of driving," Cooper said. "Hill has reached this point. There may be some kind of driving Hill can still do. But I don't know what it is."

Hill never regained his form. He raced sports cars for a few more years before retiring in 1967. "I had a premonition I was ultimately going to kill myself," he said, "and more than anything I did not want to be dead."

He was among the last drivers of his breed to leave the sport. Within a few years racing became much safer with the introduction of crash barriers, seat belts, and cockpits designed for quick evacuation. The sport also grew far more concerned with money and media. In 1968 Lotus made a deal to display the Gold Leaf cigarette logo, and it traded its traditional racing green for the brand's gold and red. Within a few years virtually every car carried a sponsor's logo.

Shortly before retiring, Hill assisted in the production of *Grand Prix,* a 1966 John Frankenheimer movie based partially on his own experiences. He advised the director, drove camera cars, and appeared briefly on camera. In a case of art imitating life, a main character, played by Yves Montand, spun off the Monza track and died, just as von Trips had five years earlier.

At age forty Hill returned to Santa Monica, where he lived as an eccentric bachelor in the house left by his aunt Helen. He surrounded himself with antiquities — player pianos and thousands of piano rolls, trumpet-speaker phonographs, and a restored violano, a mechanical instrument that reproduces violin and piano music. He started a business restoring old cars and spent evenings listening to classical music alone or with small groups of friends. He was back where he started, with music and mechanics as his primary companions.

Hill never expected to marry. The impression of family life left by his parents was too distasteful. But at age forty-four, he wed Alma Baranowski, a spirited blonde teacher. They met when she accompanied a group of former students who came to see his cars. Hill had been busy restoring a 1927 Packard when they arrived. His hands were slathered in grease and he wore an old sweater. "I opened the door," he recalled, "and thought, 'Thank you heaven!' "

When Alma's father died, Hill flew with her to Arizona for the funeral. Her parents were Lithuanians who had left Europe after the war and settled in Phoenix, where her father worked as a laborer. A reception was held in the simple, sturdy house he had built himself. Alma's mother sat by the open casket stroking her husband's forehead and greeting guests. "They were mostly these big truck-driver types who'd worked with her husband," Hill said. "They were crying and she was consoling them. She hugged and kissed these guys and, I remember, amid the tears there was laughter. She threw her arms around me and kissed me and I kissed her."

Those kisses unlocked something in Hill. His own parents had never shown affection. He had attended their funerals — and those of dozens of drivers — with steely restraint. He had always lived in a state of withholding, which served him well as a racer. Now, for the first time, Hill unclenched and opened himself to the warming prospect of love and family. In the following years he became an attentive father to Jennifer, Alma's daughter from a previous marriage, and Vanessa and Derek, the children he had with Alma. He became the kind of father that he never had.

Hill's inner development had outward expression. It was clear to his friends that his demeanor had lost its coiled tension. "When he married Alma his whole personality changed completely, his whole being changed," said Bruce Kessler, a driver who had known Hill on the circuit in the 1950s. "He was a different person. He was totally relaxed."

Even amid the happy mayhem of family life, von Trips was never far from Hill's mind. His handsome presence hovered like a shadow. Hill was asked about him frequently in interviews and at vintage car shows, as if their histories were still entwined.

Von Trips' fame grew with time. Nearly fifty years later, admirers still gathered at the mausoleum on September 10, the anniversary of his death, and they continued to leave flowers on the grassy shoulder of the Monza backstretch where he crashed.

Years after they married, Hill took Alma to Burg Hemmersbach to walk beside the ochre castle walls and view von Trips' personal effects — jazz records, driving shoes, photographs, oil portraits — housed in a museum on the estate grounds. When heroes die young, Alma said to the curator, they remain forever young and handsome in our minds.

At the end of his life Hill suffered from Parkinson's disease and multiple system atrophy, a degenerative neurological disorder. He was confined to a wheelchair in late August 2008 when Alma drove him up the coast to the Concours d'Elegance, a vintage car show held annually on the Pebble Beach golf course. After an event on Thursday evening Hill said that he wanted to see the road circuit where he had won the Pebble Beach Cup, his earliest triumph, fifty-eight years earlier.

They drove in evening light with Hill directing Alma in a faltering whisper past tents and polo fields. "He was very, very strange that night, and he wanted me to keep driving," Alma said. "And he got so upset with me, because it wasn't what he was looking for." Hill may have been searching for the road as he remembered it, the gravelly track darkened by overhanging cypress trees where he first earned a reputation for a precocious grasp of speed.

The next night, when Hill had trouble breathing, Alma called an ambulance to take him to a Monterey hospital. He died twelve days later at age eighty-one. A service was held on September 10, the forty-seventh

411

anniversary of his bittersweet triumph at Monza. His favorite classical compositions were played as guests filed into the St. Monica Catholic Church, followed by "Jesus Is the Sweetest Name I Know," the hymn his mother composed in 1925. The cemetery cortège included the 1931 Pierce-Arrow that Hill drove while sitting on his aunt's lap. His coffin was covered by a laurel wreath arranged to look like the ones he wore on the victory podium.

Of the two men, von Trips may have left the more enduring legacy. Two years before he died he bought a pair of go-karts in Florida and shipped them to Burg Hemmersbach. He had planned to build a kart track where young Germans could learn to race. In 1965 his mother fulfilled his wish by opening a track less than a mile from the family home. It was leased to Rolf Schumacher, whose son Michael took his first laps there in 1973. Michael Schumacher would become the greatest Grand Prix driver of all time. He won five of his seven championships with Ferrari, returning the marque to dominance after a fallow stretch following Enzo Ferrari's death in 1988.

Fifty years after Hill's championship season, his era has passed from modern memory into history. The headlong runs through the rutted switchbacks of Mexico, the all-night grind through the rain at Le Mans, the back-and-forth battle of 1961 — they live on in flickering YouTube videos and in the memories of a dwindling circle of survivors. These episodes seem unthinkable from the perspective of today's risk-averse culture. Formula 1 cars are now so safe that more than a decade passes between fatalities. But even today there are still some who believe, as von Trips did, that it is danger and the insistent proximity to death that most ennobles the soul.

ACKNOWLEDGMENTS

I'm an unlikely person to write a book about car racing. Like many New Yorkers, I don't own a car. Nor am I a particularly impassioned driver. No matter. I believe that dedicated reporters can write on any topic if willing to do the legwork. To my mind, nonfiction often benefits from casting against type. Sometimes the outsider is the best storyteller.

I had an embarrassment of help along my way, starting with my agent, the wise and incisive Joy Harris, who helped me think carefully about structure, character, and tone from the outset. Thanks, as well, to Adam Reed and Sarah Twombly in her office.

I'm grateful to Jonathan Karp for his early commitment to *The Limit* and for advising me on novelistic nonfiction; to Susan Lehman for her helpful observations; finally, to Cary Goldstein, who helped me across the finish line with grace and good humor. Like all great editors, Cary listens carefully and seemingly never sleeps. I also want to thank Brian McLendon for shouting from the rooftops; Colin Shepherd for graciously handling so many logistics; and Roland Ottewell for smoothing the edges.

The acknowledgments page hardly seems sufficient for the debt of gratitude I owe Michael Dumiak, a first-rate journalist based in Berlin who tirelessly interviewed, researched, and translated on my behalf — all while handling his own bulging docket of deadlines. He also delivered pitch-perfect editorial comments. Portions of this book are his as much as mine.

A number of motor sport historians were kind enough to field my unschooled questions. I benefited enormously from discussions with Doug Nye, Tim Considine, Michael T. Lynch, and Wallace A. Wyss. David Aronson read the manuscript in a late stage and offered valuable suggestions and corrections. I would like to make special mention of Thomas O'Keefe, who helped in more ways than I can mention here. His insights and explanations enriched every chapter. Robert Daley, who reported on many of the critical races for the *New York Times,* generously shared his thoughts and memories. Denise McCluggage, a correspondent for *Competition Press* and the *New York Herald Tribune,* helped me better understand the story's ironies and contradictions. I stood on their shoulders, or tried to, anyway.

Mark Patrick of the Revs Institute in Naples, Florida, greatly enhanced my research by steering me to dozens of books and publications I would not have otherwise found. It was a great pleasure to walk among those stacks.

I would like to acknowledge the help and friendship of Bruce Kessler, one of the few drivers to get out alive, who recalled his racing years with honesty and humor over the course of two long and enjoyable lunches.

My interest in Phil Hill and Wolfgang von Trips began with a book of photographs given to me in the *New York Times* newsroom. Fittingly, this project ended with a selection of photographs that hopefully tell the story visually. Sincerest thanks go to Jennifer Eckstein, a trusted photo editor (and now art consultant) who searched, sifted, and evaluated the images.

Lastly, I would like to thank my parents, Peter and Ann Cannell, for their support and encouragement over my many years as a reporter and editor.

NOTES

PROLOGUE

"This was a duel in the sun": "World Title for P. Hill," *Times* (London), September 11, 1961.

"an age of anxiety": "A Champion's Secret Thoughts," *Sports Illustrated,* November 6, 1961.

1. AN AIR OF TRUTH

"It was the first time I ever struck my father": Pat Jordan, *The Best Sports Writing of Pat Jordan* (New York: Persea, 2008), 201.

"I was awful": "Phil Hill, a Portrait in Speed," *Sports Car Journal,* August 1957.

"Jerry and I hated to let the other kids see us": William Nolan, *Phil Hill: Yankee Champion* (New York: G. P. Putnam, 1962), 19.

"Be a good little soldier": Ibid.

"I remember going down one of those hills": Tim Considine, *American Grand Prix Rac-*

ing (St. Paul, MN: Motorbooks International, 1997), 87.

"I was born a car nut": *Flat Out: Formula One in the Sixties,* DVD, 2006.

"It was as if I was trying to divorce myself": Phil Hill interviewed by Bill Pollack for the Petersen Automotive Museum, November 19, 2001.

"Phil was in awe of that car": George Hearst Jr., interview with author, January 29, 2009.

"It had only 8,000 miles on it": "A Champion's Secret Thoughts," *Sports Illustrated,* November 6, 1961.

"I peeled back the curtains": Nolan, *Phil Hill: Yankee Champion,* 22.

"I learned a hell of a lot": "Phil Hill and the Coast Crowd," *Sports Illustrated,* March 16, 1959.

"I was enthralled with cars": "A Champion's Secret Thoughts," *Sports Illustrated,* November 6, 1961.

"I've always expressed myself": Ibid.

"There was no problem": Ibid.

"a bust": "Phil Hill and the Coast Crowd," *Sports Illustrated,* March 16, 1959.

"From the time I was a little boy": "Too Slow, You Lose — Too Fast . . . ," *Newsweek,* July 17, 1961.

"My parents were apprehensive": "A Champi-

on's Secret Thoughts," *Sports Illustrated,* November 6, 1961.

"I was just a mechanic's helper": Nolan, *Phil Hill: Yankee Champion,* 27.

"I could see so much classic beauty": Ibid., 29.

"the typical American car of the day": "A Champion's Secret Thoughts," *Sports Illustrated,* November 6, 1961.

"I'd stop to talk at length": Nolan, *Phil Hill: Yankee Champion,* 29.

"Attendance was heavy for a while": "A Champion's Secret Thoughts," *Sports Illustrated,* November 6, 1961.

"Certain guys had the touch": John Lamm, interview with author, November 14, 2008.

"I loved those days": "A Champion's Secret Thoughts," *Sports Illustrated,* November 6, 1961.

"even though they told me": "High Speed, High Brow," *Esquire,* June 1961.

"He found himself": Doug Nye, interview with author, October 31, 2008.

"Every day was this ritual": Phil Hill interviewed by Bill Pollack for the Petersen Automotive Museum, November 19, 2001.

"During that final month": Nolan, *Phil Hill:*

Yankee Champion, 33.

"The limit of my ambition": "Obituaries: Phil Hill," *Telegraph* (UK), September 4, 2008.

"I drove with a thrusting kind of fever": "Long Lead at Pebble Beach," *Jaguar World,* November/December 1996.

"The first Jags had notoriously bad brakes": Phil Hill interviewed by Bill Pollack for the Petersen Automotive Museum, November 19, 2001.

"He was driving the wheels off that car": Bill Pollack, interview with author, January 26, 2010.

"That was my breakthrough race": Considine, *American Grand Prix Racing,* 85.

"Those aren't my mother's lips": "The Winner Who Walked Away," *Sports Illustrated,* March 22, 1976.

2. A Song of Twelve Cylinders

"I look for the fighter": William Nolan, *Phil Hill: Yankee Champion* (New York: G. P. Putnam, 1962), 39.

"The place seemed like a musty tomb": Brock Yates, *Enzo Ferrari: The Man, the Cars, the Races, the Machine* (New York: Doubleday, 1991), 150.

"a promising failure": Richard Williams, *Enzo Ferrari* (London: Yellow Jersey Press, 2001), 134.

"small, red and ugly": Dennis Adler and Luigi Chinetti Jr., *Ferrari: The Road from Maranello* (New York: Random House, 2006), 3.

"an ambitious dream": Williams, *Enzo Ferrari*, 126.

"the song of the twelve cylinders": Enzo Ferrari, *My Terrible Joys* (London: H. Hamilton, 1963) 41.

"I build an engine": "Count Crash," *Der Spiegel,* May 18, 1960.

"He used his position as purveyor": Mike Covello, *Standard Catalog of Ferrari 1947–2003* (Cincinnati: Krause, 2003), 31.

3. THIS RACE WILL KILL US ALL

"It's smooth, but a big sound": Tim Considine, interview with author, January 25, 2010.

"The 12-inch finned aluminum brakes": William Nolan, *Phil Hill: Yankee Champion* (New York: G. P. Putnam, 1962), 40–41.

"With Ferrari you not have to worry": "A New World Champion," *Automobile Quarterly,* 1962.

"One day we were chasing": Phil Hill interviewed by Bill Pollack for the Petersen Automotive Museum, November 19, 2001.

"This race will kill us all": "The New King of

the Mountains," *Sports Illustrated,* December 6, 1954.

"It came home to me": "Sundown of a Champion," *Saturday Evening Post,* May 8, 1965.

"Most of this stemmed from my basic uncertainty about life": Nolan, *Phil Hill: Yankee Champion,* 45.

"How do you factor in a burro": Gregg Leary, "Reviewed: *La Carrera Panamericana: The World's Greatest Road Race!*" http://auto motive.speedtv.com/article/reviewed-la-car rera-panamericana-the-worlds-greatest -road-race-by-johnny-ti/P2. Accessed February 9, 2009.

"We saw Ascari's mechanic rushing toward us": Nolan, *Phil Hill: Yankee Champion,* 46.

"They were a band of brothers": Doug Nye, interview with author, October 31, 2008.

"We were so fast on some of the stages": "50 Years Ago: Mercedes Celebrates a Sensational One-Two Victory in the Carrera Panamericana Rally," http://www.schwab -kolb.com/dc000072.htm.

"If ever there was a racing event": Leary, "Reviewed: *La Carrera Panamericana: The World's Greatest Road Race!*"

"That might be": "Le Mans As It Was," *Road & Track,* October 1978.

"I began to brood": Nolan, *Phil Hill: Yankee Champion,* 52.

"It looked like a toy tumbling in front of me": Phil Hill interviewed by Bill Pollack for the Petersen Automotive Museum, November 19, 2001.

"Richie comes staggering in": "Phil Hill: A Portrait in Speed," *Sports Car Journal,* August 1957.

"He'd yell 'LEFT!' or 'RIGHT!' ": Ibid.

"I was mentally considering": Nolan, *Phil Hill: Yankee Champion,* 56.

"We knew how deadly this spot was": Ibid.

"be driving until I die": "Racers Challenge Death in Mexico," *Life,* December 7, 1953.

"As I got towards the car": Nigel Roebuck, *Chasing the Title: Fifty Years of Formula 1* (Sparkford, UK: Haynes, 2000), 57.

"It was hopeless of course": Ibid.

4. THE ROAD TO MODENA

"the strain of inactivity": William Nolan, *Phil Hill: Yankee Champion* (New York: G. P. Putnam, 1962), 61.

"So despite my qualms": Phil Hill, *Ferrari: A Champion's View* (Deerfield, IL: Dalton Watson, 2004), 57.

"It was so dangerous back then": "Phil Hill:

Formula One Racing Driver Who Won the 1961 World Title," *Independent* (UK), August 30, 2008.

"He is not wild": "The New King of the Mountains," *Sports Illustrated,* December 6, 1954.

"A car which goes off the road": "Unscathed Auto Winner Mashes Hand in a Taxi," *New York Times,* November 24, 1954.

"Rubirosa wouldn't even sit": "Phil Hill: Formula 1 Racing Driver Who Won the 1961 World Title," *Independent* (UK), August 30, 2008.

"No blood": "The New King of the Mountains," *Sports Illustrated,* December 6, 1954.

"I'll settle for second place": "Adventure in Mexico," *Autocar,* December 3, 1954.

"Road racers are like roulette players": "The New King of the Mountains," *Sports Illustrated,* December 6, 1954.

"I was finally able to come to terms": "Too Slow, You Lose — Too Fast . . . ," *Newsweek,* July 17, 1961.

"I don't want them to get too fond of me": Enzo Ferrari, *My Terrible Joys* (London: H. Hamilton, 1963), 71.

"Whoever falters here": Denis Jenkinson, *Fangio* (London: Michael Joseph, 1973), 77.

"Be calm": Cesare De Agostini, *Castellotti: A Stolen Heart* (Milan: Giorgio Nada Editore, 2002), 29.

"You have to get straight back": Xavier Chimits et al, *Grand Prix Racers: Portraits of Speed* (St. Paul, MN: Motorbooks International, 2008), 18.

"His eyes seemed to stare at me": De Agostini, *Castellotti: A Stolen Heart,* 38.

"When I close my eyes": Chimits et al., *Grand Prix Racers: Portraits of Speed,* 112.

"Then how would you like to drive it at Le Mans": Hill, *Ferrari: A Champion's View,* 85.

"I hate Le Mans": "Le Mans Circus," *Time,* June 29, 1959.

"Just imagine": "The Tragedy at Le Mans," *Sports Illustrated,* May 12, 1986.

"We have to get some sort of signal system working": "Death at Le Mans," *Time,* June 20, 1955.

"He was torn between his fear and his ambition": Chris Nixon, *Mon Ami Mate* (Hudson, WI: Transport Bookman, 1991), 124.

"momentarily mesmerized by the legend": Ibid., 115.

"At this stage I was driving flat out": Ibid.

"I was pumped": Hill, *Ferrari: A Champion's*

View, 85.

"The crushing sound of its landing": Douglas Rutherford, *The Chequered Flag* (London: Collins, 1956), 139.

"The scene on the other side of the road was indescribable": Duncan Hamilton, *Touch Wood* (London: Motoraces Book Club, 1964), 166.

He is dead": John Fitch, *Racing with Mercedes* (Sandy, UT: Aardvark, 2006) 67.

"It was by pure chance": Jenkinson, *Fangio,* 88.

"I could see a body": Hill, *Ferrari: A Champion's View,* 121.

"Now the lock meant we couldn't get out": Ibid.

"At this point I was numbed by it all": Ibid., 122.

theatrical gesture": Robert Edwards, *Stirling Moss: The Authorized Biography* (London: Cassell, 2001), 97.

"easily build a case inside my head": Ibid., 85.

"Why test? I'm sure he can do it": Tim Considine, *American Grand Prix Racing* (St. Paul, MN: Motorbooks International, 1997), 63.

"So many women and children": Ibid.

"I spent a great deal of time": Hill, *Ferrari: A*

Champion's View, 122.

5. POPE OF THE NORTH

"The symptoms of his illness were now perceptible": Enzo Ferrari, *Una vita per l'automobile* (Bologna: Conti Editore, 1998), 149.

"I had always deluded myself": Enzo Ferrari, *My Terrible Joys* (London: H. Hamilton, 1963), 44.

"the race is lost": Ibid.

"It was watching races like that": Enzo Ferrari, *Una vita per l'automobile,* 11.

"I was alone": Richard Williams, *Enzo Ferrari* (London: Yellow Jersey Press, 2001), 17.

"I have killed my mother": "Enzo Ferrari, Builder of Racing Cars, Is Dead at 90," *New York Times,* August 16, 1988.

"There is no finer thrill in the world": "That Blood-Red Ferrari Mystique," *New York Times,* July 25, 1965.

"In later years I saw many instances": Pat Jordan, *The Best Sports Writing of Pat Jordan* (New York: Persea, 2008), 201.

"nearly always accompanied by breathtaking women": Enzo Ferrari, *My Terrible Joys,* 110.

"I don't think he liked anyone": Brock Yates, *Enzo Ferrari: The Man, the Cars, the Races,*

the Machine (New York: Doubleday, 1991), 3.

"What a ridiculous thing to say": "That Blood-Red Ferrari Mystique," *New York Times,* July 25, 1965.

"I am not an industrialist": "The Terrible Joys," *New Yorker,* January 15, 1966.

"One must keep working continuously": Ibid.

"Ferrari took a little mouthful": Phil Hill, *Ferrari: A Champion's View* (Deerfield, IL: Dalton Watson, 2004), 48.

"The violins would come out": Denise Mc-Cluggage, interview with author, May 19, 2010.

"Will God forgive me": "Only This Race Left and von Trips Was World Champion," *Paris Match,* September 23, 1961.

"man I respected": Jordan, *The Best Sports Writing of Pat Jordan,* 205.

"a Dr. No character": Doug Nye, interview with author, October 31, 2008.

"Because when a man has taken something": "That Blood-Red Ferrari Mystique," *New York Times,* July 25, 1965.

"If you go into a 100 mph corner at 101": "Life in the Fast Lane," *Orange County Magazine,* August 1982.

"nodding acquaintance with death": Rainer Schlegelmilch et al., *Ferrari* (Cologne:

Konemann, 2004), 13.

"Racing is a great mania": "Ferrari Formula for Success," *Times* (London), July 4, 1962.

6. COUNT VON CRASH

"The days of my youth": Wolfgang von Trips diary, as quoted in Reinold Louis et al., *Vom Rittergut zur Rennstrecke* (Cologne: Marzellen Verlag, 2008), 16.

"The village boys were rather rude": Hermann Harster, *Das Rennen ist nie zu Ende* (Berlin: Verlag Ullstein, 1962), 53–54.

"My friends and I did the cruelest things": Ibid., 53–54.

"We drove the car through the gates": Ibid., 54.

"Nobody had seen me fall": Ibid., 73.

"I can't remember how many corpses we carried": Louis et al., *Vom Rittergut zur Rennstrecke,* 28.

"I experienced hell": Harster, *Das Rennen ist nie zu Ende,* 73.

"From there you can follow the battle": Ibid.

"The planes were literally flying around my ears": Ibid., 74.

"We were really down": Ibid., 75.

"In a magnificent cloud of dust": Ibid., 77.

"She stood out": Ibid., 78.

"a girl who lit me on fire": Ibid.

"She was like a princess": Ibid., 79.

"He sleeps easily": "Count Crash," *Der Spiegel*, May 18, 1960.

"Man, Trips, now eat something": Ibid.

"The count was a chicken": Helmut Clasen, interview with Michael Dumiak, June 1, 2009.

"He always had accidents": Ibid.

"At the moment my dreams are haunted by Porsches": Louis et al., *Vom Rittergut zur Rennstrecke*, 131.

"I've become a different person": Wolfgang von Trips diary, as quoted in Louis et al., *Vom Rittergut zur Rennstrecke*, 133.

"Every gold medal meant 75 smackers": "Count Crash," *Der Spiegel*, May 18, 1960.

"What we need, and now possess": Alfred Neubaur to Hans-Willi Bernartz, as quoted in Jörg-Thomas Födisch et al., *Trips: Erinnerungen an ein Idol* (Heel: Königswinter, 1998), 29.

"I said, 'The Mille Miglia?' ": "Von Trips Leads Way in Auto Trials at Monza," *New York Times*, September 10, 1961.

"I was at a crossroads": Harster, *Das Rennen ist nie zu Ende*, 88.

"I was half a minute late": Ibid., 89.

"I had never seen the roads before": "Von

Trips Leads Way in Auto Trials at Monza," *New York Times*, September 10, 1961.

"The experts looked at us": Harster, *Das Rennen ist nie zu Ende*, 89.

"I'm sorry, no": Ibid., 90.

"I always had the ambition": Ibid., 73.

"I have no idea yet how to justify": Wolfgang von Trips diary, as quoted in Louis et al., *Vom Rittergut zur Rennstrecke*, 133.

"That was the hardest": Harster, *Das Rennen ist nie zu Ende*, 91.

"I thought I was struck by lightning": Ibid.

"I was strained to the breaking point": Ibid., 92.

"I request you call immediately": Ibid., 94.

"He was an amazing character": Dennis David, "Alfred Neubauer," http://www.ddavid.com/formula1/neub_bio.htm.

"world's loneliest human being": Ibid.

"I notice how the big races stay with you": Harster, *Das Rennen ist nie zu Ende*, 98.

"It would be very kind of you": Wolfgang von Trips to Stirling Moss, as quoted in Louis et al., *Vom Rittergut zur Rennstrecke*, 211.

"Can you do anything for me?": Harster, *Das Rennen ist nie zu Ende*, 103.

"The race leaders directed their gaze": Ibid.

"To climb into the cockpit of a Formula 1 car": Ibid., 104.

"was a fencing foil": "Count Crash," *Der Spie-*

gel, May 18, 1960.

"My arms were completely stiff": Harster, *Das Rennen ist nie zu Ende,* 104.

"the right front wheel flutter": Reinold Louis, *Wolfgang Graf Berghe von Trips* (Cologne: Greven Verlag, 1989), 221–222.

"I saw the tree coming at me": "Von Trips Leads the Way in Auto Trials at Monza," *The New York Times,* September 10, 1961.

"I lay on the ground": Ibid.

"He looked at me like I was a ghost": Louis, *Wolfgang Graf Berghe von Trips,* 222.

"The next day I could barely move": Harster, *Das Rennen ist nie zu Ende,* 105.

"I wanted to prove": Ibid.

"Ferrari decided that if I wanted to drive that badly": "Von Trips Leads Way in Auto Trials at Monza," *New York Times,* September 10, 1961.

"He was very fast": Enzo Ferrari, *Una vita per l'automobile* (Bologna: Conti Editore, 1998), 163.

"He conducted himself as an ordinary guy": Stirling Moss, interview with author, October 5, 2008.

"The dirtiest one there": Elfriede Flossdorf interview, as quoted in Jörg-Thomas Födisch and Christian Dewitz, *Trips: Bilder eines Lebens* (Bonn: Köllen Druck+Verlag, 2000), 140.

"His voice did not sound": Harster, *Das Rennen ist nie zu Ende,* 139.

"Anyone as intense as I was": John Lamm, *Ferrari: Stories from Those Who Lived the Legend* (St. Paul, MN: Motorbooks International, 2007), 35.

"You don't need a mechanical knowledge": Stirling Moss, interview with author, October 5, 2008.

"He is the type who does not gingerly taste the limit": Harster, *Das Rennen ist nie zu Ende,* 70.

"Most racers I know had unhappy childhoods": Pat Jordan, *The Best Sports Writing of Pat Jordan* (New York: Persea, 2008), 214.

7. GARIBALDINI

"They live in their own country": Ken W. Purdy, *The New Matadors* (Newport Beach, CA: Bond, 1965), 39.

"Peter was remarkably good looking": Chris Nixon, *Mon Ami Mate* (Hudson, WI: Transport Bookman, 1991), 186.

"Peter was a fantastic companion": Jörg-Thomas Födisch et al., *Trips: Erinnerungen an ein Idol* (Heel: Königswinter, 1998) 54.

"The ship's horn sounded": Ibid., 54.

"There he stood, wondering what to do":

Wolfgang von Trips diary, as quoted in Födisch et al., *Trips: Erinnerungen an ein Idol,* 54.

"So began a wild chase": Ibid.

"Every time I tried it": Reinold Louis, *Wolfgang Graf Berghe von Trips* (Cologne: Greven Verlag, 1989), 232.

"It took only a few laps": Hermann Harster, *Das Rennen ist nie zu Ende* (Berlin: Verlag Ullstein, 1962), 108.

"I laid my head back": Louis, *Wolfgang Graf Berghe von Trips,* 232.

" 'Go on, scram' ": Wolfgang von Trips diary, as quoted in Födisch et al., *Trips: Erinnerungen an ein Idol,* 35.

"When we came out of our air-conditioned hotel": Wolfgang von Trips diary, as quoted in Louis, *Wolfgang Graf Berghe von Trips,* 235.

"You must not give up": Ibid.

"Sheer self-preservation led me into the pits": Ibid.

"It was a blissful feeling": Ibid.

"It was love at first sight": Nixon, *Mon Ami Mate,* 245.

"He began to rejoin his racing friends": Ibid.

"He just sparkled": Louise King, interview with author, July 29, 2009.

"Phil came in and said": Denise McCluggage,

interview with author, May 19, 2010.

"It runs fine unless I do this": Denise McCluggGage, *By Brooks Too Broad for Leaping* (Santa Fe, NM: Fulcorte, 1994), 203.

"With Argentine saddles": Wolfgang von Trips diary, as quoted in Louis, *Wolfgang Graf Berghe von Trips,* 238.

"Ferrari didn't like his drivers to marry": Louise King, interview with author, July 29, 2009.

"Men are creatures of their passions": "The Terrible Joys," *New Yorker,* January 15, 1966.

"would pass other cars on the verge": Robert Daley, *Cars at Speed* (St. Paul, MN: Motorbooks International, 2007), 230.

"put courage and verve before cool": Enzo Ferrari, *My Terrible Joys* (London: H. Hamilton, 1963), 53.

"You look like a waitress": Nixon, *Mon Ami Mate,* 266.

"What a pity": Bernard Cahier, *F-Stops, Pit Stops, Laughter and Tears* (Butler, MD: Autosports, 2007), 140.

"even with the sacrifice": Stan Grayson, *Ferrari: The Man, the Machines* (New York: Dutton, 1975), 39.

"The owners see us drivers": "Sundown of a Champion," *Saturday Evening Post,* May

8, 1965.

"Without danger there wouldn't be any point": "Moss in High Gear," *New York Times,* May 7, 1961.

"The very uncertainty sharpens the appetite": Barrie Gill, *Motor Racing: The Grand Prix Greats* (Greenville, SC: Crescent, 1972), 19.

"The racers were the first ones to flee": Pat Jordan, *The Best Sports Writing of Pat Jordan* (New York: Persea, 2008), 214.

"I've been described as anxious": "A Champion's Secret Thoughts," *Sports Illustrated,* November 6, 1961.

"Hamlet with goggles and gloves": "A New World Champion," *Automobile Quarterly,* 1962.

"A racer should have": "Too Slow, You Lose — Too Fast . . . ," *Newsweek,* July 17, 1961.

"I had been to many races": "Wolfgang von Trips: One of Germany's Most Talented Driving Stars," *Vintage Racecar,* May 2003.

"I have no lack of confidence": "Too Slow, You Lose — Too Fast . . . ," *Newsweek,* July 17, 1961.

"All doubts, all anxieties, all memories": "A Champion's Secret Thoughts," *Sports Illustrated,* November 6, 1961.

"Happiness lies in mastery": Harster, *Das Rennen ist nie zu Ende,* 43.

"Once the game has become life": "Stirling Moss: A Nodding Acquaintance with Death," *Playboy,* September 1962.

"I got more column inches": "Sir Stirling Moss: Cars, Crashes and Crumpet: The Original British Boy-Racer," *Independent* (UK), July 6, 2007.

"Of course, I realize this is a foolish time": Ken Gregory, *Behind the Scenes of Motor Racing* (London: MacGibbon & Kee, 1960), 201.

"A wife would worry": "World Title for P. Hill," *Times* (London), September 11, 1961.

"Look at them": Robert Daley, interview with author, July 1, 2008.

"Here's 50 francs": "Geared to Greatness," *Observer* (UK), September 17, 1961.

"When I'm away from the track": Jordan, *The Best Sports Writing of Pat Jordan,* 208.

"If he saw a girl he liked": Louise King, interview with author, July 29, 2009.

"He always went off to some quiet place": Ibid.

"Adventure is like religion": "All in the Family," *Time,* March 25, 1957.

"a Spanish James Dean": Phil Hill, *Phil Hill:*

A Driving Life (Phoenix: David Bull, 2010), 177.

"That man was so busy with women": Nixon, *Mon Ami Mate,* 271.

"It spins so slowly": "A Man Who Was Born 400 Years Too Late," *Life,* April 9, 1956.

"The trouble with life": Daley, *Cars at Speed,* 30.

"I am considered quite an expert": "Horror in Italy," *Sports Illustrated,* May 20, 1957.

"Unless you're Italian": "Enchantment of Risk," *Atlantic,* October 1957.

"If you go into this race": Linda Christian, *Linda* (New York: Dell, 1963), 235.

"My early death": Robert Daley, *The Cruel Sport* (St. Paul, MN: Motorbooks International, 2005), xii.

"beautiful and necessary": "Count Crash," *Der Spiegel,* May 18, 1960.

"Life has to be lived to the full": Nixon, *Mon Ami Mate,* 271.

"I had to lean to touch him": Christian, *Linda,* 239.

"As I prayed": Ibid., 240.

"where the fastest cars": Olivier Merlin, *Fangio: Racing Driver* (London: B. T. Batsford, 1961), 134.

"At first I drive well": "Count Crash," *Der Spiegel,* May 18, 1960.

"I had intended to give up": "Horror in Italy," *Sports Illustrated,* May 20, 1957.

"he put his hand on the steering wheel": Harster, *Das Rennen ist nie zu Ende,* 112.

"When Castellotti and de Portago died": Nixon, *Mon Ami Mate,* 276.

8. Ten-Tenths

"I had my job to do": Reinold Louis, *Wolfgang Graf Berghe von Trips* (Cologne: Greven Verlag, 1989), 245.

"As long as you have an interest": Romolo Tavoni to Wolfgang von Trips, as quoted in ibid., 249.

"You would go": Stan Grayson, *Ferrari: The Man, the Machines* (New York: Dutton, 1975), 226.

"I began to feel": William Nolan, *Phil Hill: Yankee Champion* (New York: G. P. Putnam, 1962), 98.

"You wait and we'll see": Denise McCluggage, interview with author, May 19, 2010.

"He had a terrific feel for the soul of a car": Ibid.

"I would rather drive with Phil": "Denise McCluggage Reporting . . . ," *Competition Press,* November 15, 1958.

"Whether my open eavesdropping really made

any difference": Grayson, *Ferrari: The Man, the Machines,* 221.

"I understood now": Ibid.

"During the closing stage": Nolan, *Phil Hill: Yankee Champion,* 99.

"The turns rushed up at a far greater rate": Ibid., 100.

"That was the end of my Formula 1 introduction": Phil Hill interviewed by Bill Pollack for the Petersen Automotive Museum, November 19, 2001.

"He knew where every sex club was": Bruce Kessler, interview with author, January 24, 2010.

"It seemed only an instant": "Crash Kills 4 in Auto Race," *The New York Times,* February 25, 1958.

"A matador bears only his own risk": "Count Crash," *Der Spiegel,* May 18, 1960.

"I think we were all glad": Nolan, *Phil Hill: Yankee Champion,* 101.

"I've had a lot of bad luck": Wolfgang von Trips to Enzo Ferrari, as quoted in Louis, *Wolfgang Graf Berghe von Trips,* 265.

"If you want to speed": "The Law and Mr. Phil Hill," *Los Angeles Times,* March 27, 1961.

"We could feel the problem": Phil Hill, *Ferrari: A Champion's View* (Deerfield, IL: Dalton

Watson, 2004), 122.

"Little by little we manipulated the errant brakes": Ibid.

"The volume of rain was amazing": Ibid.

"I saw you half-lying on the road": Wolfgang von Trips to Jean Hebert, as quoted in Louis, *Wolfgang Graf Berghe von Trips,* 268.

"That was worse than the accident": Bruce Kessler, interview with author, January 24, 2010.

"I told him, 'No, no, no' ": Ibid.

"Finally I picked up a piece": Ibid.

"so high in the air": Phil Hill, *Ferrari: A Champion's View* (Deerfield, IL: Dalton Watson, 2004), 122.

"We had some laps in hand": Keith Martin, *Keith Martin on Collecting Ferrari* (St. Paul, MN: Motorbooks International, 2004), 5.

"my favorite race": Ibid.

"We all said, 'Phil, you should do that' ": Denise McCluggage, interview with author, May 19, 2010.

"At least I'd call some attention to myself": Nolan, *Phil Hill: Yankee Champion,* 111.

"Dino would say": Chris Nixon, *Mon Ami Mate* (Hudson, WI: Transport Bookman, 1991), 318.

"[Collins] had become unhappy": Ibid., 320.

"Mike always screwed up": Ibid., 316.

"Italy's last world-class driver": Enzo Ferrari, *Una vita per l'automobile* (Bologna: Conti Editore, 1998), 197.

"It was a disaster": Nixon, *Mon Ami Mate,* 326.

"I told him that it was going to be a very hot day": Ibid., 324.

"They looked like a gang of ants": "Denise McCluggage Reporting . . . ," *Competition Press,* August 16, 1958.

"A short time later Harry called": Bernard Cahier, *F-Stops, Pit Stops, Laughter and Tears* (Butler, MD: Autosports, 2007), 168.

"If you get in that Maserati": Phil Hill interviewed by Bill Pollack for the Petersen Automotive Museum, November 19, 2001.

"No one said a word": Fiamma Breschi, *Il Mio Ferrari* (Milan: Mursia, 1998), 42.

"There was no way": Bernard Cahier, *F-Stops, Pit Stops, Laughter and Tears* (Butler, MD: Autosports, 2007), 185.

"Here I started": Denis Jenkinson, *Fangio* (London: Michael Joseph, 1973), 122.

"I can remember being so gauche": Nixon, *Mon Ami Mate,* 326.

"I took his hand and squeezed it": Breschi, *Il Mio Ferrari,* 42.

"I ran for the window": "Mistress of the Maestro of Maranello," *Guardian* (UK), January 23, 2004.

"For a brief moment the hate": Breschi, *Il mio Ferrari*, 43.

"usurious, crazy, inhuman price": "Auto Road Race Ban Demanded by Italian Legislators and Press," *New York Times*, May 14, 1957.

"There was an ugly scene": Cahier, *F-Stops, Pit Stops, Laughter and Tears*, 186.

"He said I would always have friends": "Mistress of the Maestro of Maranello," *Guardian* (UK), January 23, 2004.

"He was a constructor of cars": Breschi, *Il mio Ferrari*, 45.

"One day I arrived at the factory": Cahier, *F-Stops, Pit Stops, Laughter and Tears*, 186.

"was not satisfied with the information": Breschi, *Il mio Ferrari*, 52.

"They built up such a mystique": Grayson, *Ferrari: The Man, the Machines*, 222.

"made his mark and fame right there": "Count Crash," *Der Spiegel*, May 18, 1960.

"Peter was a fun-loving and happy human being": Louise King, interview with author, July 29, 2009.

"He is one that won't die": Mike Hawthorn, *Champion Year: My Battle for the Drivers'*

World Title (London: Aston, 1959), 147.

"I had no idea what had happened": Nixon, *Mon Ami Mate,* 335.

"Mike came back to the pits": Louise King, interview with author, July 29, 2009.

"I said that's enough": Ibid.

"The doctor pulled back the sheet": Nixon, *Mon Ami Mate,* 336.

"an understood but unacknowledged waiting": Ed McDonough, *Peter Collins: All About the Boy* (Coventry, UK: Mercian, 2008), 312.

"I do remember sitting": Denise McCluggage, *By Brooks Too Broad for Leaping* (Santa Fe, NM: Fulcorte, 1994) 203.

"I had to throw the car sideways": Nixon, *Mon Ami Mate,* 336.

"A number of motor sport experts": "Peter Collins: For What?" *Die Welt,* August 5, 1958.

"almost every big-time driver": Ibid.

"This is not a sport": "After Collins, There Are Only Seven," *Die Welt,* August 9, 1958.

"I hope that your article helps": Ibid.

"That we race cannot be explained": "Therefore I Must Race On!" *Bild,* August 28, 1958.

"Ferrari wept at my bedside": Nixon, *Mon Ami Mate,* 339.

"The Vanwalls are built really high": Louis, *Wolfgang Graf Berghe von Trips,* 269.

"Von Trips must have been totally crazy": "Count Crash," *Der Spiegel,* May 18, 1960.

"I felt something like a funny bone": Louis, *Wolfgang Graf Berghe von Trips,* 269.

"What are you thinking?": Helmut Mauser to Wolfgang von Trips, in ibid., 270.

"You have the ability to love": A girlfriend to Wolfgang von Trips, as quoted in ibid., 271.

"I'm not amused": "Count Crash," *Der Spiegel,* May 18, 1960.

"We drivers of the Scuderia family": Wolfgang von Trips to Enzo Ferrari, 1959, as quoted in Louis, *Wolfgang Graf Berghe von Trips,* 278.

"The racetrack had its own aristocracy": Taki Theodoracopulos, interview with author, February 24, 2010.

"The racer is happier, luckier": "Count Crash," *Der Spiegel,* May 18, 1960.

"If your daredevil spirit knows no end": Huschke von Hanstein, as quoted in Louis, *Wolfgang Graf Berghe von Trips,* 274.

"The young ladies can rest assured": "Count Crash," *Der Spiegel,* May 18, 1960.

"We've seen a lot of great moments": Ibid.

"Only those who do not move": "Too Slow, You Lose — Too Fast . . . ," *Newsweek,* July 17, 1961.

"We abandoned this man to his despair": Richard Williams, *Enzo Ferrari* (London: Yellow Jersey Press, 2001), 213.

"I remain best of friends": Wolfgang von Trips responding to a fan letter, as quoted in Louis, *Wolfgang Graf Berghe von Trips,* 302.

"Wolfgang was once an erratic driver": Hermann Harster, *Das Rennen ist nie zu Ende* (Berlin: Verlag Ullstein, 1962), 118, citing UK journalist Louis Stanley.

9. BIRTH OF THE SHARKNOSE

"Speed is the keynote of our age": "Racing Is a Vice," *Sports Illustrated,* May 13, 1957.

"It's always been the ox": Richard Williams, *Enzo Ferrari* (London: Yellow Jersey Press, 2001), 96.

"He was unwilling for us to try": Oscar Orefici, *Carlo Chiti: Roaring Sinfonia* (Milan: Giorgio NADA, 2003), 28.

"structure is slow and cumbersome": "Count Crash," *Der Spiegel,* May 18, 1960.

"Who do you think you are": Ibid.

"Ferrari had agreed to try": Orefici, *Carlo Chiti: Roaring Sinfonia,* 36.

"I'm always afraid when I race": "Phil Hill

and the Coast Crowd," *Time,* March 16, 1959.

"Oh, I'm sorry": "The Other Hill," *Time,* September 28, 1962.

"I'm nobody": Robert Daley, *Cars at Speed* (St. Paul, MN: Motorbooks International, 2007) 230.

"The tension was excruciating": Stan Grayson, *Ferrari: The Man, the Machines* (New York: Dutton, 1975), 230.

10. 1961

"Guess where I've been": Reinold Louis, *Wolfgang Graf Berghe von Trips* (Cologne, Greven Verlag, 1989), 337.

"I've just unpacked your Christmas present": Wolfgang von Trips to Huschke von Hanstein, 1961, as quoted in Louis, *Wolfgang Graf Berghe von Trips,* 337.

"This is Hill's year": "Too Slow, You Lose — Too Fast . . . ," *Newsweek,* July 17, 1961.

"There was always an uncomfortable feeling": Ed McDonough, *Ferrari 156 Sharknose* (Coventry, UK: Mercian, 2007), 5.

"I like to feel the odds are against me": "Without Danger, What's the Point?" *New York Times,* May 7, 1961.

"The mechanic said": Stirling Moss, interview with author, October 25, 2008.

"It gave me great pleasure": Ibid.

"similar to seeing which is quickest": Doug Nye, *The Autocourse History of the Grand Prix Car, 1945–65* (St. Paul, MN: Motorbooks International, 1993), 119.

"To go flat-out through a bend": Stirling Moss, *All but My Life* (New York: Dutton, 1963), 65.

"It was a typical piece of Ferrari meddling": Oscar Orefici, *Carlo Chiti: Roaring Sinfonia* (Milan: Giorgio NADA, 2003), 36.

"What I remember about that race": John Lamm, *Ferrari: Stories from Those Who Lived the Legend* (St. Paul, MN: Motorbooks International, 2007), 134.

"It was rather like a fighter plane": "XIX Grand Prix of Monaco: What a Race!" *Motor Sport,* June 1961.

"Richie was going much faster": Bud Palmer, "Grand Prix de Monaco," http://www.youtube.com/watch?v=Qf5gZbrRe_E&NR=1.

"It's much easier to chase a man": Ibid.

"The last few laps I stopped watching": Moss, *All but My Life,* 66.

"At Monaco in 1961": Ibid., 65.

"Until I saw the checkered flag": Bud Palmer, "Grand Prix de Monaco," http://www.youtube.com/watch?v=Qf5gZbrRe_E&NR=1.

"my greatest drive": Stirling Moss, *Stirling*

Moss: My Cars, My Career (Wellingborough, UK: P. Stephens, 1987), 240.

"Embracing him, it seemed to me": Franco Gozzi, *Memoirs of Enzo Ferrari's Lieutenant* (Milano: Giorgi Nada, 2002), 71.

"No, not even worth discussing": Orefici, *Carlo Chiti: Roaring Sinfonia,* 39.

"Do you as you like then": "Confidential," *Motor Racing,* July 1961.

"calm his palpitating heart": Ibid.

"Push that thing away": William Nolan, *Phil Hill: Yankee Champion* (New York: G. P. Putnam, 1962), 181.

"all arms and elbows": Lamm, *Ferrari: Stories from Those Who Lived the Legend,* 134.

"I was going around oversteering": Tim Considine, *American Grand Prix Racing* (St. Paul, MN: Motorbooks International, 1997), 86.

"They just didn't want us ripping each other up": Ibid., 87.

"It was a big day for him": Hermann Harster, *Das Rennen ist nie zu Ende* (Berlin: Verlag Ullstein, 1962), 19.

"Trips wanted it very much": Nolan, *Phil Hill: Yankee Champion,* 189.

"more of a joke than a race": "Hill Scores in Belgian Grand Prix," *New York Times,* June 19, 1961.

"a guilty surge of pleasure": Pat Jordan, *The Best Sports Writing of Pat Jordan* (New York: Persea, 2008), 207.

"God, my car was clearly superior": Considine, *American Grand Prix Racing,* 88.

"I didn't really want to": Jordan, *The Best Sports Writing of Pat Jordan,* 207.

"take it around": Considine, *American Grand Prix Racing,* 89.

"I really let it all hang out": Jordan, *The Best Sports Writing of Pat Jordan,* 208.

"driving on a spill of ball bearings": Stan Grayson, *Ferrari: The Man, the Machines* (New York: Dutton, 1975), 203.

"I was drinking blood for about five laps": Denise McCluggage, *By Brooks Too Broad for Leaping* (Santa Fe, NM: Fulcorte, 1994), 120.

"My golden opportunity": Grayson, *Ferrari: The Man, the Machines,* 230.

"A few years earlier": Ibid., 231.

"Sometimes I lost my Ferrari": Harster, *Das Rennen ist nie zu Ende,* 63–70.

"Suddenly I saw the eyes": Ibid.

"the highest test, the high wire": Ibid.

"As I had feared": "A Champion's Secret Thoughts," *Sports Illustrated,* November 6, 1961.

"All year long it was him or me": "Phil Hill:

Formula One Racing Driver Who Won the 1961 World Title," *Independent* (UK), August 30, 2008.

"I was very aware of staying within my limits": Phil Hill, *Phil Hill: A Driving Life* (Phoenix: David Bull, 2010), 183.

"passed around the officers' club": Harster, *Das Rennen ist nie zu Ende,* 9–16.

"There was a green splash of color in the pits": Ibid.

"About 30 seconds later": Ibid.

"I guessed as much": Xavier Chimitz et al., *Grand Prix Racers: Portraits of Speed* (Minneapolis: Motorbooks International, 2008) 14.

"I noticed that I had slowly but surely fallen": Harster, *Das Rennen ist nie zu Ende,* 18–29.

"sometimes it's just too much": Ibid.

"Von Trips is to win here": "Hill Rejects 'Orders' to Lose," *New York Times,* August 6, 1961.

"Ferrari can make all the decisions he wants to": Ibid.

"starry-eyed and trembling": McDonough, *Ferrari 156 Sharknose,* 92.

"freak": Ibid.

"Out of the car he seems colder": "Hill Rejects 'Orders' to Lose," *New York Times,* August 6, 1961.

"First, the transmission is bad": Harster, *Das Rennen ist nie zu Ende,* 9–16.

"If the engine cooperates": Ibid.

"Now I know that under the same conditions": Ibid.

"If they only knew how tired I am": Elfriede Flossdorf interview, as quoted in Jörg-Thomas Födisch and Christian Dewitz, *Trips: Bilder eines Lebens* (Bonn: Köllen Druck+Verlag, 2000), 137.

"I slept three feet above the manure pile": Harster, *Das Rennen ist nie zu Ende,* 9–16.

"Now we'll start together": Ibid.

"There were so many people around": Ibid., 39.

"The calm comes over me": Ibid., 30.

"Doesn't it make a lovely noise?": "German Grand Prix," *Autosport,* August 19, 1961.

"smiling happily to themselves": "XXIII German Grand Prix: Moss the 'Ring-Meister,' " *Motor Sport,* September 1961.

"Suddenly everything was wonderfully simple": Harster, *Das Rennen ist nie zu Ende,* 9–16.

"Seeing Moss is one thing": "XXIII German Grand Prix: Moss the 'Ring-Meister,' " *Motor Sport,* September 1961.

"When Hill went past me": Harster, *Das Rennen ist nie zu Ende,* 9–16.

"We drove for a little while": Ibid.

"We were both all over the road": Lamm,

Ferrari: Stories from Those Who Lived the Legend 136.

"It was a barrage of cameras": Harster, *Das Rennen ist nie zu Ende,* 42–50.

"I screwed it up": McDonough, *Ferrari 156 Sharknose,* 96.

11. PISTA MAGICA

"A mountain stream flows": Reinold Louis, *Wolfgang Graf Berghe von Trips* (Bonn: Greven Verlag, 1989), 395.

"I feel like a thousand eyes are on me": Hermann Harster, *Das Rennen ist nie zu Ende* (Berlin: Verlag Ullstein, 1962), 47.

"If I drive fast, I'm so calm afterwards": Ibid., 139–140.

"Every driver has a place deep inside": "Death in Auto Racing: It's Predictable," *New York Times,* April 8, 1968.

"This could all end tomorrow": Robert Daley, interview with author, July 1, 2008.

"I love motor racing": William Nolan, *Phil Hill: Yankee Champion* (New York: G. P. Putnam, 1962), 202.

"Worse yet, nobody would believe me": John Lamm, *Ferrari: Stories from Those Who Lived the Legend* (St. Paul, MN: Motorbooks International, 2007), 137.

"Everything's gone wrong with my car": "Last

Race for Count Crash," *Sports Illustrated,* September 18, 1961.

"Are you sure there isn't something wrong with your foot?": Tim Considine, *American Grand Prix Racing* (St. Paul, MN: Motorbooks International, 1997), 94.

"Just change the damn engine": Ibid., 95.

"We may be teammates": "Last Race for Count Crash," *Sports Illustrated,* September 18, 1961.

"a stumble to it": Considine, *American Grand Prix Racing,* 95.

"shifted sideways": "Von Trips; 11 Fans Killed," *Los Angeles Times,* September 11, 1961.

"I didn't really want to go over": Eric Dymock, *Jim Clark: Racing Legend* (St. Paul, MN: Motorbooks International, 2003), 138.

"Ladies and gentlemen, dear listeners": Louis, *Wolfgang Graf Berghe von Trips,* 43.

"He lay there": Jörg-Thomas Födisch and Christian Dewitz, *Trips: Bilder eines Lebens* (Bonn: Köllen Druck+Verlag, 2000), 328.

"We have lost": Brock Yates, *Enzo Ferrari: The Man, the Cars, the Races, the Machine* (New York: Doubleday, 1991), 231.

"a warming relief": Ibid.

"He muttered something": Ibid.

"At the risk of seeming to be callous": "A Champion's Secret Thoughts," *Sports Illustrated,* November 6, 1961.

"He knows that his victory has been so submerged": "Hill Finds Taste of Auto Racing Victory Bitter," *New York Times,* September 12, 1961.

"I bow my head before him": "12 Killed in Italian Car Race," *International Herald Tribune,* September 12, 1961.

"Easily and quickly he died": Harster, *Das Rennen ist nie zu Ende,* 139.

"There was a certain amount of guilt": "The Sad Hero," *Motor Sport,* September 2001.

"it would be criminal to allow": "The Accident of the GP of Monza," *Le Figaro,* September 12, 1961.

"fatigued and hollow-eyed": Yates, *Enzo Ferrari: The Man, the Cars, the Races, the Machine,* 233.

"It was an emotional moment": Ibid.

"For all the Germans": Nigel Roebuck, *Chasing the Title: Fifty Years of Formula 1* (Sparkford, UK: Haynes, 2000), 54.

"I have never experienced anything": "A Champion's Secret Thoughts," *Sports Illustrated,* November 6, 1961.

"About you, Wolfgang Graf Berghe von Trips": Harster, *Das Rennen ist nie zu Ende,* 141.

"I had felt it before": "A Champion's Secret Thoughts," *Sports Illustrated,* November 6, 1961.

"I sensed, as we spoke": Ibid.

"He was slipping home": "The Thoughtful Champion," *Autoweek,* August 19, 1991.

"I was really sick about that": "The Sad Hero," *Motor Sport,* September, 2001.

"Not at all": Albert R. Bochroch, *Americans at Le Mans* (Tucson: Aztex, 1976), 82.

"Perhaps I am oversensitive": "A Champion's Secret Thoughts," *Sports Illustrated,* November 6, 1961.

EPILOGUE

"I don't know": Phil Hill, *Phil Hill: A Driving Life* (Phoenix: David Bull, 2010) 125.

"If this is how you feel": Mattijs Diepraam and Felix Muelas, "Angry at Laura," http://www.forix.com/8w/ats.html.

"He said, 'I'll make it' ": Stirling Moss, interview with author, October 25, 2008.

"What are you going to do?": "A Bloody Go," *Time,* May 4, 1962.

"He's pushing it": Ibid.

"Connie, vous étes une belle fille": Ibid.

"We must inevitably replace it": Enzo Ferrari, *My Terrible Joys* (London: H. Hamilton, 1963), 42.

"It will be a better car some day": "Ferrari:

Race Cars Are His Life," *New York Times,* August 19, 1962.

"I knew where I was psychologically": Brock Yates, *Enzo Ferrari: The Man, the Cars, the Races, the Machine* (New York: Doubleday, 1991), 234.

"Your great champion": "No Regrets," *Motor Sport,* October 1994.

"There comes a time": "Sundown of a Champion," *Saturday Evening Post,* May 8, 1965.

"I had a premonition": "The Winner Who Walked Away," *Sports Illustrated,* March 24, 1976.

" 'Thank you heaven' ": "Obituaries: Phil Hill," *Telegraph* (UK), September 4, 2008.

"They were mostly these big truck-driver types": "The Winner Who Walked Away," *Sports Illustrated,* March 22, 1976.

"When he married Alma": Bruce Kessler, interview with author, January 24, 2010.

"He was very, very strange that night": Alma Hill, interview with author, January 26, 2010.

ABOUT THE AUTHOR

Michael Cannell has written about sports for *The New Yorker, New York Times Magazine, Sports Illustrated,* and *Outside,* and was editor of the *New York Times* House & Home section for seven years. His previous book was the critically acclaimed *I.M. Pei: Mandarin of Modernism.*

The employees of Thorndike Press hope you have enjoyed this Large Print book. All our Thorndike, Wheeler, and Kennebec Large Print titles are designed for easy reading, and all our books are made to last. Other Thorndike Press Large Print books are available at your library, through selected bookstores, or directly from us.

For information about titles, please call:
    (800) 223-1244

or visit our Web site at:
    http://gale.cengage.com/thorndike

To share your comments, please write:
    Publisher
    Thorndike Press
    10 Water St., Suite 310
    Waterville, ME 04901